ASPECT PATTERN ASTROLOGY

A New Holistic
Horoscope Interpretation Method

Detailed descriptions of
over 45 Aspect Figures

Bruno & Louise Huber
Michael-Alexander Huber

HopeWell
Knutsford, England

Originally published in German entitled 'Aspektbild-Astrologie'
by Bruno & Louise Huber, Michael Alexander Huber
Copyright © 1999 API-Verlag, Adliswil/ Zürich (Switzerland)

First published in English in 2005 by HopeWell
This second, revised edition published 2019 by HopeWell,
with full colour illustrations

HopeWell,
130 Grove Park, Knutsford
Cheshire WA16 8QD, U.K.

English translation
copyright © 2005, 2019 HopeWell and Louise & Michael Huber.

Translated by Heather Ross
English version edited by Barry Hopewell

Jacket: aspect pattern in Bruno Huber's horoscope
Graphics: adapted from originals by Michael-A. Huber
Horoscopes: Huber-Method
(drawn up with MegaStar software)

ISBN 978-0-9956736-4-9

Acknowledgements

Special thanks to David Kerr and Joyce Hopewell for checking the translation for accuracy and the terminology for consistency with current English usage, and to Sue Lewis and Joyce Hopewell for helping to improve the second edition.

The following acknowledgements appear in the original German edition:

We would like to offer our deepest thanks to all our friends for their contribution to the preparation of this book. They took care of the proof reading, production of diagrams, audio tape transcripts, text correction, preparation of manuscripts, and gave additional advice and suggestions. In particular I would like to thank Martin Kannenberg from Berlin, who produced the coloured horoscopes in this book with a special calculation and drawing method using his Astro-Sys Programme software, thus making our work a lot easier.

We are now delighted to have finished this teaching book at long last. We are convinced that all those who have already waited so long for this book will find their patience rewarded. We would like to thank the following individually for their collaboration on this book:

Daniel Cuny
Taomir Ebersold
Monika Gubler
Elke F. Gut
Joyce Hopewell
Michael-Alexander Huber
Martin Kannenberg
Annegret Kaufmann
Johanna Kohler

Richard Llewellyn
Edith Sager
Hans-Peter Sauerwein
Rita Schafroth
Barbara Schmidt
Ruth Schmidthauser
Beatrice Solér
Gaby Thür
Barbara Zollinger

Planetary Symbols

Sun	☉	♂	Mars
Moon	☽	♃	Jupiter
Saturn	♄	♅	Uranus
Mercury	☿	♆	Neptune
Venus	♀	♇	Pluto
ascending Moon Node	☊		

Sign Symbols

Aries	♈	♎	Libra
Taurus	♉	♏	Scorpio
Gemini	♊	♐	Sagittarius
Cancer	♋	♑	Capricorn
Leo	♌	♒	Aquarius
Virgo	♍	♓	Pisces

Abbreviations Used

AC	= Ascendent	MNH	= Moon Node Horoscope
IC	= Immum Coeli	HC	= House Cusp
DC	= Descendent	LP	= Low Point
MC	= Medium Coeli	IP	= Invert Point
AP	= Age Point		

Aspect Colours

Trine and Sextile	= Blue	△ ✳
Square and Opposition	= Red	□ ☍
Semi-Sextile and Quincunx	= Green	⊼ ⊼
Conjunction	= Orange	☌

Element colours

Fire	= Red	Earth	= Green
Air	= Yellow	Water	= Blue

Numbers in (round brackets)

Refer to books in the Bibliography on page 259, e.g. (2).

Contents

Foreword

Dear Readers,

This book arose from the need for holistic guidelines for astrological-psychological horoscope interpretation. Up to now, nearly all interpretation books have simply described individual aspects, which often contradict each other. Even when the individual aspects are carefully interpreted one after the other, it is extremely difficult to get an overall picture from them. Too often, what is said is not consistent. Even computer text programs just create a string of separate sentences which do not do justice to the person's character. This book should enable you to learn to interpret the horoscope as a whole.

This book is founded on the revolutionary discovery that aspect patterns in themselves, (i.e. without planets), have an important motivational significance. They are of overriding importance and serve as synthesizing generic terms for the interpretation of the individual planets contained in them. For example, Jupiter in a Learning Triangle has a different influence on the development of the intelligence than Jupiter in an Achievement Square.

In this book, we describe the psychological influence of the overall aspect pattern and of more than 45 aspect figures that provide a new holistic perspective on the influence of aspects in the horoscope. We begin with the classical theory of aspects and then present a systematic and thorough description of how the aspect pattern as a whole can be broken down. This includes the knowledge of the laws of geometric aspect patterns, whose detailed interpretation constitutes an important part of Aspect Pattern Astrology. Towards the end of the book we deal with the many triangles and quadrilaterals that constitute the different component aspect figures. At the back of the book, you will find both an alphabetical and a pictorial index of the aspect figures.

We hope that for many astrologers *Aspect Pattern Astrology* will provide the key to holistic horoscope interpretation and to the understanding of people's true essence. We are convinced that in the future the cosmic, universal knowledge of astrology will become ever more widespread and understood as a path for development, synthesis and unity, to which our book is our attempt to contribute.

Adliswil, April 1999   Bruno, Louise and Michael Huber

Editor's foreword to Second Edition

We are delighted that it is now possible to produce this second English-language edition of *Aspect Pattern Astrology* with full colour illustrations at a reasonably economical price. In this second edition, the reader can now see these illustrations as originally intended by the authors, and can gain a better appreciation of the role played by colour in the charts of astrological psychology. The opportunity has been taken to update and improve readability of the text.

1. Wholeness and Synthesis

1.1 From Analysis to Synthesis

In recent years, many astrologers have been looking beyond the analytical-psychological use of astrology for more holistic methods. They have recognized that it was not enough to incorporate psychological techniques into astrology, while at the same time remaining bogged down in the old, analytically-oriented use of astrological symbols. Instead they needed to develop visually comprehensible methods that correspond to the needs of modern man and are easy to understand. This new development requires a rethink, an embracing of the laws of spiritual growth, which are closely connected with evolutionary ideas and with esoteric truths.

This rethinking moves from analysis to synthesis, from detail to the whole, thus giving rise to a philosophy in which structure and content, expression and quality, form and colour balance each other. A visual symbolic way of thinking (Jupiter) must be added to the analytical mind that registers every detail (Mercury). Only when both ways of thinking work together is it possible to combine the details and the whole in a meaningful relationship, i.e. developed holistic thinking can enable one to grasp the connections and the inner meaning of a situation.

Astrologers have always dealt with the interpretation of symbols. Symbols are external and visible forms of spiritual realities. Their study leads inwards, from the external perception of a thing to its inner meaning. If someone possesses the ability to discover the truth and meaning lying behind a specific form, this means that the intuition is awakened. Students of Astrological Psychology develop their intuition almost automatically, along with the ability to access the subjective truth through the form. Astrological study helps them to think holistically and spiritually, accelerates the flow of intuition and encourages a sensitive reaction to human nature. There are various ways of activating intuition; one of the most useful and effective is the study and interpretation of astrological symbols.

Before we go into specific holistic astrological methods, we would like to define the term *synthesis* more accurately. Synthesis means bringing together all diverging energies and turning them into a whole. If we are able to perceive and review all component parts as a whole or a functional entity, we also get a total picture. To see a total picture the necessary distance is required, in psychological terms: objectivity, neutrality and impersonality. It is easier to appreciate how everything belongs and works together if we stand back from it. From a certain height, like a bird's eye view, there is a wider range of visibility than from close up. The astrological perspective naturally enables such an elevated standpoint, namely a cosmic point of view. Because it works according to the law of analogy, it reflects the cosmic order in ourselves and our world and teaches us to see ourselves as part of the whole.

The concept of wholeness and synthesis can and must be realized in modern times. Analytical ways of perceiving the human condition are not sufficient. Networking and globalisation and the connection between nature, man and the cosmos are the ubiquitous buzz words. The truth is emerging, that we are just a small part of a cosmic network in which everything is included and everything participates. We recognize that every organism and every person is an integral part of a greater whole, yet still a self-contained living being. In order to comprehend this, we need the development and cultivation of a new global awareness with which this mutual interrelatedness can be perceived.

The Law of Love and Understanding

From another point of view, synthesis is the Law of Understanding, the Law of Love, of higher reason or the "as-well-as" philosophy of the modern man – and the Age of Aquarius – that leads to the experience of wholeness, as opposed to the "either-or" of the past, which separates the parts. That is why both the understanding of cosmic laws and the serious consideration of details belong to the experience of wholeness. It is the hermetic fundamental law *as above, so below, as within, so without*, which holds true for all esoteric teachings as well as for astrology. This law of analogy allows us to recognise the connection between the large and the small, and thus to see the sense and meaning of our existence.

It is exactly so with our horoscope, in which the great and the small merge together; it is the depiction of an all-embracing micro-macrocosmic framework in which everything that makes up our life is contained and combined. We can only make out a pale image of the grandeur and the depth of this functional interplay; we can just get a vague idea of it and be moved by it. This approach puts our small analytical understanding humbly back in its place.

Contribution to New Thinking

The rules for comprehending aspect patterns present a very important contribution to these new developments. The new Aspect Pattern Astrology offers a concept for the comprehension of wholeness, which provides both a psycho-synthetic and an analytical approach to the horoscope. The interpretation of the aspect pattern reveals the structure of the consciousness and gives an insight into an individual's life motivation. This brings us much closer to his integrity. *Moon Node Astrology* (18), which works with three horoscopes, also develops the understanding of wholeness. It enables the inclusion of both the present and the past in the horoscope and incorporation of the so-called shadow personality.

This new direction in astrology is consistent with evolutionary events and the spirit of the age. You can see these links in the following quote from Alice A. Bailey's book *A Treatise on White Magic* (8), (page 439). It is astonishing that this book appeared back in 1934 and even then made a clear reference to this new development in astrology.

Alice A. Bailey writes:

"Astrologers will eventually realise that it is necessary to cast three horoscopes or three charts: one purely physical dealing with the body of nature; one primarily emotional, and dealing with the quality of the personality and with its sensitivity, or state of awareness; the third will be the chart of the mental impulses and conditions.

It will be found that these three charts will take certain geometrical lines, the lines of energy will form patterns. These three charts, superimposed one upon the other, will give the personality diagram, the individual life pattern.

Amazing symbolic charts and linear forms will be found to emerge when this is done, and the "geometry of the individual" will grow out of this, for it will be found that each line will function in relation to another line, and the trends of the life energies will become apparent. Eventually, even in this department of knowledge, "the star will shine forth". This will constitute a new branch of psychology and its due exponent for our age will be duly found. I but indicate the lines of the future astrology in order to safeguard the present".

The Tibetan.

1.2 Bruno Huber's Research Work

Autobiographical Notes

I originally turned my attention to astrology purely in the spirit of research. It seemed to me to be an extremely promising, if unusual, tool for explaining basic questions that concern people like "Where do I come from?" "Where am I going?" What I found more than exceeded my expectations. For example, a clear concept of human nature, which incorporates all current psychology – and at the same time a delicate tool to diagnose every individual character and its specific problems. There are no other known disciplines or methods that can offer anything so valuable.

Barely one year after I started learning astrology from books, I gave it up again, because I didn't like the contradictions that the different methodical elements produced, so I gave away all my books and plunged back into the study of psychology. But that brought me again and again to key terms that I had found in the astrology books, which eventually brought me back to astrology, admittedly now with the clear intention of getting to the bottom of the subject.

1ˢᵗ Phase

This initially required the clarification of terminology, for it soon became clear that linguistic confusion reigned in this discipline. This was quite obvious throughout the whole history of astrology, due to its passing through different cultures and religions. I found myself repeating the question "where does this term come from?" so many times that historical research became necessary. In the years that followed, this led to clearer and clearer wording of the meaning of the basic symbols in explicit, well-defined concepts. For any overlap in terminology (e.g. the same concept used for two different planets) led directly to a lack of clarity, which was not and should not suffice from a psychological point of view. This was highly intellectually-disciplined work that kept me in suspense for years, and which I know I only coped with because I had been taught to think clearly and analytically by the Jesuits, which made it easy to examine speech and writing for flaws and inconsistencies.

In this first phase, I had already begun to work on the unsatisfactory horoscope display format. Charts were confusingly overcrowded with numbers, symbols and lines which intersected each other although they came from different systems and levels. In addition, the aspects showing the connections between the planets were not visible; they had to be worked out from abstract numerical equations. The resulting universally used Aspect Step was anathema to me from the start – it was not graphic enough. I wanted a chart that the senses could comprehend – from which everything important could be understood at a glance. The further the clarification of terminology and my basic research progressed, the clearer the design of my horoscope became. The form that I finally found has now become widely adopted. After recently being adopted by various astrology software designers, with small variations, it could soon become the norm.

2nd Phase

The next phase – the basic research – also began with clarification of terminology, and the question of what the horoscope was really made up of. This was not made clear in the literature – partly as a result of the lack of astronomical knowledge of the authors concerned. It soon became clear that the elements of the horoscope originated from four different levels, and that this must also be meaningful for the interpretation. The planets, their aspects and the signs in which they lie, belong to the sky and therefore have no direct access to the human consciousness – we cannot manipulate them. The houses, on the other hand, represent the earth-bound perspective from which we interpret the sky. For example, we can manipulate them by moving around or by the passage of time. For us they are the space and time in which we move, dimensions in which we are at home. But our displaced earthly interpretation has no effect on anything in the sky.

This first geo-cosmic distinction is enormously important in the interpretation, because the planets, aspects and signs represent the most deeply innate that we bring with us into life. The reflexes determined by the flesh of our parents and ancestors are responsible for our earliest childhood reactions to the conditioning attempts of the environment, which wants to give us quite specific interpretations of life. It is easy to see how different these reactions are in children from the same family. What the conditioning will provide is determined by the time and space-determined earthly view of our parents' generation. That is the perspective view provided by our house system.

Sign/House Distinction

The question of which is more important in the horoscope, the houses or the signs, has long been a matter for dispute among astrologers. The question cannot be answered validly and for everyone from the horoscope. It must ultimately be established for each individual case by talking to the subject. It is important to clarify this, as it can then be established whether the person concerned is more conditioned by nature or nurture, and this influences how the horoscope is interpreted. People who are conditioned by nurture (i.e. by the house system) are generally better adapted, or at least try to be. Only in later research did I find out how such distinctions can be obtained at least partially from the horoscope itself.

Even the sky must be divided into levels. It is obvious that the horoscope deals exclusively with the solar system, and that this system is perceived and experienced from the earth. For the planets subjectively move on a clearly delimited path around the earth, on the same path as the sun and the moon. This path is not physical. We have divided our year (=1 revolution of the sun) into twelve months. The solar and planetary orbits are also divided into twelve segments, in each one of which the sun stays for around a month as the definitive timekeeper. That is our zodiac system. It does not exist in outer space, only for the earth. It rotates not around the sun, but around the earth's axis, which is tilted and does not revolve around the sun like the planet itself but remains (almost) rigidly fixed to an (unknown) cosmic stopping place. The zodiac is probably a function of the earth's magnetic field, whose orientation is partly influenced by the orbiting of the earth around the sun. We therefore distinguish the different qualities of twelve magnetic field sectors, which we call zodiac signs, and to which we attribute various qualities based on thousands of years' experience. It is said – and

I believe it – that the zodiac contains the archetypal qualities, or to put it another way, the projections of the hopes and fears of humankind since the outset are assembled and concentrated into twelve basic personality types.

The Signs of the Zodiac

The zodiac works like a filter for the energies that emanate from the planets, which move in their very own characteristics outside the terrestrial system. So when we say that Jupiter is in Scorpio, then Jupiter's colour – let's say green – takes effect through the, let's say blue, Scorpio filter, which naturally makes the green of Jupiter appear a lot more severe (blue-green) than it would alone – or a lot deeper than the lighter, rather more superficial yellow-green that would be formed on its course through the yellow sector of Libra. This means that we hardly ever see the planet's qualities as they really are, but always coloured, i.e. changed due to the filtering effect of the signs. They are therefore subject to constantly changing interpretation by man's changing projection. They appear to us to be something distant, untouchable. It is not for nothing that they used to be seen as unfathomable gods. Or else they were firmly woven into ethnocentric concepts, and adjustments then had to be accepted by history (culminating in the exchange of principles, as happened with Mars and Saturn in the transition from Babylon to Greece, for example). The planets cannot be embodied, as they are actual principles of cosmic magnitude. Therefore they had to be represented as abstract principles and not as human qualities. For this reason, the defining of terms is also very important for planets. The overlapping of terms soon leads to misinterpretations, for principles are unique and indivisible; the diversity of forms of our sensory phenomenal world arises only from their combined influence.

The Planets

Aspect patterns show us the combination of planetary influences. It is the aspects that make the arrangement of planets in signs and houses appear meaningful. Aspects forge relationships between planets. They show an interaction of the principles in order to form a concrete function, which in life equates to a task. A planet in one sign is not yet a task, but merely a point of view and therefore arguably the range of certain opportunities (selection).

1.3 The Horoscope in Five Layers

To illustrate this idea, the colour chart is used in which the individual layers are presented separately as reference levels so that they are clearly visible. Each layer is a self-contained unit and influences the whole. For each level of consciousness there are precise basic principles of interpretation that must be coherent. So a planet in its zodiac sign is interpreted as investment potential, its position in a house shows the

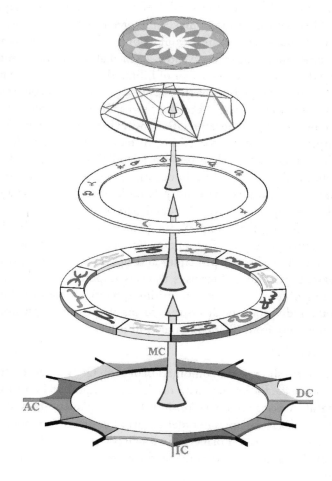

The Five Levels of the Horoscope

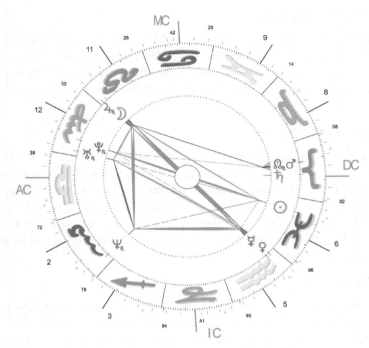

Foundation chart of API Switzerland
12.3.1968, 20.05, Zürich/CH

influence of the environment and the aspects derived from it modify it according to its inner motivation. We illustrate this with a horoscope.

This horoscope was calculated and drawn up according to the Huber Method. The twelve signs of the zodiac are shown in the colours of the elements: red: fire, green: earth, yellow: air, blue: water and the aspects are shown in red, blue and green. When seen from the inside working out, the five layers represent the following: the circle in the centre is the core of the personality, the higher self of the human soul. Then come the aspect pattern, the planets arranged in a circle, the twelve signs of the zodiac and outside on the edge the twelve houses. Seen like this, the horoscope is a mirror image of the whole person.

1. The Centre Circle

In the centre circle is a free space, which we leave untouched and in which aspects never appear. We leave this space free out of a certain respect for man's inner being. This circle also symbolises the immortal soul that lives eternally. It is the Higher Self and as such the root of our existence.

2. The Aspect Pattern

Around the core personality there is a relatively wide space in which the aspects appear, together forming a complete pattern that represents the structure of the individual consciousness. This includes a central life motivation and corresponds to the causal body in Alice A. Bailey's esoteric astrology. This is the deepest level in man and barely, if at all, accessible to the unaware, even though the whole life is governed by this motivating life energy.

3. The Planets

The planets appear in the next layer. They form aspects according to their position in the zodiac, and can be treated as actual tools. Planets are the tools with which we react and act, perceive the environment and can influence it. The ring of planets represents an important layer, because it is our first point of contact with the environment. All ten planets are available to each one of us as tools, but they are in different positions for everyone, i.e. in a certain zodiac sign and in a certain house and even then, they still have different aspects. If one planet is badly placed, then it is an effort to assert the corresponding life functions. In interpretation, we must always eventually consider the planets as a supporting set of tools for the personality.

4. The Zodiac

This is a circle divided into twelve parts, through which our sun moves in space during the year. The zodiac is therefore a cosmic framework and stands for nature and her laws (20). The zodiac signs reveal an individual's hereditary disposition. They indicate genetically-inherited structures that we carry inside us as potential from birth and must then develop, use and implement during the course of our lives with the help of the environment.

5. The Houses

The houses represent the environment. All the influences from our surroundings are recorded in the twelve houses. The environment conditions our behaviour through our upbringing; it motivates us to make the best use of the planets as tools. Of course, sometimes certain existing abilities are not understood, and they are blocked instead of being developed. These influences, so-called sensitisations of the environment (education and environmental effects), can be seen in the position of the planets in the houses. In adults, the houses above all represent the reactions and behavioural structure by which we influence the environment, which helps or hinders us (16). More details on this can be found in house horoscopes (13).

That is a brief summary of the five-layer horoscope. You should always keep this in mind as we analyse individual horoscope features separately. We must be careful not to lose the overview and the context. We must always go back to the principles, the essentials, to the motivation and develop the interpretation from there.

This interaction can be illustrated well with a theatre analogy.

Example of a Theatre Performance

Imagine a theatre stage on which a section of the revolving stage is visible; this represents one of the twelve houses, the backdrop represents the signs of the zodiac. Every actor is a planet, the script is the aspect pattern and the director is the core personality. They perform a play, which requires certain facilities. We see a section of the revolving stage with the backdrop, the actors perform the play according to the script (aspect pattern). If one actor is missing, in the horoscope this means re-casting on the horoscope, if there is no planet present in a house and sign, there is no action. With no planets as tools we can neither react nor act in this area of life. In this section of backdrop we can hardly make out what kind of play is being performed. In an empty house and sign, the spectator (the environment) can only see minimal, stereotyped reactions. For the director, this scenery without actors is not an interesting area of life. Only the actor (planet) can act, the backdrop (signs) cannot replace him, they only form a frame for the action.

Conclusion: a really accomplished play can only be performed when all five layers of the horoscope are working as a whole.

2. Aspect Theory

2.1   Introduction
2.2   Aspect System
2.3   The Seven Major Aspects
2.4   Aspect Influence according to Colour
2.5   Planetary Influence on the Aspects
2.6   Four-Dimensional Aspect Interpretation

2.1 Introduction

Aspects used only to be given in tabular form, and were rarely displayed directly in the horoscope as in modern astrology. Now we see a graphic image, a pattern whose very uniqueness is significant, irrespective of the planets which form the pattern and their house and sign position.

In traditional astrology, aspects were always shown separately, so that if someone had a trine between the Sun and Jupiter, it was considered a lucky aspect. Other aspects were not considered in relation to it, even when they considerably reduced the positive effect of this aspect or completely contradicted it. In Aspect Pattern Astrology we very rarely consider aspects in isolation, instead they are always interpreted in combination with the whole aspect pattern.

Aspectarium

When you read astrological literature, you will often find an aspectarium, in which each different planetary aspect is described in detail (29). An aspectarium is a list of all the aspects that are identified as being influential in a birth chart, or all the aspects that are formed within a certain timeframe, for example in Ephemerides or in predictive astrology. The corresponding texts refer to individual aspects like conjunctions, sextiles, squares, trines, oppositions, etc., between one or more planets.

Just as with a computer horoscope, these texts usually provide unconnected and even contradictory information, and do not do justice to the whole person. It is a kind of reference work, where you can look up the meaning of, e.g. a square or an opposition between the Sun and Saturn. The definition will be mainly negative, to the effect that the

individual is unteachable, he gets his own way, has to fight against strong opposition and his undertakings only succeed at the second or third attempt.

If such judgemental statements are taken seriously, they will undoubtedly inhibit personal development. Many people make themselves dependent on such statements and lose freedom because they regard them as unalterable facts, although they actually only relate to a small part of their lives.

Even in astrological research, aspects are always treated separately, analysed statistically and compared with psychological questionnaires. There have been various attempts of this nature, where for example the behaviour within a partnership has had to be diagnosed and classified. Defining love for other people based on traditional aspect interpretation is very questionable. It turned out that nothing came of this and neither could any proof be found for the accuracy of astrology. Even comparing so-called "bad" aspects with accidents, illness or catastrophes was not supported by the research. It was recognised that when individual aspects are compared statistically with a person's real life the results are not consistent.

Whole Aspect Pattern

So, for psychological aspect interpretation, we should never consider one aspect in isolation, but always the whole aspect pattern, plus the sign and house position of the planets concerned. As already emphasised, aspect pattern reading enables a previously unattainable holistic understanding of the horoscope. When we are dealing with human beings, we cannot work with templates and give recipes for their behaviour. We always have a whole aspect structure in front of us, an aspect pattern, in which the planets are mutually connected. Extracting individual aspects and defining them in isolation is wrong in principle, because they are part of the whole interdependent structure.

Our way of presenting a horoscope is to portray the whole aspect pattern in different colours. It used to be done very differently: the aspect degrees were just noted around the edge of the circle and no colours were used and there was certainly no graphic presentation. Nowadays, the graphic layout of the aspect pattern structure reveals deep-seated life motivations.

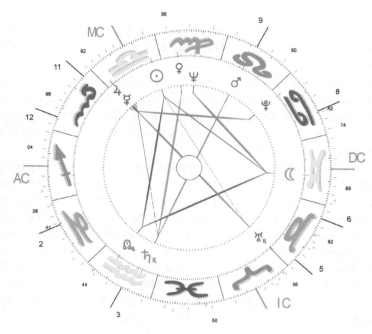

Brigitte Bardot, Actress
28.9.1934, 13.15, Paris, France

As you can see in the above horoscope, aspect patterns are clearly marked inside the horoscope circle. In every horoscope we can see several distinct patterns or figures; each one relates to the expression of a characteristic of the person's individuality. Close observation shows geometric figures: large, all-encompassing triangles, small triangles, polygons and lines.

2.2 Aspect System

What are Aspects?

The word aspect comes from the latin *aspicere* and means look. If an aspect links two planets, they are looking at each other; there is a relationship between them. They are connected to each other and have to deal with each other whether they like it or not. An aspect can also be compared to a telephone line. If someone calls, the person at the other end must react. If a planet is called in a certain life situation, the call is immediately transferred to all the other planets connected to it. Aspects are a sort of communication network between the planets. As every person's aspect pattern is different, each one also has a different communication network. In the modern sense, one could say that aspects are like circuits in an electronic device. In the horoscope, the aspect structure is like an internal circuit diagram, representing the structure of a person's consciousness. It can nurture, diminish, modify or increase the function of the planet concerned depending on the quality of the aspect and its angle. Primarily, they show the relationship function of the horoscope factors, particularly of the planets as essential forces between themselves. When these and their inter-relationships are seen as a whole, the overall aspect pattern gives the astrologer a picture of the connections and the different functional areas in a person's consciousness, which defines the life motivation. This gives rise to a correctly proportioned picture of the character of the person concerned, which is why it is important to learn to interpret aspect structures as a whole and not just individual aspects.

However, in aspect reading we must gain a thorough knowledge of the individual elements. To begin with, we should know that every gap between two planets is not necessarily an aspect. They must be calculated and ascertained very accurately according to the appropriate rules. Technically speaking, aspects are standardised angles between planets in multiples of 30 degrees.

30 Degree Intervals

Aspects are basically 30 degree intervals measured around the zodiac. Each zodiac sign also covers 30 degrees. Basic empirical research has led us to use only angular divisions of 30 degrees or multiples of 30 degrees, i.e. 30, 60, 90, 120, 150, 180 and the special case of 0 degrees. They are

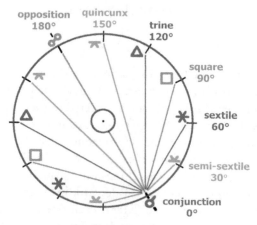

Ptolemaic Aspects

angles that are ordered according to the same system as the zodiac signs. The 30 degree division is based on empirical results that goes back to the origins of astrology. Ptolemy had already suggested this aspect system back in the year 120 AD.

From the point of origin, aspects can run forwards or backwards in the zodiac. They also don't have to correspond exactly to the above-mentioned number of degrees. There is a little leeway, depending on the planet concerned, which is called the orb. Different astrological schools have conflicting views on both the size of the orb and which point outside the planets is still aspected (1). In the API school, only the aspects between planets, plus ascending Moon Nodes, of multiples of 30 degrees are considered valid. No aspects are drawn to the ascendant [AC] or to the midheaven [MC] and also no house cusps are drawn through the central area of the chart as they distort and falsify the whole pattern.

Aspect systems

The greatest difference between the various schools lies in the range of the aspects to be considered, as there are differing opinions on how the circle should be divided. Below are summaries of the two main tendencies:

1) The Bisection Method is actually the oldest of them all, and already existed in the Babylonian era. In those early days, when there were still no geometric instruments available, the simplest solution was to bisect the circle (180°, opposition), to bisect the semicircles (90°, square) and likewise the quarter (45°, semi-square). Even the first attempt by the Babylonians to construct an eight-house system follows this principle. This eight-house system (octopodos) was not very widely used in astrology, although the astrologer Manilius was still propagating it in Roman times.

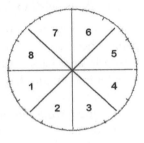

Octopodos

The Chinese *I Ching* is also based on this simple division of the halving and doubling of an original duality. There, the basis of the system is the eight original trigrams, which are doubled to form hexagrams and then the sixteen halves are fleshed out to create 64 hexagrams. Chinese astrology was also based on this method until Jesuit missionaries introduced the western 12-house system in the 15th century.

2) In the second century A.D. Claudius Ptolemy, the famous geographer, mathematician, astronomer and astrologer suggested **dividing the circle into 12 parts** as a way of organising the aspects. He was thus following the Babylonian system of dividing the zodiac into 12 parts developed in

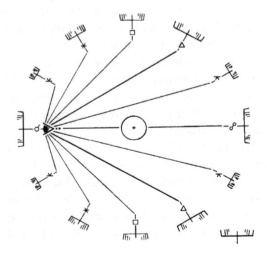

the 8th to 5th centuries B.C. This produced a 30° interval between each aspect, thus giving the seven different possible angles within the circle:

Aspect Types with Orbs

These seven aspects provide twelve possible aspect positions for each planet, because the five aspects between 30° and 150° can run both forwards and backwards in the zodiac. This Ptolemaic model with Babylonian origins has been the most commonly used, with a few modifications.

It is interesting that nearly every author who recommends it or who has recommended it in the past, has not mentioned two out of these seven aspects, or their interpretation is vastly underrated: the semi-sextile and the quincunx – although Ptolemy clearly mentioned and defined both of them. Unfortunately, his own explanation contributed to this neglect. He was convinced that the aspects must form symmetrical shapes. So, four squares make a rectangle, three trines make a triangle, six sextiles make a hexagon. However, the fact that twelve semi-sextiles make a dodecagon and 12 quincunxes also make a symmetrical shape obviously escaped him. So he just mentions briefly these two aspects with the term unrelated signs, "as they do not look at each other, do not order or obey each other and do not possess the same energy" (26).

It is quite obvious that Ptolemy has in fact chosen the correct system, even the division into 12 parts, but his reasons are based on a different logic and as a result there is no coherent explanation for the system. The real reason for Ptolemy's explanations should really lie elsewhere, i.e. in the fact that at his time there were no psychological or philosophical concepts for the qualities of the semi-sextile and the quincunx. From the point of view of the history of psychology, at that time the abilities of self-awareness, of the conscious sensitive perception of the environment and the critical-analytical understanding, were at most cultivated mainly by a brilliant minority and were therefore not really definable from astrological experience. It is precisely these abilities that are associated with the 30° and 150° aspects.

Consequently, in the Middle Ages, the assessments of the two remaining aspect groups were expressed purely in black and white terms: the square and opposition (red) were unlucky, bad or even evil aspects, to some extent the conjunction too; the sextile and trine (blue) were lucky, good or even divinely gifted. Not until the twentieth century did a certain dissatisfaction with such dogmatism and absolute either-or judgements take hold. Traditional astrology began to express itself more moderately: bad became tense or difficult; good became relaxed or soft. But nevertheless, the duality of this mediaeval point of view had still not disappeared and the psychologically necessary non-judgmental differentiation was still not yet possible. This could only be found in the already existing 30° and 150° angles, the semi-sextile and quincunx aspects (green), which correspond to an awareness-forming thinking function.

Calculating the Aspects

Aspect type	Symbol	Degree	Colour
Conjunction	☌	0	Orange
Semi-Sextile	⚺	30	Green
Sextile	✶	60	Blue
Square	☐	90	Red
Trine	△	120	Blue
Quincunx	⚻	150	Green
Opposition	☍	180	Red

Although nearly all horoscopes are calculated by computers and displayed in colour, every student of astrology should know how to calculate and plot the aspects (15). Aspects are calculated as follows: the zodiac circle is divided into twelve equal segments; a point is fixed in the horoscope, for example, Mars, and you then move forward 30°. If there is a planet at this point, then there is an aspect between the two. We can measure the exact angle by counting the number of degrees separating the two planets around the outside edge of the horoscope, which is divided into degrees. In this way we measure the angle formed between one planet and another and on the birth chart we draw a connecting line in a particular colour between the two planets concerned.

Square Sun/Saturn

In the example on the right, there is a right-angled aspect between the Sun and Saturn, it is a 90° aspect called a square and is drawn in red.

Trine Venus/Jupiter

If a planet (Venus, in the following example) lies at 5° of the sign Taurus and Jupiter at 8° of the sign Capricorn, then an angle of approximately 120º is measured around the 360° circle, which we call a trine.

A trine normally occurs between two signs of the same element, i.e. from earth sign to earth sign, from water sign to water sign, fire sign to fire sign, air sign to air sign. A 90° angle, or a square, normally occurs within the cardinal, fixed and mutable cross, likewise an opposition, which connects opposite signs, unless the aspected planets lie on the cusp between two signs, when the aspect must be accurately calculated.

Area of Influence of the Aspects (Orbs)

Planets almost never lie at the same number of degrees; this would actually mean that the angle between them would be exactly 30° (or 60° or 90°, etc). In practice, there is rarely an exact aspect between two planets. That is why astrology allows a tolerance of influence of a few degrees on either side of the aspect angle, within which the aspect is still effective. This area is called an orb (from the Latin: orbis = radius). This varies according to the astrological importance of the planets and the aspects concerned. So when calculating the aspect, we must find out exactly what orb a planet has. There are tolerance limits that differ depending on the planet or aspect concerned, as you will see in the Huber Orb Table on page 24. The orb allows us to plot an aspect when it is not exact, but still falls within the tolerance limits.

Different Orb Methods

Individual schools of astrology have different opinions about the size of the orb (radius of influence of the aspect). About 10° has been the norm for the Sun and the Moon, with smaller orbs for the rest of the planets. In the API school, every aspect has a precise area of influence, as in the Huber Orb Table. This is the result of many years of empirical research using countless sample cases.

It was decided that the criterion for the orb limit was that a planetary relationship is only an aspect if the definable influence is permanent. If it is only sporadic, it lies outside the permanent orb. In powerfully stimulated situations, an aspect lying outside the permanent orb can be acceptable for a short time, but it is not a characteristic ability of the individual concerned. This is most noticeable with one-way aspects.

These days, a wide range of programs is available from computer software companies, which are not secured and can often even be modified by the layman. Although they are interesting for advanced astrologers to use for their own research purposes, there is still the danger that lay people will not be able to use them correctly. The decision as to whether to plot an aspect or not (Huber Orb) was tested over a 30 year period at the Astrological Psychology Institute. More than a thousand active astrological consultants all over the world put the aspects in horoscopes to the test almost daily in personal consultations with their clients.

So with good reason we can state and demonstrate that the aspect definitions (Huber Orb Table) developed by Bruno Huber have proven themselves many times over. We therefore recommend that you use these orbs when you chart aspect patterns.

In aspect patterns drawn up with other orb systems, the interpreted life motivations almost never correspond to the person concerned! But every serious student should find this out and test it for himself. After all, all astrologers are researchers. The use of computers in astrology makes the calculation of data easy and is very useful for astrological research. It is safer and more convenient if you use the Huber-Koch method when you draw up the horoscopes by computer (4).

Huber Orb Table

The table on the next page shows the orbs relating to each individual aspect and planet. We see that the different planets have orbs of different sizes: so that the Sun and the Moon have a larger orb than Uranus, Neptune and Pluto. The Sun and Moon orbs are 9° for the conjunction and opposition, 8° for the trine, 6° for the square, 5° for the sextile and quincunx and 3° for the semi-sextile. At the other end of the scale, we find that for the three outer planets Uranus, Neptune and Pluto the orbs are reduced as follows: 5° for conjunctions and oppositions, 4° for trines, 3° for squares, 2° for sextiles and quincunx and 1° for semi-sextiles. In between lie the orbs for the other planets.

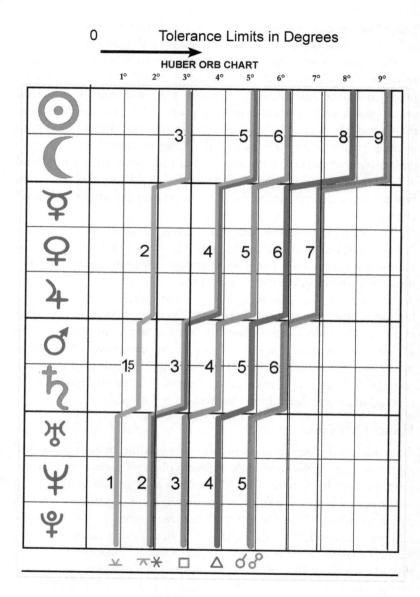

Huber Orb Table

Sun/Moon Opposition

For an opposition between Sun and Moon, there is an orb of 9° on both sides. That means that if these two planets are opposite each other, the opposition aspect is still valid within a range of 9° from the exact position. In this case it means that intervals of between 171° and 189° are oppositions.

The orb allowed for an opposition between Neptune and Pluto is only 5°. So the aspect only exists when these planets are separated by an angle of between 175° and 185°. The orb for a semi-sextile aspect between the Sun and the Moon is only 3°; if the angle were 4°, there would be no aspect. Aspects to the ascending Moon Node are allowed, but the Moon Node itself has no orb, so the orb of the planet aspected to it is used instead.

Goodwill Aspects

You can be confronted with situations where two planets lie just outside a mutual aspect, let's say an arc minute too far from each other. We would like to plot these aspects, but think that at the outer limit the influence is very weak, so it is better to leave it out. Some people call these goodwill aspects and note them on the calculation sheet but not in the horoscope. Eventually an aspect pattern emerges from the aspects that must be accurately calculated and plotted, to ensure the correct astrological interpretation of the consciousness structure and of the life motivation. Just one wrong aspect can change the pattern considerably.

One-Way Aspects

If we see aspects that have incomplete lines, this means that one planet lies outside the tolerance limit. As explained above, every planet has a specific area of influence, a radius of tolerance. It can happen that for one planet the orb is sufficient for an aspect, but not for another planet. That is a one-way aspect. So a connecting line is only drawn half way and then dashes are drawn up to the planet lying outside the orb. This is significant, as it is a planetary relationship that only works in one direction, i.e. from the complete line to the dashed line.

As you can see on the Huber Orb Table, a certain aspect does not always have the same orb. An opposition from the Sun has a 9° orb, an opposition from Pluto only 5°. A square from Venus has an orb of 5°

while the same aspect from Saturn has only 4°. This is significant when we come to plotting the aspects in the birth chart.

Example 1

Let us assume that the Sun stands at 27° Capricorn and Pluto at 20° Cancer, thus creating an opposition with a deviation of 7°. Here the Sun definitely makes an aspect to Pluto, but Pluto (with an opposition orb of only 5°) does not make one to the Sun. The half aspect line from the Sun to the centre circle is shown as a continuous red line, the aspect from Pluto to the centre is just shown as a dashed line.

Example 2

When Mercury stands at 10° of Leo and Mars at 16° of Sagittarius, and we look at the orb table, it shows that a trine aspect is formed from Mercury, which has an orb of 6°, while Mars' orb is only 5°. So here we have another dashed aspect as there is an angle of 126°. That is why the line going from Mars is dashed, but continuous from Mercury.

Example 3

The Sun lies at 7° of Sagittarius and Jupiter at 15° of the same sign, thus forming a conjunction. On the orb table we see that this angle forms a conjunction for the Sun, but is not sufficient to form one for Jupiter. This is known as a "one-way conjunction".

Strength Differences

There are even differences in effectiveness between continuous aspects. If an aspect is exact, e.g. it goes from five degrees to five degrees in any angle, it is very effective. In this case it is drawn thicker in the middle of the horoscope, as shown in the drawings on the next page. Exact aspects showing low tolerance are also drawn thickly, while an aspect that moves right at the tolerance limit is drawn with a very fine line. Medium

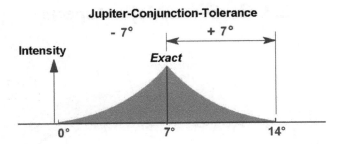

Jupiter-Conjunction-Tolerance

strength aspects are drawn with a medium line. This produces a sort of proportioned line pattern with strongly prominent aspects that catch the eye and others that recede into the background. The former must naturally be considered stronger, they play a greater, more important role and contribute to the profile of the aspect pattern. This starts to give the aspect pattern a more vivid effect.

Width of Aspect Lines

Another important reason for drawing the aspects thicker or thinner according to their orb-related strength, is that it makes it obvious at first glance whether the aspect's influence is significant or not. This provides a four-dimensional picture of the structure of the consciousness and enables us to identify colour and depth with colourful, vivid aspect patterns, thus facilitating the holistic understanding and interpretation of the horoscope. In the different Huber software programs, the lines are presented as follows:

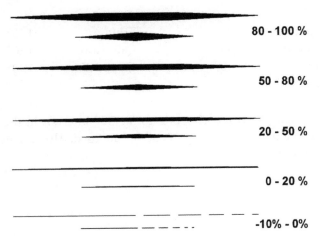

2.3 The Seven Major Aspects

Conjunction	0°	Trine	120°
Semi-Sextile	30°	Quincunx	150°
Sextile	60°	Opposition	180°
Square	90°		

The seven major aspects correspond to the 30° intervals in the zodiac. As already mentioned, only aspects of 30° are used. They are described briefly in the following.

1. Conjunction: Angle 0°, Glyph: ☌

Colour orange, Planetary quality Sun/Moon

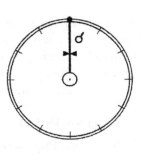

In a conjunction, two or more planets lie together. A conjunction is a zero degree angle. The quality of a conjunction depends on the planets involved. In general, it corresponds to a combination of different components that are hard to differentiate or separate. This often causes a mainly unconscious, inner tension. The conjunction also corresponds to an embryonic state and indicates latent talent that must first be developed.

2. Semi-Sextile: Angle: 30°, Glyph: ⚺

Colour green, Planetary quality Mercury

This small green aspect goes from sign to sign in 30° steps. It connects two qualities with differing characters. The semi-sextile indicates a need to experience, learn, discuss, read and be informed about new things. Objectivity and indifference merge in the process. This aspect is called "the small thinking step".

3. Sextile: Angle: 60°, Glyph: ✳

Colour blue, Planetary quality Venus

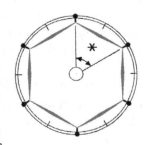

The sextile corresponds to the Venus qualities of harmony-seeking and willingness to compromise. It is accepting, adaptable and able to attract and to assimilate substance. There is usually a passive defence against the loss of a state of harmony and often a fear of conflict.

4. Square: Angle: 90°, Glyph: ☐

Colour red, Planetary quality Mars

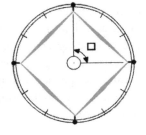

The nature of the square is fiery and dynamic. It originates from the combination of the three cross qualities (cardinal, fixed, mutable) and is an energy aspect. There is usually a deployment of strength or supply of energy, which nearly always causes an increased readiness for action and motivation. There is a lot of strength available for assertion and defence. Of course, the square also generates conflict, friction, crises, stress and sometimes also a tendency to aggression.

5. Trine: Angle: 120°, Glyph: △

Colour blue, Planetary quality Jupiter

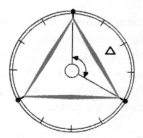

This aspect has a relaxed and harmonious effect. The trine connects the separate elements in a 120° angle. It is a material aspect that tends towards abundance, luxury and enjoyment and gives sensual pleasure. Sometimes it indicates perfectionism or obsessive behaviour.

6. Quincunx: Angle: 150°, Glyph: ⚻

Colour green, Planetary quality Saturn

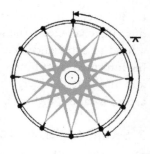

The long green aspect causes insecurities on the one hand and on the other the urge to achieve an imagined future goal. Sometimes it is also called the "longing aspect". It often brings decision crises, uncertainty, and eventually the challenge of restricting oneself to a single goal, in which case it aids decision-making. It is called "the big thinking step".

7. Opposition: Angle: 180°, Glyph: ☍

Colour red, Planetary quality Saturn

This aspect is formed when two or more planets lie exactly opposite each other in the zodiac. The planetary principles concerned often contradict each other, which is experienced as inner tension and often an energy blockage, stress or postural rigidity. An opposition also generates inner strength and endurance, particularly relating to the subject of the axes. Sometimes there is an increased tendency for repression, in which lateral aspects are compensated.

Aspect Interpretation

0°	consolidation, connection, germination
30°	cognition, communication, informing
60°	striving for harmony, growth, assimilation
90°	friction, stress, deployment of energy
120°	perfection, abundance, fruition
150°	longing, decision, development of informed opinion
180°	pressure, tension, repression

Aspects Compared to the Growth of a Plant

If we go back to the basic character of the aspects to try to understand them, we discover an essence behind them. They are obviously related to an already familiar system, i.e. the zodiac, to the twelve divisions, as well as to the planets that rule the signs. This statement reveals how coherent the basic structure and way of thinking of astrology are; even aspect reading draws from the same sources and builds on the same basic structure.

The aspect layout presented in the Seven Major Aspects diagram on page 28 can be compared with a tree or a plant with long leaves which goes through several development stages as it grows. When the year comes to an end, the plant dies and leaves seeds behind, which fall to the ground and initially hibernate. Within the seeds there is a germinating potential, a construction plan in the form of a genetic structure. If the seeds receive the right environmental conditions, like light, water and warmth, in spring they will open out and start to germinate and a new plant is born. It is a cycle of growth and death.

Compared with our aspect sapling the germinating soil of this imaginary plant lies between Cancer (Moon sign) and Leo (Sun sign).

Conjunction = Sun/Moon Aspect ☌

When two planets lie together, they are like a seed; everything is contained within them: aptitude, potential, future possibilities. But they cannot actualise them by themselves; they are barely able to react to each other or to be active with each other. For this they need external help. They just constitute a seminal power in which much is latent. When, for example, a conjunction stands alone in a horoscope, i.e. has no aspects to other planets, it is difficult for this individual to transfer the qualities and energies available in both planets. They are latent and can often lie dormant for a lifetime. To learn how to analyse and evaluate these energies requires an understanding of the way these planets work and a knowledge of what they mean, otherwise they will never be awakened, just as the seed that lies in the soil can do nothing by itself. It needs outside influences: light, warmth and moisture. To be effective, the conjunction needs an external stimulus or trigger. In astrological terms, this means that a conjunction will only develop if aspects to other planets are present.

Semi-Sextile = Mercury Aspect ⚹

Next comes the semi-sextile, which triggers the growth of this seed. In the chart, this aspect runs in from 0° Leo in both directions to both the Mercury signs Gemini and Virgo. If the energies from the environment act on the seed in the spring, its inner life is kindled by warmth and moisture and it starts to germinate. A pale seedling grows cautiously and stretches out diffidently into the world. This state is a kind of experimental stage. The conjunction sends out a kind of tentative feeler, in the form of the semi-sextile. It is a neutral attempt to test out the situation and to find out what the environment is like. If all goes well for a while, it can continue to grow. In the psychological sense, this is an information stage. Everything that happens in a semi-sextile aspect provides information and is of a temporary nature. Everything is possible, much remains indefinite and brings no results and nothing conclusive, a lot can still happen or happen quite differently. This aspect aids perception, to receive a picture of what the possibilities are. In this state you cannot expect nature to provide support. Two planets connected in this way are in an information exchange, and that corresponds exactly to the quality of Mercury. This is why we call the semi-sextile a Mercurial aspect.

Mercury is generally known as our information mechanism. When we talk to each other, we exchange information. Sometimes this can lead somewhere, sometimes not. There is nothing conclusive about information, it is just available to us, we can do experiments and little tests with it. So the semi-sextile is the first step in the growth process. In the above example of the plant, it means that if the weather is warm, the plant grows and turns green and moves onto the next stage, which in the aspect structure is the sextile.

Sextile = Venus Aspect ✶

The sextile is a Venus aspect. In the Seven Major Aspects diagram (page 28) we see that the sextile aspect runs on both sides to the two Venus signs Taurus and Libra, and that the sextile stage of our plant is the flowering stage. What is a flower for? On the one hand, we enjoy its beauty and on the other it wants to be pollinated so that it can bear fruit later, survive and reproduce itself. The Venus aspect is receptive to every kind of impression. It is an important and beautiful stage. A flowering plant is a feast for the eyes and usually has pleasant connotations for most people. But this stage can also bring problems; they are subtle problems that are not so easy to detect. What we have imagined to be so beautiful and harmonious can be broken with a flash of lightning or a hailstorm. This aspect cannot easily tolerate hardship. The sextile avoids conflict and keeps to the sunny side of the street.

Square = Mars Aspect ☐

The next stage will not feel very pleasant. After the pollination of the flowers, the plant must bear fruit. The plant is at its most active stage, which involves the transformation of a great deal of energy and reserves. The energy balance is optimally increased and energy expenditure is maximised. Ensuring these two processes requires a lot of reserves and energy. The plant now has to work and cope with a hard task requiring dedication and effort. This is why the square aspect is called a Mars aspect. With a square, difficulties can be surmounted and effort can be generated. Energy is transformed, resulting in the growth of the plant and, for people, achievement. In the summer it is often hot and water can be in short supply, there are gales and electrical storms that shake the plant. The plant must withstand all these natural influences, while at the same time continuing to grow and allowing the fruit to ripen.

In life, too, squares are there to tackle possible difficulties, to have the strength to struggle through them and achieve things or just to work. Work is done with the square, not with the sextile. With the sextile we enjoy, with the square we work. A square in a horoscope is an achievement aspect and the planets involved are achievement tools.

Interestingly, in the past, the blue aspects, the sextile and the trine, were called the "lucky" aspects and the red aspects were considered "bad". There are people with almost exclusively red aspects in their horoscope who are very hardworking. Problems only occur when they don't recognise when it is time to stop working. Generally the red aspects prepare the person for effort, while the blue aspects are quieter and more harmonious and tempt one into pleasure. This is also the case for the following blue aspect.

Trine = Jupiter Aspect △

The plant has now gone through its fruit-ripening stage and it is time for the harvest. The plant has fulfilled its fundamental destiny. Its fruit is ripening and with that its succession is assured. The trine and the planet Jupiter, always regarded as the lucky planet, belong to the fruitful stage. Of course, this is not really the case; there are no good or bad aspects. They must be considered as obsolete valuations. The red aspects are achievement aspects, while the blue ones are referred to as talent aspects. Neither is better nor worse than the other, it is just that we tend to value one more than the other. It is harvest time, when we rejoice, have fun and take the fruits to be stored in the barn. Afterwards, we need exert ourselves no longer, all we need is there and we just have to enjoy it. Harvest and abundance both correspond to Jupiter and the trine in the horoscope.

But there is a dark side to this too. When one has everything that one needs and lives in abundance or after a great party, one can easily get a hangover. The delight goes and nothing really satisfies. Such over-saturation often leads to a mental crisis.

An individual with many trines in his horoscope usually likes convenience, he doesn't want to make an effort and can be proud, conceited and self-satisfied. He doesn't to want face reality and refuses to admit to mistakes or to recognise when things are wrong. There are plenty of people with many trines who are ill, resigned and mentally weak. So this aspect carries no guarantee of good luck.

Quincunx = Saturn Aspect ⚹

We have now reached the penultimate stage, the long green quincunx aspect. This aspect is analogous to autumn, which inevitably follows the harvest. In a certain sense it is also a beautiful phase in which the leaves change colour and when nature still shows herself in all her rich colouring, like the last fling of the life force. But it is also the phase of dying off, the end of the growth process, the valediction. We all know what this means. Autumn evokes a melancholy mood; we become contemplative and tend to turn inwards. We know that spring is not far away from autumn, but there is a long winter in between where nothing grows, nothing is green. We are almost snowed in, as it were, and thrown back onto our own resources. In summer we live more outside, now we bring ourselves back indoors. But an inner knowledge remains that spring is definitely coming around again. Hoping and longing are qualities associated with this long green aspect. The consciousness anticipates better times, we think of other things that we would like. We wish for good and beautiful things, and imagine them as tangible in our fantasies. It is a projecting thinking power, imaginative ability that can make things happen. Wishes and hopes are also connected to this aspect. On the understanding level, thinking ahead that wanders far afield, planning ahead or striving for knowledge which is not yet there but which one is working towards.

In autumn, nature just ticks over, annual plants die and trees revert to minimum sap circulation. It is just enough to survive the winter, but not enough to generate any life. That is the Saturn part of the quincunx aspect, the knowledge of reductionism, of the not quite arrived at. There is not enough strength to get where we want to go, resulting in a great longing for what we would like to have.

The quincunx is also called the longing aspect. On our table, you can see that it leads to Saturn signs on both sides. This means that we must get used to the idea that it lasts a long time. We should arrange to plan very carefully, to consider everything thoroughly, not to rush into anything and not to think that we already know everything. Every situation must be thoroughly thought through, all facets of a problem weighed up and worked through. This is what winter is for, for everything to be reset to zero. Then we can ponder in peace and quiet.

The long green aspect in a horoscope points to long deliberation, the prolonged thinking process that could lead to a better outcome. This process often causes insecurity and crises of indecision.

Opposition = Saturn Aspect ☍

The last stage comes when everything is hibernating and nature is seemingly dead. The annual plant dies off, leaving its seeds behind. The tree stands like a stone statue. This is the opposition, a final state, a rigidity that can no longer move under its own strength.

On our aspect table the opposition leads to a point where both Saturn signs, Capricorn and Aquarius virtually trap the aspect. To the left and right is Saturn, meaning hardship, coldness, standstill and crystallisation. In the natural world, ice and snow cover and protect the ground. This means that even when Saturn is cold, it represents a form of protection. It is a strong, impenetrable cover, providing defence, blockade and immunity. Although the opposition represents standstill and scales down the life functions to a minimum, it is not absolutely a zero state. We are in a waiting stage and preparing for a new cycle. Waiting belongs to Saturn; it always had an affinity with the concept of time. Saturn the timekeeper, the Chronos. With Saturn we have to be patient, and with the opposition likewise.

This pattern demonstrates the qualities of the seven aspects in a particular way. It corresponds to the astrological point of view originating in primitive times. Astrology expands all principles from the small to the great. For example, what happens to the plant during a year happens to a person during their lifetime, however long that life may be.

2.4 Aspect Influence according to Colour

Three Types of Aspect

The grouping of the aspects into three colours is another way of classifying them. These three colours are red, blue and green. According to the three primary colours they should be: red, blue and yellow, but unfortunately yellow shows up very badly on the page as we cannot see it properly. We have therefore made a practical compromise and called it green.

Red, blue and green are three colours that are analogous both with the major planets and also to the crosses. Red corresponds to the Sun, blue to Saturn and green to the Moon. We find the same analogy system in the three crosses and the graphic aspect patterns. Red is called the Energy aspect, blue is the Material aspect and green is the Awareness aspect.

Analogy Table

Red	Blue	Green
Achievement	Pleasure	Sensitivity
Energy	Matter	Consciousness
Cardinal	Fixed	Mutable
Linear	Quadrangular	Triangular
Sun	Saturn	Moon

Red Aspects

Square: 90° angle, Opposition: 180° angle

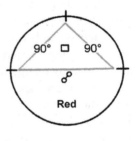

The difference between the Mars and the Saturn aspects is clear. The red aspects are always an expression of an inner dynamism, vitality and motor energy. A lot of red aspects in the horoscope give strength and energy that make specific achievements possible according to which planets are involved. Even the so-called weak planets, i.e. the Moon, Mercury, Venus and Jupiter are positively activated by a red aspect. They trigger energetic processes in us and in our environment, which can cause significant changes in our way of life.

Red aspects are energy aspects, relating to strength and achievement. They transport energy from one planet to another, or both planets transfer energy. It is the act of working where the targeted use of energy produces performance. The red aspects require a readiness to do something, to apply ourselves to something, to be active, not just an attitude. They influence our way of doing things, not our inner reserves like the blue aspects, and stimulate our readiness for action and motivation. That is why red aspects should be accepted as positive, they enable us to achieve something in life, to overcome resistance and to reduce inhibitions and fears. They give us the courage and the strength to do what is necessary for our development and inner liberation. The red aspects enable us to unblock deadlocked, untenable situations, whether they are in close relationships, at work or within ourselves. In any case we should be prepared to take on possible conflicts with the environment. Often inner changes provoke external resistance. But with the red aspects we also have powers of self-assertion to cope with them. When things get us down and we can't do what should be done, then we can get into internal and external conflicts.

That is also why the red aspects were seen as negative in traditional astrology. No one wants to suffer voluntarily; no one wants to overexert themselves if things go wrong. Our resistance to effort, work or exertion is the problem, if we have problems with these aspects. We very often compensate with resulting feelings of guilt in hectic, inane compulsive activity. We take refuge in work, almost blindly wasting the dynamic red aspect energy, pushing our strengths to depletion without achieving satisfactory results. Because we act rashly and without control, we make little mistakes that come back to haunt us and for which we have to pay. Then we will probably blame it on the red aspects and decide that they are bad. But it was my own fault, because my rash reactions, obstructiveness, or defiance prevented me from accepting the challenge and I used my energy unwisely.

With the red aspects, it is particularly important to really understand what they want from us. We should make a thorough study of the aspected planets in search of corresponding ideas on how to develop and round our personalities. Then we can undertake new activities intelligently, consciously and joyfully and experience positive results in terms of the planets involved.

Red aspects to the hard planets Sun, Mars, Saturn, Uranus and Pluto naturally have a stronger influence, as they are similar to them. Depending on the way they are aspected by other planets, their problems can be increased or aggravated or weak planets can alleviate them. Either we tend to blockages or hardened attitudes or in the best case to a consolidation of the available essential energies. With enough self-discipline, the same aspects can lead to one's own abilities being used for the good of others, especially when the aspects are to the spiritual planets of Uranus, Neptune or Pluto. Tension that brings down some people is redeployed by others who, with insight, spur on their development by shouldering larger tasks or responsibilities to resolve internal conflict.

The square as a Mars aspect is generally very helpful for further development. It activates us more strongly than the opposition does, but also makes us more aggressive. The energies stimulated from outside and inside us provoke us and call up hidden desires, but problems can appear, depending on which planet or aspect figures are involved and in which house and sign the planet is situated.

It can happen that our activities and goals meet with resistance, usually inciting us to still greater efforts. A square often makes us dissatisfied with the status quo, and awakens our revolutionary impulses, independence and defence of freedom. This is particularly likely when hard planets (Sun, Mars, Saturn, Uranus, Pluto) are connected by squares. In squares to weak planets (Moon, Mercury, Venus, Jupiter, Neptune), there can be exaggeration and excessive behaviour. Sometimes the square has a drastic character whose influence can extend to external events. In profiled planets, i.e. those lying near a main axis or those singled out by the aspect pattern, red aspects act as strong stimuli and put these planets under excessive tension, just like stress planets (16).

Blue Aspects

Sextile: 60° angle, Trine: 120° angle

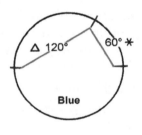

In contrast, blue aspects are concerned with material things; they are bearers of abilities and qualities. Planets connected by a blue aspect have a material relationship and are equipped with optimal substance. This frequently includes a particular talent that requires no effort (Talent Triangle). There are people who have talent but do not commit themselves as the situation does not require it. These talents can remain latent for a long time. The blue aspect gives no stimulus, except for the stimulus of pleasure! That is why red aspects should always be available to get things moving.

From this point of view, a blue aspect is not particularly "good". Even habits (both bad and good) can hide in the blue aspects. Obligations are dealt with in a reflex manner, which does not necessarily mean that the reflex suits the situation.

The sextile and trine correspond to Venus and Jupiter respectively. The sextile could also be defined as a talent still in the process of growth, the trine as a mature talent, comparable to the fruit at harvest time. A trine indicates the ripened stage of a talent, the reaching of completion, while in the sextile, the talent is still being developed. Interestingly, the striving for perfection is a property of the sextile. There is still movement in this matter, it is striving and still growing. Harmony and perfection are the measure of all things in the blue aspects. Maturity is a perfect or harmonious and resting state. That is also the reason why we prefer the blue aspects. They give us satisfaction, we need do nothing more, we don't need to make any effort. The sextile = growth, the trine = fulfilment. Sometimes with the sextile there is an exaggerated need for harmony, and with the trine perfectionism or addictive tendencies.

Because blue aspects penetrate the reserves deeply, every disruption is frequently perceived physically – in certain cases even as illness. When something is wrong, for example in the case of ingrained habits, crystallised states or tensions, blue aspects want to make them flow again. That can cut right to the quick. When we have become too comfortable, lulled into security, wanting to rest on our laurels, we are roused out of this tranquillity. Situations often crop up in life in which we must show character; without this we will not be taken seriously nor will our true worth be recognised, which is naturally hurtful. It should already be obvious that blue aspects are not just good aspects, they can actually demand a lot from us. Of course the evaluation depends on which type of planet is aspected and how this aspect is integrated into the whole pattern.

Sextile Aspect

A sextile to a planet supports the release of existing tensions. Sextiles are Venus aspects, so they make us more open to new relationships and mainly to the pleasant side of life. We are more adaptable, tolerant and can understand other people better, even forgive them. The sextile often has a problem-solving effect, creates new possibilities for compromise in situations of conflict. Our aesthetic sense is also sharpened, which can also lead to anxiety. According to the planet, house and sign involved, we react hypersensitively to disruptions, to the undesirable, to the ugly and to noise. We don't want to lose a previously attained state of harmony; we want to enjoy it on an ongoing basis. This often causes separation, anxiety and fear of conflict, with the willingness to back down and adapt. Many people do not want to change and want to be left in peace; they are ready to compromise and unable to tolerate conflicts. If this aspect is activated by the Age Point (17), a kind of assimilation process takes place. Now we often have the necessary time to process or to "digest" previous experiences, or to assimilate new things without tension.

Trine Aspect

Planets connected by a trine aspect show their best properties. They are real benefactors and compensate for many things; they bring us the fruits of our labours. People with trine aspects find a way out of many difficulties; they are optimistic and look for the highest and best in everything. It is a "Jupiter aspect" that promises the optimum and usually has enough reserves to keep those promises. It protects against unpleasant experiences and magnetically attracts what is good for it. In this aspect, reserves are accumulated that can be drawn on at any time.

But there are dangers lurking here too, if we rest for too long on our laurels and are not aware that life goes on in an eternal interplay – demanding new adaptations, changes and conversions of us on a daily basis. If we possess too little character, we will be made painfully aware of this lack. Everything fake and untrue should now be rejected; things should start moving and bring us joy again. It is no fun any more to pretend that we are happy with everything. It is well-known that indulgence, tranquillity, comfort and satiety can lead to boredom and to a so-called "over-saturation crisis"

Green Aspects

Semi-Sextile: 30° angle, Quincunx: 150°
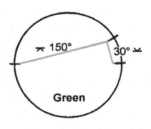
The green aspects are called sensitive or information aspects. Up to now, only the API school has given these aspects the attention they deserve. Although they are relatively weak and have a correspondingly small orb, they have a completely different systematic relationship with the traditional aspect interpretation than other equally weak aspects like the semi-square (45°), the sesquiquadrate (135°), the quintile (72°) and the bi-quintile (144°), with which they are often associated.

The colour green was actually only arrived at in the 20th century, via the third principle called 'information' in physics. Behind every process there is an aim and an intent that scientists call information. Wherever we come across patterns in nature, there is pattern-forming information hidden behind them that wants to construct something very particular according to a specific information pattern out of the available energies and matter.

Nowadays, for example in further mathematics, they are trying to unravel this information model to find out why certain patterns, substances and energies always behave in the same way. What intention lies behind man's use of naturally occurring materials and use of energy to produce tools, for example? They are man-made artefacts that are used for the purpose for which they were created. A quite conscious information technology lies behind it. We think of something and produce it; that is why we need energy and matter. We let energy act upon matter in a specific way, thus creating the object we need.

The green aspects in a person's horoscope do not relate to pure information, but to awareness. The green aspects are awareness aspects. Awareness has many different unconscious forms, for example sensitivity and even a feeling is a kind of awareness. It does not matter whether we are aware of this in our daily consciousness or if it is a subliminal but still available awareness process.

Semi-Sextile (small thinking step)

The 30° semi-sextile is the Mercurial division that we call the small thinking step. It is an attempt by the consciousness to understand something. Although it still need not have to have any consequences, one is open to everything. Mercurial means: being neutral and not taking a stand, also to have no tendency to judge or to evaluate, but just the curiosity to want to be informed. Let us take the example of a journalist, who must make neutral reports of everything that happens so that the reader gets an objective picture of the situation. It is a non-binding process and in principle absolutely neutral. When we read the paper and something is wrong with one article the information can be denied or repressed by the consciousness. When we like something we can spread it around everywhere. But that is a subjective reaction. The impressions and information that the small green aspect brings can, in principle, be used as one wants; the aspect itself contains only information, it is up to the ego to evaluate it. The aspect characterises the factual assimilation of information and its communication. There may be interest and curiosity relating to an issue, but there is no judgement; in many cases there is also indifference. This may be caused by their own objectivity towards the issues, there should be more emotional involvement in them, or they are not interested in the things because they are too far removed for them to reach. Or they are too close at hand, apparently too mundane and the topic is already familiar because it is ordinary.

Quincunx (big thinking step)

As previously mentioned, we call the long green aspect the big thinking step. Our consciousness tries to extend itself and reach a goal, to strive for knowledge or experience. When we go through a thinking process with the consciousness and reach an intellectual goal, it is called deduction.

That is a possible way for the long green aspect to achieve awareness. The quincunx aspect also evokes longing (which is also a process), for example when we long for spring in autumn. The process of consciously striving for something that we do not yet have, and longing for it with all our hearts until it arrives so that we can then enjoy it, is also caused by the long green aspect.

The green aspects are also concerned with our awareness of the environment. There are consciousness processes that aspire towards something. It is the long drawn out striving, the reaching and longing of the consciousness for unfamiliar ways, waiting for something. It is both a feeling and an intellectual process that wants to work hard for a result. Not until the long green aspect decides on a specific goal does it become a factor in decision-making.

When trying to reach a decision by thinking, we have to work through different cognitive processes and experiences before making a decision. From this point of view, the quincunx is a decision-making aspect and therefore an important one, for decision-making is a very important process; it makes people strong. It is also a Saturn aspect though. How many times do we have to renounce the many opportunities available to us in order to concentrate our energies on one single goal? Both green aspects are active from the purely instinctive level up to the highest spiritual processes.

The quincunx aspect enables us to see the awareness-forming quality of the mutable cross to which it corresponds. The big thinking step brings a new quality into the old world view. Up to now this was determined by polarities (cardinal = active energy / fixed = passive matter) and limited to perceptions of black-white, good-evil, etc. Since the start of the 20th century and the formulation of the Theory of Relativity by Albert Einstein, a new dimension in human thinking has been established by the development of psychological thinking, with the experience of the relativity of values. This fact also helps us to understand why Ptolemy had not yet defined the green aspects, despite specifically mentioning them in the *Tetrabiblos*. This new quality can be experienced in the quincunx. The old black-white divisions are no longer sufficient; it represents a third dimension, a neutralising or transcending of opposites.

Although people with quincunx aspects look for causality and reasons for everything, they also look for finalities, i.e. they try to discover the direction and meaning of developments. The quincunx aspect is a longer intellectual process, with which we can discover our direction in life. If we look at the position of the quincunx (150°) in the "The Seven Major Aspects" (page 28) between the Jupiter-influenced trine aspect (120°) and the hard, tension-laden opposition aspect (180°), it corresponds to the soft side of Saturn, i.e. the willingness to assimilate, cultivate and be interested in the long-term development of things, events and information.

The quincunx aspect also responds to the demands of Jupiter, which asks questions about meaning, context and perspective. So the quincunx's quality as a longing and searching aspect is as clear as its decision-making function. We have a vision – often just a projection – try to achieve it, but find out quite soon that the goal is a long-term one. We must develop our willpower if we don't want to give up half way. The longing and searching should give way to efforts to achieve personal intellectual results. The aspect then has a decision-making influence, causing developmental processes that can transform the whole personality.

Green aspects work directly on our consciousness. Consciousness, a much broader term than thinking, is formed by processing all experiences, including thought processes, sensory perceptions, feelings and sensations that arouse the intuition and supply the consciousness with inner knowledge. Green aspects make us sensitive and receptive to new thoughts.

Both green aspects have a particular significance in developmental psychology, because they are the primary switch points of consciousness, in which acute learning processes take place. Learning therefore also means achieving decision-making processes and abilities. The green aspects provide many opportunities for decision-making. They are mainly about acts of cognition: bringing about spiritual purification, achieving awareness and making decisions.

Colour Choice for Conjunction 0°

It is hard to attribute a colour to the conjunction because it can be red, blue or green, and in our computer horoscopes we actually draw it in orange. The choice of colour depends on the planets involved, for example Venus and Jupiter for the blue aspect and a red aspect for Mars to symbolise the energy present. Green suits the Mercury/Jupiter conjunction, it always sees both sides of an issue. Even clearer is the Mercury/Saturn conjunction; it is neutral. This planetary conjunction does not really stand for anything, it just notices objectively, factually and thoroughly. Attributing colours to the conjunction is not as important for the interpretation as understanding planetary qualities.

In a conjunction, two components have an undifferentiated connection. The qualities of the two planets are so close together; it is as if they were stuck together with glue. It is hard for the human consciousness to separate them. For a person with a conjunction in their chart, this feels like a new planet that has not existed before. It is as if two planets disappear and then merge to form something new. The interpretation given to this quality by the person concerned is crucial as to whether it helps him or hinders him.

A conjunction can make one compulsive. One acts under compulsion because one has no interior knowledge at all to differentiate, and is then simply compelled to act. Many conjunctions have the effect that we make quite specific evaluations and have no idea where they come from.

Close and Wide Conjunctions

There are close and wide conjunctions, and the limit lies at around 3°; beyond that is a wide conjunction. With a wide conjunction, it is easier and quicker to separate the components. The greater the distance between two planets, in general the more clearly one can distinguish between them and keep them apart.

For example, if the conjunction lies on one side of an opposition aspect, which is the furthest distance between two planets, then the tendency is just to observe the planets in the conjunction and not to live them. The conjunction planets mostly remain latent. The distance between two planets shows how clearly they can be differentiated.

A Basic Rule is that distance creates overview and visibility. The conjunction is the worm's-eye view; the opposition is the bird's-eye view, and in between are variations.

2.5 Influence of Planets on the Aspects

In the aspects, the different planetary principles generally influence each other and are in a reciprocal relationship. One of the best presentations of this subject is in the book by Thomas Ring: *Astrological Anthropology*, volume III, Combination Theory (27). The evaluation of the aspect generally depends both on the rules explained above and on the linked planetary qualities. To clarify this, we must make a meaningful classification of the planets.

Feminine, Masculine and Neutral Planets

With this classification we can immediately establish whether planets harmonise with each other or have different qualities. On the Planet Table on the following page the planets are organised into three columns, showing us which planets are compatible and which are not.

The planets on the left, i.e. Venus, Saturn and Uranus are considered feminine; Mars, Sun and Pluto on the right are considered masculine; Mercury, Jupiter, Moon and Neptune in the middle column behave neutrally. Planets in the same column are similar in quality and motivation and complement or support each other, although they can be quite different in their way of functioning and reacting. Planets that form aspects to planets in other columns have conflicting qualities and cause problems and tensions that reflect this.

Hard and Soft Planets

There is another important distinction in aspect interpretation, which is that the ten planets are separated into soft (sensitive) and hard (achievement-orientated). This distinction also shows us whether or not the basic qualities of planets are compatible or not.

    a) Soft, sensitive planets:
        Moon, Mercury, Venus, Jupiter and Neptune
    b) Hard, achievement-oriented planets
        Sun, Mars, Saturn, Uranus and Pluto

Aspect Influence on Soft Planets

Soft planets react harmoniously with blue and green aspects, as they correspond to their character. They sometimes only really get a look in with red aspects because these have an activating influence upon them. But it is more common for the red aspects to irritate the soft planets and

Planet Table

	CREATIVE INTELLIGENCE	ALL – LOVE (Christ)	SPIRITUAL WILL
DEVELOPING AREA / ASPIRATIONS / **SPIRITUAL GROWTH** — Spiritual Level / Superconscious Realm	MOTHER ⛢ IMAGO — Occultist / Methodology / Ideal of the perfect world / Organising	CHILD ♆ IMAGO — Mystic / Mediation / Ideal of unconditional love / Serving	FATHER ♇ IMAGO — Magician / Metamorphosis / Ideal of the perfect human being / Creating
PERSONALITY (EGO) / ROLES OF THE EGO / Interests and Motivation — Personal Levels / Daily awareness	**BODY** Self-Confidence — Immunity housekeeping MOTHER ♄ Security closing heteronomous	**FEELING** You-awareness — Sensitivity learning CHILD ☽ Sympathy opening ambivalent	**MENTALITY** Self-awareness — Vitality growing FATHER ☉ Mental capacity radiating autonomous
Drive-Instinct = Achievements / **LIFE-SUSTAINING FUNCTIONS** — Animal levels / Subliminal realm	**Enjoying** AESTHETIC ♀ — Assimilation Selection Woman Fruitfulness	**Learning** SENSORY — DEDUCTIVE ☿ Formulation Information / Human Receptivity / Evaluation Perception ♃	**Achieving** MOTOR ACTIVITY ♂ — Achievement Activity Man Potency
	Feminine / Matter / Holy Spirit / Shiva	Neutral / Awareness / Son / Vishnu	Male / Spirit / Father / Brahma

© API

lead to bad reactions, hypersensitivity and exaggeration. Of course, it depends on whether we want to develop ourselves or whether we oppose internal or external change that can totally change everything.

Aspect Influence on the Hard Planets

Hard planets react particularly strongly to red aspects because their characteristics are compatible. The intrinsic strength of these planets is activated and can be used appropriately in the outside world. Green and blue aspects irritate the hard planets; they often paralyse them or evoke feelings of anxiety. They can also have a refining effect though, thus softening their harshness. Some people do not react to them at all.

Unaspected Planets

There are planets that are not aspected. There is much discussion about this and the way they are evaluated largely depends on how they are approached. It is a fact that an unaspected planet lies in isolation with its psychic power and has no connections with other planets to modify it. It is neither repressed nor stimulated and can be itself. As it has no connection to the rest of the aspect pattern, its contents also remain a mystery to the person. This planetary quality is not incorporated into the structure of consciousness, so the person concerned does not experience it as an integrated part of his core. Even in this case, a clear concept can be obtained with a four-dimensional interpretation.

On the first level, the material, there is mostly an unconscious essential strength. We have no idea that these planets exist; such a planet just functions as an autonomous mechanism and is to a large extent experienced by the environment. In the partnership comparison, these planets want to click with a partner, which we can see from the Click horosocope (14). In the case of the spiritual planets Uranus, Neptune, Pluto, in many cases there is a superego, which enforces collective norms, which this person is subject to without thinking about it.

On the second level, the feeling level, this planet is experienced as a failure, an inability or a deficiency in conflictive situations. We notice that something is missing and start to be interested in it, thus starting what is often a painful learning process that awakens awareness.

Only on the third level, the mental thinking level, have we gathered enough knowledge about it to enable it to be used freely, without being "distorted" by aspects with other planets. It has been statistically established that such a planet works brilliantly.

The fourth transformed level is demonstrated by a successful female author with an unaspected Mercury in her horoscope. She dealt mainly with the problems of mankind, and skilfully wrote about the path of evolution and development, thus preparing the hearts of men for the spirit of the age. So she should have reached the transformed fourth **level**, in which the personality takes on the luminosity of the unaspected planet.

Aspect Interpretation in Nine Steps

As you can see, the evaluation of the aspect depends on different factors. It is best to proceed as follows:

1. Establish the angle 0, 30, 60, 90, 120,150, 180
2. Which of the three colours is the aspect?
3. With which planets is it connected?
4. Does it have an aspect to one single planet?
5. Is it part of an aspect figure? If so, which one?
6. Is it a detached single aspect?
7. Does it project as a line from the aspect figure?
8. Is this person working consciously on himself?
9. What degree of freedom has he reached?

2.6 Four Dimensional Aspect Interpretation

Another method of holistic interpretation is a three or four-dimensional view, as we have already introduced in other horoscope elements. This consists of a division of our sensory universe into four levels: physical, emotional, mental and spiritual. In this four-dimensional view, we are not interested in planets and figures, but in aspects themselves.

We interpret the aspects initially according to the three levels of our experience: 1. from undifferentiated physical impressions, 2. from the psychic and emotional constitution, 3. from the autonomous mental consciousness. The fourth level is reached after the transformation of selfish motives into humanitarian goals or, in other words, when our awareness has transformed from the small ego to the higher self. In this way, we can also see this four-dimensionality as a gradual development process that first has to be understood.

Stages of Development

The first stage corresponds to physical awareness; here we should be concerned with the preservation of our existence. This stage is used for self-preservation and the satisfaction of our natural needs. If the awareness is anchored at this stage, one is largely controlled by circumstances, dependent on others, and takes what is available. Many people do not even realise that they could free themselves from impulses, but rather take them for granted. It is the saturnine level.

At the second stage, we come into conflict with existing norms; we wake up and rebel against determining conditions, e.g. regulations, bans and claims. It is the rebellion against internal and external pressures; we want to free ourselves from the chains that bind us, which leads us into conflict. It is the stage of antagonism and duality, throughout which we are embroiled again and again in bitter disputes. It is a fruitful learning period in which more information can be gained about reality. Nothing is stable here, all is flux. The stage corresponds to the feeling level and thus the lunar phases of ebb and flow.

The third stage brings us to the mental area, where we start to understand, to think and to be able to make our own decisions. The will is awakened and is activated by the increased sense of identity. A phase of self-awareness, self-examination and identification follows. In the awakened consciousness, we learn to be creative and to build our own destinies. We make free space for our own development and are mainly preoccupied with actualising our own plans and goals. It is the phase of autonomous, self-contained solar energy.

The transformation stage (4ᵗʰ stage) requires a certain separation from the attachments, desires and compulsions of the three personality levels, so that the aspect influence relates to transpersonal goals and tasks that serve society. The transformation stage raises the effect of the aspect to the spiritual area, where personal creativity, responsibility and investment in the evolutionary plan are required.

We can derive many rules of interpretation from these laws of development, which represent a rich source for the correct connections. We learn to see for ourselves on which of the three levels our consciousness is stuck and in which direction we should develop.

We would now like to extend the aspect theory and to describe it in detail on the four levels. This is only a theoretical presentation of the aspects, not an interpretation of their content.

The Conjunctions on 4 Levels ♂

On the physical level, the 1st stage, a conjunction is perceived as inner strength. There is a doubling, a strengthening, which is why a concentration of energy is felt as a physical experience. The conjunction then resembles a bundle of energy that convinces the person concerned that he has an enormous reservoir of energy inside him that he can easily put to use when the time is right. But when energies work so closely together, they can be hard to distinguish and it is very easy to overestimate their strength.

On the emotional level, the 2nd stage, the conjunction evokes a strong egoism or subjectivity. This also affects some people as mental inflexibility and lack of differentiation. It convinces many people that they possess special abilities that other people cannot appreciate. They imagine that they have a special hidden power that they will use when the time is right.

On the mental level, the conjunction causes a powerful increase in energy; giving the idea that one is a very special person, unique and unequalled. From the consciousness and the mental area comes the impression: "I am powerful and possess magical charisma; no one knows who I really am. I will show you when the time is right".

The transformed conjunction works as a reservoir of abilities in the mental area and as a source of inspiration. Suddenly energies can awaken and flow out into creative works as inspiration. Those around us are astonished at the inspirational abundance that has suddenly appeared. But not necessarily, for inspiration and creative activity require the deployment of higher levels of consciousness, as they come from above, as the phrase poetically goes. Sometimes the energy potential is also activated by fateful events, but is only available while the situation lasts, only to sink back into the subconscious afterwards.

The Semi-Sextile on 4 Levels ⚺

On the physical level, the 1ˢᵗ stage, the semi-sextile, being the Mercurial small thinking step is not suited to starting large operations. It is at the experimental stage and easily loses perspective, is easily influenced and cannot see the wood for the trees. So on the physical level, this Mercury aspect makes people insecure and irritable. The small green aspect is like a quicksilver messenger that runs around and collects information, without passing judgement and misjudging. It constantly relativises and neutralises and throws everything into a pot and easily loses the overall perspective.

On the emotional level, the 2ⁿᵈ stage, the semi-sextile aspect is pure curiosity. The effect of this emotional component is that such a person is driven around all over the place and absolutely must be in on everything in order to keep his curiosity satisfied. If this works emotionally and his curiosity is satisfied, he leaves it at that. There is frequently emotional insecurity, and one never knows exactly what one wants. Many people let themselves be influenced, blinded and misled by a stronger will. In many issues, the person concerned lacks a firm point of view, often changes opinion and asks everyone for advice.

On the mental level, the 3ʳᵈ stage, this Mercurial aspect is rational and adaptive. Knowledge is gathered with the hope of being able to use it at some point. These are similar qualities to the sign of Gemini, as Mercury is the planetary ruler of this sign, resulting in the ability to combine and the desire to pass on what has been learnt and to exchange information. Although much information has been collected, it is easily forgotten. What was previously said or promised is also often forgotten.

The transformed Mercury aspect can be seen as a very special source of information. Wherever the thinking is directed, it receives exactly the information it needs. We are often led there unknowingly and in the bookshop find just the right book that has something to say to us. We are also ready and willing to pass on all information so that it can benefit the general public and not just ourselves.

The Sextile on 4 Levels ✶

On the physical level, 1ˢᵗ stage, a sextile creates the desire for material comfort. One tends towards complacency and lets others do all the work. One does not want to be torn away from harmony and complacency and reacts sensitively to any disturbance. That is why there is often a significant demand for consistent procedures, for a fashionable appearance and for money, possessions and affluence.

On the emotional level, 2ⁿᵈ stage, a sextile aspect mainly feels the attractions of beauty and harmony. One is in touch with the female libido, the feminine and the Fine Arts. The feelings are attuned to perfection and to the "certain something" that makes life worthwhile. "Only the best is good enough" is often the motto for people whose Ego planets (Sun, Moon, Saturn) are connected with this aspect. No arguments or unpleasantness are tolerated, and are in fact studiously avoided. People with a sextile on the emotional level are good company, due to their love of harmony; but they are also critical and dismissive of other's ugliness, imperfections and mistakes. They avoid roughness and do not tolerate aggression or conflict.

On the mental level, the 3rd stage, the sextile is experienced as a certain aestheticism. There is a search for harmonious relationships and an aesthetic philosophy. There is a desire for the happiness derived from the merging of minds to be expressed in an ideology or in art. This results in aesthetic endeavours and idealistic pretensions. This harmonious, cultural way of thinking of the Venus aspect can easily be influenced by a strong personality. If the style and the forms agree, the influence is not so easily avoided, but they are rejected at the slightest disagreement.

The transformed sextile effectively leaves behind the ego area of the three-dimensional world. Here the sextile conveys the ability to present things as perfectly, precisely and clearly as possible. It is the ability to find a certain synthesis in all things and to show conformity. Love between people is proclaimed and perfection and justice are pursued intensively. This harmonious, Venusian philosophy is easy to deal with, and conveys trust and fairness once a false willingness to compromise has been overcome.

The Square on 4 Levels □

On the physical level, the 1st stage, this aspect has the physical energy, strength and the ability to achieve. Top sports people need this aspect, as do soldiers, who must obey orders blindly and do what they are told without questioning. On this level, this aspect is undifferentiated activity, the unquestioned turnover of energy. It is like an engine that transfers energy. That is why people with a lot of squares on this level are fighters. Of course it also depends on the planets that are connected in the square. But the square itself is already masculine; there is a virile strength that wants to get things done. On the physical level, the square has a rather undifferentiated Martian influence, a strength that is used whenever conflict or fanaticism prevail.

On the emotional level, the 2nd stage, the square has a stimulating and mostly unbalancing effect. The feelings are excited and stimulated by a square. When nothing is happening, we become uneasy and have the feeling of having missed something, often driven by anxieties and also by feelings of guilt. These people are self-driven and never come to rest until they have done everything asked of them. On an emotional level, they react with a certain sensitivity to possible setbacks, and with euphoria and passion to contact and love. There is a hunger for success that drives them uncontrollably and embroils them in conflict. The fighting spirit can also be excited, when provoked.

Only at the mental level, the 3rd stage, is the square experienced as energy-tension. It mostly provokes consciousness processes, so that we learn on the thinking level how to handle conflict. It is mostly a matter of a confrontation of the forces of polarity, which are handled intelligently. This is more a function of thinking than of feeling. The conflict is then a necessary consequence, above all when one is dealing more closely with existing intellectual problems. There is a desire to know why things are not right and make an effort to find ways to get out of the conflict. If the horoscope shows several squares, there can be a certain enjoyment of conflict. Such people often need a conflictive situation to win something. They tend to create conflicts because they think that otherwise nothing is happening. Only by asserting resistance or opposition can they come to a real dispute. If a person has no squares in his horoscope, he lacks this strength and avoids disputes and conflicts.

The transformed square is free from the libidinal uncontrolled activity impulse. Energy is not dissipated, but used intelligently to achieve goals and accomplish something that did not exist before. They want to find solutions for existing problems and do away with old states, they get things and people moving to make improvements, no effort is spared to eliminate problems. The economical and intelligent use of energy always achieves something. It is a feature of the successful entrepreneurial spirit to have mental energy. The transformed square gives an energy-charged thinking power and even convinces dissenters.

The Trine on 4 Levels △

On the physical level, the 1st stage, with the trine, the blue Jupiter aspect, there is a pronounced need for calm and well-being, for the maintenance of the status quo. It is a question of security. They would like to maintain and enjoy everything just as it is. This leads to a certain physical inertia. Someone who is in an optimal situation does not strive for improvement, because the existing one is actually good enough. This leads to satiety, and often to idleness.

On the emotional level, the 2nd stage, there is a very pleasant trine. This lucky and enjoyable situation can be fully savoured. The feeling of luck is the reason why in traditional astrology the trine was called the lucky aspect. But for many people, the trine causes a state of stagnation and listlessness. If one already has everything, effort is no longer required and there is a danger of becoming passive, easy-going or even resigned. Some take it for granted that their fellow men will serve and help them.

On the mental level, the 3rd stage, the trine signifies the ripened fruit, the perfection of a state or a talent. When two or three planets function mentally in a trine, there is complete balance and transcendence. But also on the mental level, the state of abundance leads to stagnation and standstill. So the person thinks they already know everything; nothing surprises them any longer and they know everything in advance. This leads to complacency; mental pride and the refusal to develop oneself further because one thinks one has already reached the highest level of development.

The transformed trine yields the fully ripened fruit of all preceding efforts. This aspect pours its horn of plenty over us, raises awareness, provides an overall picture and allows us to discover transpersonal connections. There is therefore a positive and healthy reaction to all external and internal processes. Abilities can be optimally and abundantly implemented and exploited. Success is possible right down the line. There is freedom from personal desires and thanks to this serenity one gains the trust of one's fellow man. If one is no longer driven by ambition, aspirations for power or any kind of deficiency, one reaches an optimum stage, a state of perfection, balance and happiness, but also wisdom.

The Quincunx on 4 Levels ⚻

The quincunx aspect is, like the semi-sextile, a thinking aspect and also a three-dimensional one. Because thinking aspects are hard to understand, and there is hardly any information in the literature as to how to evaluate them, they are particularly interesting. We have already written about them in the previous chapter, and in *Life Clock* (17) a whole chapter is devoted to them.

On the physical level, the 1st stage, the 150° angle is a factor of insecurity. As a thinking aspect, it is not easy to implement physically. People with many green aspects very often just leave work they are asked to do; they put it off for a better day. On the physical and emotional levels, the quincunx generates digressive thoughts, unclear goals, illusions, projections and castles in the air. This delays and unsettles the fulfilment process. Things that they want to tackle are postponed again and again, and are only completed after much indecision and rumination. Often, it is enough just to visualise a goal, a place or a situation. The visualisation is important, but it is not necessary to reach the goal. They like to wallow in their thoughts and fantasies and often find that satisfying enough. Without knowing what they should do exactly, they have the vague feeling that they were born for something better. They are easily influenced and mostly only do what others expect from them. They willingly submit to a stronger will – at least until they know what they want. They are seekers, driven on by an undefined longing.

On the emotional level, the 2nd stage, it has the effect of a longing aspect, as described by Thomas Ring in his books (27). It is a feeling in which all one's wishing power tends towards an undefined state that is actually a goal but cannot really be aimed for. One either underreaches, or overreaches in the case of excessive longing. It is a reaching out for something out of a vague longing.

On the 2nd **stage** we find ourselves in a doubting phase. Although at first we enjoy our dreams and projections, with time we are seized with a nagging doubt as to whether everything is right as it is. Then we start to think, to ask and to philosophise. An almost Faustian struggle starts, with all the doubts and corresponding crises of belief. The truth has so many faces; we see so many possibilities and easily lose ourselves in relativising. We cannot decide at all what is less valuable than the best and most beautiful that we can imagine, and fall into an intense crisis of indecision.

On the mental level, the 3rd stage, the long green thinking aspect has a particular awareness-forming effect. It activates uninterrupted thinking processes. Making a choice requires decision-making ability. That is why the acquisition of this ability is worth aspiring to, and is something everyone should develop. It is the most important function of thinking and the whole development of intelligence. The large thinking step of the quincunx aspect collects and extracts the essence of many experiences. Not until the individual has gone through crises of indecision and has dealt intensively with existing conflicts or objects can he make a choice and separate the significant from the insignificant. What happens next is very interesting. Decisions are only made when the will is activated. The will function on the mental level of the quincunx aspect is what makes choices and opts for what is important for personal development; everything else is rejected and eventually eliminated.

But there are dangerous obstacles here too. If we do not undergo this three-stage development process, and do not decide according to the laws of inner growth, a long green aspect can take the decision away from us with an incident corresponding to the quality of the planet concerned. In modern astrological literature, the quincunx aspect is also called "the Finger of God" and it has often brought harsh blows of fate to bear on the unreasonable or the indifferent. It is advisable to adapt oneself early on to the developmental quality of the quincunx aspect and especially to prepare oneself for Age Point aspects (17).

The transformed quincunx aspect means the ability to carry out independent thought processes and to find creative, inventive solutions. At this stage we are both flexible and autonomous. We recognise that it is up to us whether we achieve a goal or not. Now we can confine ourselves to one thing, one matter, even if this means limiting our freedom, our fantasies or our ideal vision. Here the long green aspect becomes the Will aspect. The increased concentration intensifies thinking on a specific issue, brings everything together that belongs together and rounds off the whole thing. It is a new, synthetically-orientated thinking process, where the accumulated knowledge yields results both in the detail and in the context. We do make progress down a long, hard path though, which is why this is also called the Development aspect.

The Opposition on 4 Levels ☍

On the physical level, the 1st stage, there is a real polarity; after all, the opposition is formed by two planets lying opposite each other. In the horoscope it is shown as a red line. It works as a blocking aspect at the level of physical experience, and produces a feeling of rigidity, of being stuck. One feels rooted to the spot. In life that can manifest itself physically in many possible ways, such as stubbornness, mistakes, misjudgements. If one easily identifies oneself with one pole, the other is suppressed and thought of as the enemy. The polarity calls for combat, in which the energies are channelled in the wrong direction. Depending on the house axis, this produces anxieties, defensive behaviour and fanaticism, which have nothing at all to do with reality. Tilting against windmills, fighting against imagined enemies, defensiveness as a form of attack: all of these are bad attitudes that result from an unresolved opposition.

On the emotional level, the 2nd stage, the polarisation is already a little weaker, because there is some flexibility from the feeling element. The Moon is changeable and is classified as a water principle. There is an oscillation, swinging from one pole to another, when the polarity becomes a real duality. One is victimised from both sides, according to which planet is stronger at the time. Because the opposition passes through the core, one often feels penetrated and suffers from anxieties. But the opposition, as a red aspect, contains a lot of energy that can sometimes erupt explosively and cause both disasters and creative power. But at this stage the energy discharge is nearly always provoked by anxiety.

Only on the mental level, the 3rd stage, does the opposition as a source of energy lead to intense intellectual conflict, in which the tension felt inside would like to take over. Firstly there is an either/or attitude. People with strong oppositions are very argumentative. They are uncompromising; things are either black or white and there is nothing in between. This tension can be unbearable and painful, and the mental consciousness develops a process of seeking liberation from it, culminating in its repression. As already mentioned, the opposition is also a repression aspect. With the power to block, freeze and stop, the painful situation can be repressed from the mind into the subconscious. Only when other elements in the horoscope cooperate with it, when it is pondered long enough or the opposition is diluted by blue or green aspects in the horoscope, comes the realisation that the polarities in life do not represent these combating forces but that they are an antagonism.

The transformed opposition is a real source of inner strength. It gives backbone, solidity and stable behaviour. The opposition no longer runs straight through the core personality and does not cause pain and anguish, but instead now receives a powerful energy supply directly from the inner core. Antagonism has given way to complementarity; one pole needs the other and they can only be used in a creative and constructive way if they work together.

Brief Overview

The brief overview of four-dimensional aspect reading that follows is a short definition that everyone can add to. Everyone should try to check, investigate and experience these statements for themselves, for every astrologer is also a researcher after all.

Conjunction
1st stage: Egoism, concentration, complex formation
2nd stage: Sensation of power, lack of differentiation, latency
3rd stage: Magical power, source of inspiration
4th stage: Reservoir of strength, creativity, budding

Semi-Sextile
1st stage: Excitability, nervousness, insecurity
2nd stage: Curiosity, adaptation, eager to learn
3rd stage: Lively interest, intelligence
4th stage: Source of information, intuitive knowing

Sextile
1st stage: Need for comfort, fashion sense, convenience
2nd stage: Striving for harmony, fear of conflict, compromises
3rd stage: Perfectionism, aesthetic, beauty
4th stage: Fair attitude, synthesis and perfection

Square
1st stage: Energy, achievement, activity
2nd stage: Arguing, conflict and fighting
3rd stage: Physical strength, euphoria, assertion
4th stage: Intelligent use of energy, realising goals

Trine
1st stage: Need for peace, inertia, satiety
2nd stage: Enjoyment, feeling of luck, pleasure
3rd stage: Optimal abundance, transcendence, serenity
4th stage: The horn of plenty runs over, inspiring trust and goodness

Quincunx
1st stage: Insecurity, wandering around, projecting
2nd stage: Longing, doubt, slight irritability
3rd stage: Crises of indecision, decision-making
4th stage: Creativity, finding solutions in the context

Opposition
1st stage: Blocking, freezing, repression
2nd stage: Polarisation, either-or attitude
3rd stage: Reserves of strength, antagonism, backbone
4th stage: Transcending polarity, the middle way

3. Aspect Pattern Astrology

3.1 Holistic Astrological Methods
3.2 Traces in the Sands of Time
3.3 Rules for Aspect Pattern Interpretation
3.4 Basics of Aspect Pattern Astrology

3.1 Holistic Astrological Methods

It is well-known that astrology, like other disciplines, is based on asking questions. This means that we develop appropriate methods to know what we want from the horoscope. It is obvious that questions about luck and success require different methods than do the solving of psychological or mental problems.

Over the centuries, the questions and hence also the astrological techniques and schools have changed continually, according to shifting cultures and the condition of man's awareness. Along the way, many have become out-dated and a hindrance rather than a help. Nowadays there is a whole range of schools offering different methods, which can often be confusing for those interested in astrology. Choose a type of astrology by answering the initial clarifying question "What do I want to know from the horoscope?" not according to whether one type is "better" than the others.

New Questions - New Methods

Nowadays people are asking new questions. More and more people are studying astrology in order to gain a better understanding of themselves and those close to them. They are interested in astrology because life no longer satisfies them, and they hope to be able to solve their problems with the aid of astrology. Others want to go deeper and find the meaning of life, their true identity or their higher self. They want to discover their karma and understand the destination route of their incarnation.

They strive for inner growth and the rejection of incorrect ideas and behaviour patterns; they shoulder rejections and crises, purification phases and transformation processes in order to reach the essence of their being. They are interested in all conformity to natural laws that relates to this, and they are enthusiastic readers and learners. For a holistic and profound psychological horoscope interpretation, integrative methods must be used which answer questions like "Who am I? Where am I coming from? Where am I going to?"

The Huber Method

The concept of astrological psychology expressed in the Huber Method is based on holistic principles. The psychological background is the knowledge of depth psychology, along with humanistic and transpersonal psychology. It is closest to Roberto Assagioli's psychosynthesis. In astrological psychology, we work from a psychosynthetic concept of an organic, self-regulating and thus subjectively healthy being, not clinical pictures. Values such as good and bad are avoided on principle. We have abandoned the outdated and contradictory methods of traditional astrology.

The Huber Method of horoscope interpretation is mainly concerned with the integrative, i.e. holistic understanding of the individual, not with the analytical process. The astrological-psychological methodology follows the holistic requirement that all parts must balance and complement each other. As such, the method has internal coherence, but is not closed to further developments and refinements. One of the most important innovations to be developed by the Astrological Psychology Institute is Aspect Pattern Astrology. It has been tested and corroborated in a teaching and consulting context over many years. Aspect Pattern Astrology is the interpretation of the aspect pattern as a pattern for consciousness and motivation.

The Complete Aspect Pattern

Aspects are the angles that separate the planets from each other; they have been known in astrology since ancient times. They used to be given mainly in tabular form, and rarely plotted directly on the horoscope. They now give a direct overview, a pattern, a model, whose very uniqueness makes them invaluable, without even considering the planets which form the pattern and their house and sign position.

These aspects were formerly only categorised as good-bad, harmonious-inharmonious, tense-easy; this approach is now rejected as psychologically unsound. There are no "good" or "bad" aspects; instead each aspect possesses certain defined qualities that are seen as challenge, opportunity, talent or sensitivity. As explained in the previous chapter, the 30 degree angle and its multiples have proved to be fundamental in the character structure of the individual. Intermediate angles (45, 72, 135 degrees) are not plotted in the API School, they are recognised as gaps in the horoscope and can be interpreted accordingly. The aspects are not interpreted in isolation, but rather in their figurative connection to other planets.

Diagram of Consciousness

The aspect pattern as a whole can give immediate information about the proportions and profile of the personality of the individual. It is understood as a diagram of consciousness, showing the deep, unconscious motivations of the individual. The aspect pattern of most individuals is unconscious, as this structure lies directly around the centre of the character. It is concealed beneath the layer of the twelve signs of the zodiac, far removed from the house system, which is the sphere of the daily consciousness. We spend almost all day living in the house system. From the moment we wake up in the morning and open our eyes, we are relating to an environment in which we remain until we go back to sleep. It is no wonder then, that the aspect pattern of many people is not accessible, in any case until it is dealt with consciously, hence the importance of learning something about the deeper meaning of the aspect pattern.

Uniqueness

First of all, we must know that the overall aspect pattern represents the individual in its uniqueness and individuality. It shows the "inner picture of the person", is something hidden that would like to develop and manifest itself in this world. In the aspect pattern, we find the building blocks available to each one of us to structure our lives in our own way; to cope with our problems, discover our talents, to use our learning aptitude and to become a responsible individual. The aspect pattern reveals the inner life, the predispositions and also how this inner life can be exteriorised. It shows in which areas the person is successful and where he is blocked or feels misunderstood. It is the art of the astrologer to interpret this pattern both in its complexity and in its wholeness.

Form Evaluation

In the overall view of the aspect pattern, a basic theme can usually be established that is either more dynamic or more static. In this classification one can and should trust one's intuition and aesthetic sensitivity. Quadrilaterals have a static character, triangles are dynamic, and with aspects not forming closed figures the so-called linear figure represents an increased dynamism. The symmetry of an aspect pattern is also important; the more symmetrical it is, the more static. The more asymmetrical a figure is, the more dynamic is the individual's character.

Colour Expression

In this splitting into three of the dynamic-static approach, we again find the three basic motivations cardinal, fixed and mutable, which exist as crosses in the signs and houses and act as qualities via the planets and aspects. These motivations are immediately recognisable in the three-colour presentation of the aspects: the red aspects (opposition and square) are cardinal energy aspects, the blue (sextile and trine) are latent vehicles for talents (fixed) and the green, mutable (semi-sextile and quincunx) are information and consciousness forming sensitive aspects.

To analyse the whole structure we use a form, colour and spatial code. The latter is the result of the position of the aspect structure in the quadrants, so that a more conscious, awareness-orientated way of life (above the horizon) is distinguished from a more unconscious, action-orientated (below). In the combination of the form and colour codes, for example, latent blue aspects which stand on their own can have a dynamic character in linear figures, while square red figures can act statically. However, it cannot be emphasised enough that a final evaluation can only be made by the most accurate observation and reflection. We will deal with this in more detail later on.

Relationship to the Centre of Being

We now consider the relationship between the inner centre (core of the personality) and the aspects involved with it, especially the opposition, as it passes through the centre. The nearer the aspects point to the centre, the more the subject matter of the inner personality can be recognised and detached; the further they point outwards, the stronger the influence of the environment on the configuration of that subject matter. The aspects are also to be understood as antennae for communication from the inner core (divine radio) to the everyday personality, to which its wisdom and energy are transmitted.

Therefore, especially in the opposition, there is a permanent decision to be made as to whether to open up to the influences of the core or not. By taking up these energies one can better understand the subject matter of the axis and transcend it. By denying the inner essence, the problematic nature of the opposition is fought against and the ego is trapped in its selfishness. This splits the polarity into a duality, from which the individual suffers and is eventually caught at one pole and represses the other pole out of his consciousness. This is how the opposition aspect becomes an energy blockage and takes on the character of a blockade of the soul that may possibly be compensated for by other aspects. The other aspects should then be considered in order of their distance from the inner core.

What does Kepler say about this?

It is interesting what Kepler has to say about the aspects: *"An aspect is effective when the radiation from two planets forms an angle, which is able to stimulate the nature of the earth under the moons and the lower powers/faculties of animate beings so that at the time of this configuration have an increased activity."* From further remarks by Kepler, it emerges that it is not the aspects themselves that are effective, but people's reaction to them. Their effect lies outside the senses; it is transcendent, i.e. extrasensory or psychic. The aspect resembles sensory perceptions only insofar as it can be compared to signals that flash rhythmically. The only ones to react to the signals are those that are inwardly deeply moved by them. So as such the aspect lies outside the general relationship of cause and effect. This potential existence of the aspects, with their character of only existing in the event of reactions, was interpreted by Kepler to the effect that the aspect is a geometrical relationship between two light rays here on earth and can therefore not be physically comprehended, a connection of special quality and energy. So the whole aspect pattern represents a structure of the consciousness of the person concerned. It is an energy field with a specific radiation. Every aspect figure has its intrinsic value. One way of clarifying this is to compare it to the laws of music.

Analogy with Sound

For example, in the Dominant Triangle (page 187), consisting of a square, a quincunx and a trine, we have a very special chord, the dominant chord. Kepler's genius was to explain harmonic relationships in mathematical terms. So he succeeded in discovering his three basic planetary laws. As the harmony of the planets is revealed in the aspects, aspect figures are the most important means of illustrating this. In the *"Harmony of the World"*, Kepler developed his third and most important planetary law from the observation of the harmony of the planets that play within the intervals of the third, quarter-tone, quintuplet, etc. It is not far-fetched to compare the whole aspect pattern to a composition in which we recognise a basic melody that accompanies people throughout their lives. From the aspect pattern, the keynote, the building blocks and the person's life motivation become visible. Particular abilities and possibilities are contained in individual horoscope aspect figures, likes and dislikes, questions that stir a person again and again afresh and also involve him in the appropriate fateful events.

3.2 Traces in the Sands of Time

Conception Horoscope

Astrologers often ask whether the conception horoscope, which is charted from the moment of conception, is not the true, correct one for the character and destiny. The issue has never had a valid, universally acceptable answer. This is not only due to the problem that in most cases people have no idea of their time of conception, although special methods for determining it do exist.

If we trace theoretically what happens in the planetary dance after the moment of conception, we see how in the nine months of pregnancy each one moves on in its own rhythm in the cosmic space around planet earth. Their comings and goings form many new aspect connections between planets. This means that the gravitational pattern (the gravitation field attracting all planets in the solar system to each other) is constantly moved and altered. Eventually, after the required 273 days, a form has been reached that leads to the birth of a quite distinct human being.

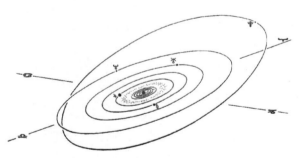

Planetary System

It is certainly correct to presume, even if it has not yet been researched scientifically, that the gravitational pull in the planetary system affects all the material existing in the system at any one time. This can be seen in the behaviour of the earth during drastic planetary configurations, e.g. volcanic eruptions and earthquakes, or of the sun in sun spot and flare activity. Quite specific patterns have quite specific effects. That has always been the astrological view. Individual patterns come and go. They do not remain as patterns but fade away again.

Some of them leave behind traces in the sands of time, in which they give certain materials such a fixed form that they take shape and remain for a relatively long time. If we apply this to human beings, we can say that we are traces in the sands of time that only exist for a short time in cosmic terms; newly-formed volcanoes live much longer!

Birth Chart

So the birth chart is the representation of the forces that form a person at the moment of birth, when he leaves the protection of the womb and is released into the influences of the world. The horoscope reveals the formative power potentials (the planets), their cosmic orientation (position in the zodiac) and in their terrestrial or geocentric radiation direction (position in the houses). The gravitational pattern that at this moment binds the power potentials together in a certain behaviour pattern, and therefore also controls them, is also represented in the birth chart in the form of the aspect structure or the aspect pattern.

In physics today, it is assumed that everything we can observe in the cosmic or earthly dimension in the way of processes and states can be reduced to the co-action of three principles.

Energy

Mass　　　　**Information**

For centuries, it was assumed that the energy – mass polarity was the all-explaining principle ("everything in the cosmos is either energy or mass, or an interrelated process"). That is why in astrology also the birth constellations are interpreted exclusively in terms of a concept of energy and, as such, were one-sidedly interpreted only as effects of energy. It will be clear from the author's previous comments that information can also be read in the horoscope, specifically in the aspect pattern!

Aspect Pattern

Interpreting separate aspects as relationship functions between two planets has been in current use in astrology since the time of Ptolemy. Some aspect figures, like the Grand Trine, Cosmic Cross or Dragon have been known to us since the Middle Ages. These were initially obtained by comparing degree numbers of different individual aspects, which naturally entailed additional work in the reading. Not until the 20th century did a new form of plotting the horoscope (round form) slowly catch on, which allowed the aspects to be incorporated into the birth chart and thus to be visible. Only in this way was it actually possible to understand the aspect structure as a whole.

It has been known for a long time then that a planet that is aspected to other planets is not to be interpreted in the same way as if were standing alone. Of course, every planet has its own character, which is modified by its position in a sign and house. One could characterise this as a colouring or also as a differentiation. So as humans we never experience a planet in its original pure quality. For it is well-known that it works differently in a summer sign than in a winter sign and incites us differently if it shines directly from a house above the horizon than if – because it lies below the horizon – it is first filtered through the earth below us.

This spatial orientation of individual planets gives us information about the "how" of their effectiveness, but not about the "why" of their location. We humans always ask why though, because things in life must always have meaning and sense for us. This is why the old esoteric saying went: "Whoever stops asking the question 'why' stops living". And another, equally ancient, insight said that sense can only be understood from the context, not by listing and describing the individual parts (however ample and precise this description is).

Astronomical Perspective

If it is tidy and methodical, the horoscope is a truthful image of all the important bodies in the solar system from a geocentric, i.e. subjective or earthbound point of view. The description of the individual parts says nothing about the whole solar system and what it is like. For if one wanted to draw conclusions from the character of the huge methane planet Jupiter for the whole solar system, the image would look substantially different than if it came from arid little Mercury, overheated due to its proximity to the Sun. If the two definitions were placed next to each other, the image of the planetary system would clash irreconcilably, and the inclusion of every other planetary analysis would not clarify the picture, but instead make it more unclear. So much for the astronomical point of view as an example.

Astrological Approach

With the astrological approach it is no different. The birth chart is the image of the whole person, and the isolated interpretation of all individual constellations eventually brings us to a very conflicting and therefore inconsistent image of a person, if we do not possess the generic terms that allow us to discover the position of the parts in the whole in their meaningful context from a higher perspective.

Structures

The aspect structure provides this superior perspective. It is like a diagram that makes sense of the arrangement of the planets in space by highlighting their functional interconnectedness. It is possible to identify the significance of this particular planetary configuration in this complex arrangement and control system of powers and substances. In other words, the aspect pattern is a relationship diagram in which the various communication paths between the planets enable certain characteristic reciprocal dependencies and interactions. All such co-operating units can and should produce achievements corresponding to their form.

The Aspect Pattern

The aspect pattern should not simply be seen in terms of energy like a plumbing or wiring system through which energy passes. Its function is much more special: it creates qualitative connections, it informs, orders and controls. Aspect structures can be viewed in isolation, i.e. without the planets inside them; they contribute information that cannot be provided by the definitions of planetary positions in signs and houses because they belong to another level that works according to different laws to those of energy and matter – or even those of information mentioned above. Aspects condition each other if they touch each other in a figure.

The laws that regulate aspects are geometrical or graphic, and the patterns can be linear, triangular or polygonal. Their significance is that they reveal motivations, how one wants to use the characteristics of the planets they contain, what kind of goals they aim for, what kind of qualities will be taken from life. As the lowest common denominator, the aspect structure can, on the whole, be seen as a direct impression of the individual's life motivation, in which the personal will to live can be identified or the meaning of a certain human life can be felt.

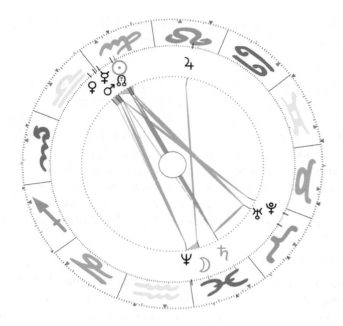

Swiss horoscope, Federal Constitution
12.9.1848, 10.42, Bern/Switzerland

Interpretation

The interpretation of the aspect pattern is firstly a visual, or graphic thing and secondly one of simple geometric logic. To be able to make valid, correctly proportioned statements, two different approaches must be cultivated:

1. The aspect pattern as a whole (also called aspect structure) must first of all be correctly understood and laid out, for as such it is the overriding genus. It shows us three basic types of motivation and their multiple possible combinations. Five criteria can be used for this.

2. Individual aspect figures, which have a more or less closed character (so-called functional circle), should in fact be defined in isolation, but only be interpreted under the generic term of the whole aspect pattern. More than 45 such aspect figures have been researched, written out and named up to now. They are the building blocks of the aspect pattern and will be described in detail in the following chapters.

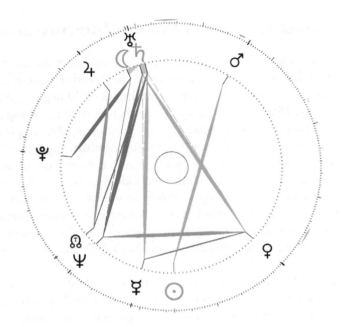

Arthur Garfunkel, American pop musician
5.11.1941, 23.00, New York/USA

The total statements that we can make about the aspect pattern and its constituent figures have great psychological importance and consequences. They cannot be made at all with the classical means of horoscope analysis. In the above example we can see clearly that the quincunx aspect between the Sun and Mars is separate from the rest of the aspect pattern. This fact alone is already significant for an individual's state of consciousness. In it we identify two different functional circles, or modes of behaviour, that are mostly experienced in alternation. In the life of this individual, this is expressed in a contradiction, now he lives in one figure, now in the other. This doesn't mean that the individual is schizophrenic. The two-fold motivation can be lived in alternation without too much difficulty. A large fund of experience has been developed over more than thirty years' work with aspect patterns and figures.

3.3 Rules for Aspect Pattern Interpretation

The rules for aspect pattern interpretation given below are essentially only true for horoscopes in which all angles concerned correspond to the classical zodiac division into twelve by multiples of 30 degrees (0°, 30°, 60°, 90°, 120°, 150° and 180°). Aspects which, for example, belong to the harmonic divisions, like the semi-square, quintile, septile, are products of other systems and should not be considered in this approach. Using them leads unfailingly to misinterpretations that do not correspond to the reality of the personality of the individual concerned. Of course it is conceivable that these angles also form aspect patterns that could be interpreted, but this would require a new code of interpretation. For example, the Harmonic System, originated by Englishman John Addey, is to some extent just such a code. Such different systems should definitely be used separately.

When reading aspect patterns, mixing of methods would lead to vague definitions, as each method is known to be geared towards certain questions. Our approach requires charts generated according to the Huber-Koch method.

Aspects to the AC, MC

What is more, it is not advisable to use aspects to the Ascendant (AC), to the Midheaven (MC) or to other house cusps, for they would lead to a distortion of the aspect pattern, which could not fulfil the rules given here. Having said that, many years' experience have shown that the ascending Moon Node should be included in the pattern. This is a pragmatic conclusion, for which the author cannot find a satisfactorily logical reason.

Aspect pattern reading is firstly an art, and also a science. It is an art because we identify a pattern with our eyes and can interpret it with our intuition. One can often allegorically establish similarities of shape with structures from nature; occasionally there are also associations with human artefacts. It is also scientific in that the mind keeps learnable rules consistent in the context of a simple geometry and an added dimension of chromatics. These are the laws that we would like to present here.

Geometric Shapes

The first and most important difference that we must make is that there are only three basic forms that are important and which make basic statements: the line (or a combination of them – a linear figure), the triangle and the quadrilateral (or polygon). In this context the polygon grouping includes the pentagon and the hexagon.

Heptagons and above form a Diamond figure (page 207), in which a maximum of eleven sides, including aspects to the Moon Node, are possible.

| LINEAR | TRIANGULAR | QUADRANGULAR |

At first sight, an aspect pattern initially shows whether the figure as a whole roughly resembles a triangle, or a quadrilateral/ polygon, or whether it is exclusively composed of aspects arranged separately. These three main forms correspond to three types of motivations: 1. the linear type, 2. the triangular type, and 3. the quadrangular type. This is the basic distinction that we can make between people. The three are internally deeply formed by an innate attitude towards life that differs fundamentally from that of other people, and which has specific expectations from life and corresponding main objectives. These three different forms in the aspect pattern enable the identification of an individual's personal philosophy and motivation, even when this is often only partly known or even unconscious.

Linear Type

According to the law of graphics, the line represents a movement (from A to B). The linear type is therefore a person who is instinctively convinced that life is movement. So he always wants to be moving, will make an effort to accomplish something, wants to better himself, to achieve something and seeks expansion, growth and development. The well-known proverb "The devil makes work for idle hands" must come from this type, for states of standstill, quiet and lingering enjoyment make him downright nervous or even angry after a short while. He fails in his own efforts (and likes to blame others for it). So, according to his type, he can produce feats of physical, emotional or mental power or endurance that astonish others. But he needs recovery phases, which for him are not states of rest, which is why he likes to fill them (e.g. holidays) with activities like games and sports or cultural activities.

This judging oneself by one's achievements is not the same as the achievement philosophy acquired by our society and typical of our culture; instead it is the individual urge for action of the linear type. If there is peace and quiet for too long, something must happen, as symmetry and stillness are suspicious. It stinks of the rigidity of convention, of laziness behind the attractive façade, of the corruption of an oppressive system. Fighting against such states can lead to an enhanced experience of desire. But hell-raising can also degenerate into an end in itself.

This example for this type shows the linear figure in the horoscope of Wolfgang Amadeus Mozart. Mozart lived his whole life under a tremendous pressure to achieve. He created a large number of compositions, more than 40 symphonies and operas, many of which were masterpieces of the first order. His work was characterised by the richness and virtuosity of its melodies.

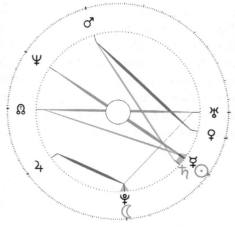

Wolfgang Amadeus Mozart
27.1.1756, 20.00 LT, Salzburg/Austria

Linear and Cardinal

If you are familiar with the three crosses of the zodiac, you will diagnose Mozart's horoscope as a linear figure and compare it to the cardinal cross. But this is only conditionally correct. There are also motivations to establish in the cross, but this is a question of the characteristics of a shape, not of motivation. Aspect pattern and crosses are on two different levels. On comparing the achievement motivation of linear types and cardinal types, it is clear that the urge to achieve of the cardinal cross is always goal-oriented; it is the final effect or the end product, reaching a goal, that is the motivation. So the achievement process can even be imperfect or superficial, as long as the result is ok!

This is not true of the linear aspect pattern, where the interesting thing is the process of movement itself. People of this type argue, sometimes almost philosophically, with sayings like "life is movement, perpetual change; what does not change is dead; all life is growth and expansion". Of course, movement can soon become an end in itself, and the search for change can become annoying for those around. Where there is a detached linear aspect pattern, it can lead to restlessness or fidgetiness and absent-mindedness (restless straying); dispersal of energy often leads to a loss of energy.

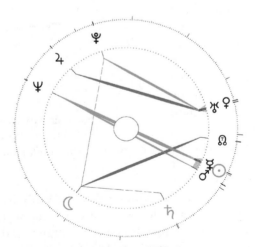

Elizabeth Taylor, Film actress
27.2.1932, 19.56, London/GB

Quadrangular Type

The quadrilateral or polygon (square, oblong, trapezium, trapezoid, pentagon, hexagon) is the symbol of the stable form; it is a clear representation of order. It is not for nothing that people build everything that must be stable (e.g. chairs, tables, houses) as a square or a polygon.

The quadrangular or polygonal type is the diametrical opposite of the linear type; it seeks peace and quiet, and values nothing more highly than the harmony of a well-ordered and secure life. That doesn't mean that he opposes all change on principle, or that he is lazy. He can be extremely hardworking if he wants to establish or restore calm and order. Everything should always be sorted out quickly. Whoever wants to change the existing order will initially be seen as a troublemaker. This generates fundamentally conservative behaviour, in which conscientiousness and the upholding of rules are defining factors.

This example, belonging to former French President François Mitterand, shows a quadrangular aspect pattern. For him, the criteria for everything were stability and maintenance of the status quo. "Somewhere along the way there must be a valid system that people can rely on", is the ever-present hope that can incite an even too exceptional effort/ performance. Underlying this basic philosophical principle championing the preservation and support of life lies the condition, "at any price". For the weakness

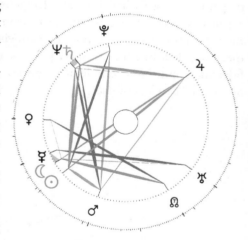

François Mitterand
former French President
26.10.1916, 04.00, Jarnac/France

of this type is their need for harmony that can easily become an end in itself, and can then have the effect of opposing anything new or changing. The quadrangular then becomes an admirer of the strong and powerful, who adhere to his philosophy of life (might before right), often making him a supporter of injustice. He then becomes a master of looking the other way, and his philosophy shifts to that of an ideal world. That's why the quadrangular type is also vulnerable to ideologies and cults that endorse his philosophy.

A strongly blue aspect pattern (predominantly harmony aspects of 60° or 120°) reinforces this tendency, as it boosts the inertia; likewise the parts of the figure that do not join up closed quadrilaterals (e.g. one side of a quadrilateral is missing, or one of the angles does not quite close). The 'ideal world' philosophy helps in the repression of disappointments that result from the continual failures of their own desire for order. A typical example is the horoscope of Jean-Paul Sartre, the existentialist philosopher.

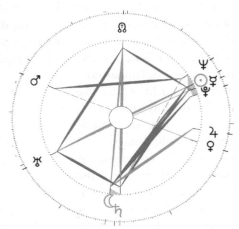

Jean-Paul Sartre
Existentialist Philosopher
21.6.1905, 18.45, Paris/France

Quadrangular and Fixed

The quadrangular type is remarkably similar to the fixed cross in the zodiac, but here the motivations are different. In all fixed signs there is a basic need for acquisition (striving for possessions), profit making and economical thinking; these do not appear to feature in the motivation of the quadrangular type. The quadrangular aspect pattern is concerned with one of the three basic possible consciousness-forming models, which has quite abstract ideas of life and is detached from realities of life in its own world. This is because his own needs for peace and order matter more to him than the state of the world. In the structure type, it is exactly this connection with reality that enables him to think and act with such efficiency.

Triangular Type

This type is similar to the mutable cross. The trinity typifies the triangle. In the triangle there is no polarity, as there is always a third point of view to relativise or to search for meaning. This type is an observer, a discoverer and a learner. He experiences the world not as an actor who is either moving or at rest, he experiences himself with the awareness that movement and static states are intrinsic aspects of the world. This awareness just wants to "understand why the world works like that". For only then can it be safely and successfully negotiated – and maybe even meaningfully changed. A good example for this is the horoscope of Boris Yeltsin, who seemed irrepressible as he continued his political tasks with a seemingly unfounded optimism after his heart operation.

Because it is an observer, the triangular type is a receptive or even passive participant in life. To him it seems that both other types

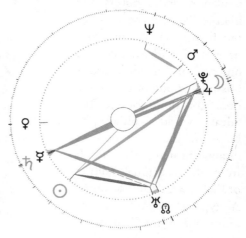

Boris Yeltsin, ex Russian President
1.2.1931, 06.07, Butka, Russia

construct the world according to their rules, just because they want to. Because he rejects this, he very quickly becomes an adaptation specialist (the cat that always lands on its feet). Anyway, it is always difficult for him to associate himself either with the dynamic approach of the one or the static approach of the other, for his nature is inclusive (both... and). He is mainly interested in interpersonal relations, the protean processes that occur between people – for him what matters is quality, not quantity, and one of his magic words is **love.**

Triangular and Mutable

Like the mutable cross, the triangle enables this type to cope with the changing circumstances of life. For him, the world is like a tripod, it cannot wobble. It is a potpourri and, although he does participate in life's constantly changing mixture of action and rest and would actually like to enjoy it, he can never inwardly identify with it because, for him, polarities are not a true reflection of reality.

Adaptation

In the case of a mixed aspect pattern that is therefore hard to integrate, he can become an adaptor. Then he is like a weather vane. If his environment manages to cancel out the effect of the triangle, i.e. it forces him to identify with one or other extremes, that goes against his nature and he loses the sensitivity that makes him such a nice person. If he commits himself to the dynamic motivation, he will become competitive and possibly ruthless. If he is overcome by the sense of guilt of the ordered world (static), he will become a fanatical fighter, and will judge those who sin against justice, order and convention.

The effect of the former is often that it is not possible to form a sufficiently stable identity, which means that the character is weak and that it takes refuge in all kinds of addictions in difficult situations. In both latter cases, there is a long-term danger not only of loss of identity, but also illness, because one is actually living someone else's life.

The types presented here are pure types, which are actually very rare. Out of the aspect pattern samples given here, only Mozart is a pure linear type. Aspect patterns normally contain a mixture of types.

Colours Speak Too

The second most important thing to consider in the total aspect pattern, before looking at it in detail, is the colours within the pattern, for they make a significant statement about the quality of life of the individual concerned. Colours play an important and varied role in our lives, and we give them different meanings according to the context in which we find them.

We have drawn on the theories of colour psychology in our choice of aspect colours, which is logical because we are practising astrological psychology. And as there are three different basic types of aspect, it seemed appropriate to choose the three primary colours from the visible spectrum, i.e. red, blue and yellow. We are referring to the subtractive spectrum of selective light reflection by the various substances and materials in our world, and not to the colours of the light in the additive spectrum.

If you already know how horoscopes are used in the API School, you will be wondering what happened to the colour yellow, as green is used instead. There are simple practical reasons for this. When we began training in astrological psychology, students always found it difficult to find yellow felt tip pens (it was still difficult back in 1968!), and the few who did manage it complained that the yellow couldn't be seen clearly on our white paper forms. The latter is still true today, which is why green was chosen. Since then it has become so familiar, that many people don't realise that it should actually be yellow.

The Meaning of the Colours

Red

We use red for the 90° and 180° aspects. Our definitions of the square and opposition are not judgmental, as is still unfortunately the tendency today with terms like 'hard' or 'tense' (they were previously even classed as 'bad' or 'evil'). Psychologically, such aspects are energy-transporting links between planets, and red is the appropriate colour for the handling of energy or power, for it represents psychologically expansive, outward-going (extrovert) energies. Energy transfer (work, performance) is not bad in itself though, as it was said to be in the past, but rather something quite natural in our lives. It is just that it is not always easy to handle energy wisely, particularly in our civilisation where effort is inextricably linked to all kinds of ambition and pressure to achieve. This results in many mistakes vis-à vis property, situations, nature and the human environment which then bring emotional distress (environmental degradation).

Blue

We use blue for the sextile (60°) and trine (120°); it creates a restful, rather inward-looking (introverted) and statically-inclined mood, which is appropriate for the blue aspects. We call them substance-carrying angles, which show that two planetary functions have a material connection. In our experience this means that they get on well together (easy going). We naturally prefer this to the effort the red aspects demand of us, which explains the good reputation of these aspects in the past. We cannot accept that blue aspects are considered good aspects based only on their past glorification. We know from experience that blue aspects can also show pride and mental laziness.

Green

As mentioned above, yellow is theoretically the colour that should be used, but it did not stand out enough, hence the use of the colour green. In astrological psychology, a lot of importance is attached to the 'green aspects' semi-sextile (30°) and quincunx (150°), although they are hardly used in classical astrology. They are very relevant for modern man.

Yellow is the colour of connection, contact, exchange and communication (the colour of the postal and telecommunications services in most countries in the world is yellow!) Yellow neither expands nor contracts, it is neither extrovert nor introvert but ambivalent and versatile and adaptive. Its sensitive nature transmits neither energy nor matter, but varying levels of awareness. The function is comparable to that of the central nervous system and the sensory organs. Green (yellow) aspects show receptiveness to stimuli and are highly sensitive. They are curious and also alert. As these are ideal preconditions for learning, not in the sense of swotting but as alert, interested perception, they are also called learning aspects.

Red and Blue

Red and blue form a natural polarity: the outgoing, showing-off ego of red and the retiring, inward-looking blue. Yellow completes the trinity. The experiences of the handling of energy and matter are interpreted by the consciousness in humans (as opposed to animals). Consciousness is therefore what makes us human. We recommend reading Kandinsky's *Concerning the Spiritual in Art* (25). This master of colour writes about colour in a deeply psychological way.

3.4 Basics of Aspect Pattern Astrology

By way of illustration we would like to go over the most important basic rules of astrology once again and show you sample horoscopes. We also distinguish between five visible layers of the horoscope (see diagram on page 10) in the holistic reading, which correspond to the structure of the human being.

1. The Centre Circle   Inner Self/ Soul/ Spirit
2. The Aspect Pattern   Consciousness structure
3. The Planets   Tools
4. The Signs of the Zodiac   Genetic structure
5. The Houses   Environmental conditioning

They are carefully separated from the inside out in astrological psychology horoscope design. The interpretation records their interaction. You can read about this in more detail in Chapter 1, in *The Astrological Houses* (16) and in *Transformation* (13).

Orb Table

To enable the aspect pattern to be understood visually, aspects must be calculated accurately according to the Huber Orb Table (page 24) and drawn in the appropriate colours. We repeat: there are no aspects to the ascendant, to the MC, to the planetoid Chiron, to the black moon or to Lilith; only to the ascending Moon Node and the ten planets. Due to the basic significance of the aspect pattern for finding the life motivation, a precise procedure for the determining of the aspects must be followed.

Charts and software

Horoscopes should be calculated (usually by computer or online service) using the *Huber Koch Method* (4). The computer calculates all the aspects carefully and the aspect pattern looks vivid, because the aspects are drawn with different thicknesses according to the influence of the orb, which is very valuable for visual understanding.

Koch House System

It is important to clarify that in astrological psychology we only use the Koch house system. Mathematically this is a time system that can calculate the intermediate houses (2, 3, 5, 6, 8, 9, 11, 12) exactly according to the place of birth, while Placidus and other systems relate the intermediate houses to the centre of the earth. The main axes (AC, IC, DC, MC) are the same in all house systems. We obtain the best results in horoscope interpretation with Dr Koch's so-called Birthplace Houses.

Dr Koch's house system provides answers to clearly different questions to that of Placidus or Campanus, for example. An equal house system that is oriented towards the AC has a different perspective than one based on the MC, etc. When choosing a house system, the important thing is not whether it is *better* than the others, but whether it is appropriate for certain questions or perspectives.

Visual Perception of Aspect Structure

Looking at aspect patterns with carefully drawn colours stimulates our senses. The aspect pattern represents a kind of symbol or mandala, and possesses an energetic vibrancy with the rare power to stimulate the intuition. The clearest way to imagine the aspect pattern is as a fiery field of energy or vibration containing a basic model of the life plan and the individual development goal. In astrological psychology, we interpret the aspect pattern as the structure of the individual consciousness.

When we have learned to read the aspect pattern correctly, we see a deep inner world that is never directly accessible, but that reveals unconscious approaches and deep life motivations. They cannot be grasped rationally, but require a higher thinking function, i.e. the intuition or sensitive perception. By association, combined with exercises for the imagination and horoscope meditations, we teach the visual perception of the horoscope that opens up new perspectives to us. We perceive the horoscope as whole, and that leaves an impression behind. Aspect patterns reveal some familiar images, for example a ship, a mountain peak, a deck chair, etc. The whole picture of the horoscope has just the same effect on us as when we meet someone for the first time and we have a certain impression of them that we remember.

The graphic structure, the colour, the shape and the size of the aspect pattern evoke visual associations. These are reflected upon and serve as the introduction to the deeper meaning of the horoscope. Looking and associating is in reality a natural and simple method. Everyone possesses this ability within them that can be brought out. When looking we shouldn't try too hard and just have a sensual, almost playful approach to understanding the connections. Jupiter is astrologically appropriate for this. Jupiter involves all sensory perceptions and plays an important part in intuitive visual thinking.

Metaphorical Imagery and Intuition

Carl Gustav Jung described the human pictorial imagination as a plunging into the world of metaphorical imagery. There we enter archetypal areas/spaces that reflect our inner life. Jung said that "thinking in pictures and colours" was the language of the soul. The human aspect pattern can actually be considered as a picture, an artwork of the soul. Just as artworks, such as drawings and paintings, count as the creative expression of a particular person, aspect patterns with their total creative power can also become the speech of the soul. If we direct our meaningful perception inwards, associations emerge from the world of metaphorical imagery that awake our fantasies and intuition and want to communicate something. The images arising in this way are not thought out or planned, but they carry a message from the inner world with archetypal content.

If these patterns are considered seriously in astrological psychological consultations, together one can identify their meaning and trace the stories they tell. This liberates a transforming energy. It is an ancient law of human life that we can only be changed by what we look at, and therefore objectify.

In astrological psychology we try to create such effects deliberately in self-awareness groups, with the aim of releasing one's own essential strengths, qualities and energies, using visualisation exercises and thereby training the intuition.

Individual Seed Thoughts

Recently, we have started developing individual seed thoughts or motivation formulae from the consciousness structure of the aspect pattern, with the aid of a special group exercise. This can be a kind of life guide for the person concerned, like a mantra. It is a new, revolutionary way of experiencing the horoscope personally. This method initiates the transformation process from visual understanding (Jupiter) to verbalised knowledge (Mercury), allowing the symbolic power of the aspect pattern to evoke images in us that come from the depths of our own souls. Through images we evoke the language of the soul and the aspect pattern starts to talk to us. The seed thoughts are generated in us as verbal associations and are the key to the holistic understanding of the individual. The formulation of the seed thought becomes an intensive group process in which the validity of cosmic laws is revealed in the individual's experience of his life motivation.

Association

Before we start on the interpretation of a horoscope it is important to consider the aspect pattern as a whole, without paying attention to astrological rules. If possible, we should temporarily forget everything we have learned about astrology, so as not to inhibit our sensory perception and intuition.

Maybe as a child you were able to make out patterns or scenes in the embers of a glowing fire. The clouds in the sky sometimes look like a dog, sometimes like a dragon. With a bit of imagination, you can transform the shapes of the clouds into patterns. This is exactly how we should approach the horoscope. If we train our intuition, we will be able to find the core of the personality, by letting the perceived patterns influence us.

- Hold the horoscope at arms length, or place yourself so that you can see the whole thing properly.

- Look at the aspect pattern through half-closed eyes and try to avoid logical thoughts. If you wear glasses, take them off to make the pattern lose sharpness.

- Hold the horoscope upright, do not turn it.

- You can make a template out of cardboard that covers the planets, zodiac signs and houses, leaving only the aspect pattern visible.

- Give yourself time to look. The pattern can provide a lot of information: a blossoming flower, a tent roof, a pyramid, a butterfly, a space rocket, an open book, a sailing boat, a flag, etc.

- Perhaps you don't see anything at all in the aspect pattern, but are struck by the colours. Maybe the aspect pattern is very spread out, compact or one-sided. Even if you can see no concrete pattern, something will make an impression on you.

The Jupiterian Approach

When we work with the Huber Method, we look at the aspect pattern for a long time before we go on to analyse it technically. This is a Jupiterian approach; we use our eyes and our intuition. Only then comes the analytical phase in which the Mercurial interpretation of further details and facts are examined. For us, the Jupiter-inspired total picture is the corner stone that must be laid if we want to find the way into the horoscope. We will illustrate this with a few examples:

This aspect pattern looks like a tornado. It has an opening to the sky (gap between Jupiter/ Sun and Venus). The unaspected Mars lies in the centre in the eye of the storm as master of ceremonies. The Moon lies at the foot of the tornado on the earth. The other aspects are scattered, as though they have been swirled around by the storm and then sucked out. This is the horoscope of the boxer Mike Tyson, known for his aggressive and erratic behaviour both in the ring and in his private life.

Mike Tyson, Boxer
30.6.1966, 12.00, New York/USA

Even when we stick to the above guidelines, it can be difficult to see a pattern immediately in the above horoscope. Nevertheless, we get an intuitive impression of the personality.

The next aspect pattern seems to vibrate and reminds us of the wing beat of a hummingbird in slow motion, of something that seems still but in reality is extremely strong and vibrates at high frequency. This is the aspect pattern of the violinist Yehudi Menuhin. Even if it is not easy to see a recognisable pattern in it, we do get an impression of the vibration of violin strings, which played such an important role in this man's life.

Yehudi Menuhin, violinist
22.4.1916, 23.30, New York

In the final example the pattern appears broad. Perhaps, as we look, a big shape comes to mind standing with both feet (Saturn and Jupiter) on the ground. It is wearing a blowing cape, whose tails are formed by Mars and Pluto. The figure seems to be making a dramatic entrance, as if it wants to shout "here I am!" This is the horoscope of the composer Johann Sebastian Bach. His *Toccata and Fugue in D Minor* for organ has exactly this theatricality

Johann Sebastian Bach
31.3.1685, 11.30, Eisenach/Germany

of the grand gesture that we notice in this aspect pattern. Some of his other works evoke the same impression.

Aspect Patterns without Planets

For a better understanding here are three more examples, this time without planets. They are covered with a ring (2), so that only the aspect pattern is visible.

On looking at the aspect pattern in Example A, words like diamond, tent, mountain and angular peak come to mind. They are stable objects that, like the aspect pattern, are firmly anchored. The whole aspect pattern gives an image of protection and security. The high position means that the need for security is not material, but spiritual, more like security through trust. On the

Example A
13.10.1953, 14.28, Zürich/Switzerland

outside, the aspects are mainly peaceful and easy-going blue. On the inside, though, they are red and green, which are more indicative of reflectiveness and energetic, fiery tensions that the person concerned doesn't want to show outwardly. It is important that these energies are correctly implemented, so that there is no build-up of pressure or even an explosion. Varied, naturally meaningful activities can transform these energies.

Aspect patterns with a large surface area have many opportunities to gather experiences. It often takes a long time for these people to give everything a try and find what suits them. They are usually known as late bloomers.

In example B, we see what could be a crab with an antenna or a deckchair with several short legs. It is a small, simple and quick pattern. While in the previous pattern problems are slowly mulled over, in the small pattern they are dealt with quickly and not worth mentioning. The position of the aspect pattern in the second quadrant means that the person reacts instinctively. The many blue aspects give a peaceful influence, like a calm sea. One senses a depth of character that must be aroused, as there is little energy (red) available; aroused but not overwhelmed. One senses from example B that one must proceed carefully, not like a bull in a china shop. Otherwise the crab will be crushed easily.

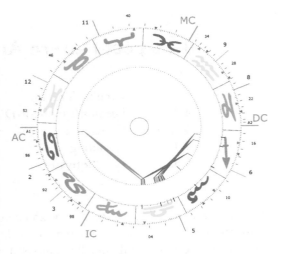

Example B
15.10.1982, 21.10, Dielsdorf/Switzerland

The aspect pattern in example C represents a sailing boat with a red sail. The protruding blue mast balances the catamaran in the storm. This person has more red. They can and want to be pushed. Of course, it depends on which planets are connected by red aspects. In this case the subject is a schoolgirl who, with this planetary layout, is suited to the modern Mercurial educational system. In spite of the red aspects, she can adapt when she has to.

Example C
13.2.1985, 17.38, Kilchberg/Switzerland

4. Aspect Pattern Analysis

4.1.	Graphic Structure
4.2.	Position/Emphasis/Direction
4.3.	Coherence
4,4.	Colouring
4.5.	Life Motivation

If we treat the overall aspect pattern as an energy model of the human consciousness, it can be compared to a human fingerprint that constitutes a constant, individually composed, personality model. The aspect pattern contains abilities, ways of reacting, characteristics, typical models, mental qualities and motivational forces that are quite different for each individual. It has an individual code stored in it, like the DNA in every cell in the body. Bringing out these individual codes is a main purpose of aspect pattern analysis.

The first analysis concerns the difference between the three levels of our lives. If we look at the aspect pattern on all three levels as a kind of diagram, it affects the physical level as an activity model, the emotional level as an inner map of the psyche, feelings and the unconscious, and the thinking level as an adornment of the mentality that indicates the objectives of opinion-forming and decision-making.

But the aspect pattern does not reveal one's destiny or even events or external things. It is a deep inner dimension in which the life motivation is hidden, which consists mainly of a mixture of the qualities of the three crosses, which are primordial motivations. Primordial motivations have archetypal characters and most strongly affect the feelings. That is why the analytical process only brings correct results when we first let ourselves be affected by the whole aspect pattern. As already mentioned, the perception of the horoscope as a pattern is a first step in sensing the symbolism of the aspect pattern and thus arousing the intuition. Only then can we start to analyse the aspect pattern according to the above five rules of interpretation.

4.1. Graphic Structure

Static or Dynamic: Linear, Triangular, Quadrangular

After the sensory perception of the aspect pattern, the next step is to establish whether it is static or dynamic. Often this distinction can only be made emotionally. The following rules can be observed though: triangular and linear figures are always dynamic, all quadrangular and polygonal figures are static. If the figure is large and triangular, the movement or dynamic is more undulating, but movement is always present if the figure is a triangle. Quadrilaterals and polygons indicate a static consciousness. For these people, there is a marked tendency to support themselves on different points so as not to lose stability. Of course at this stage only a subtle distinction can be made between dynamic and static. There are thin triangles and wide ones. For example, the large blue triangle comprising three trines tends to be static because of the colour blue, although it is a triangle and as such could be dynamic. But as it is equilateral and therefore absolutely symmetrical, it tends more towards stability. On the other hand, there are quadrilaterals that basically tend towards stability, but which are very irregular and are therefore classed more as dynamic. There are oblique quadrilaterals that are trying to break out of the static form, and which as such should be classed as dynamic and moveable.

Symmetrical and Asymmetrical

As a rule, we can assume that: because dynamic and static yield to each other, when the quadrilateral is asymmetrical there is nevertheless in it a dynamic presence; if it is symmetrical it is completely static. In a blue triangle, the colour has a static influence and the shape a dynamic one, whereas a linear figure is always dynamic.

Comparison with the three Cross Qualities

Once we have ascertained this, we can then differentiate between three different graphic forms: linear, quadrangular, triangular figures. They constitute three basic different types with differing life motivations. As already described, we can compare these three categories with the qualities of the three crosses (cardinal, fixed and mutable). The cross qualities are basic human traits and not life motivations. The latter are only visible in the graphic structure of the aspect pattern. However, in principle, the motivating forces of the cross are the same as those of the three graphic structures of the aspect pattern. It is helpful for the purposes of interpretation to know the cross qualities according to the law of analogy. It is generally known that the three cross qualities represent three basic principles in life and in all of creation. These are reflected in all trinities by a chain of correspondences. The astrological interpretation code always proceeds from the theory, from wholeness, so every astrology course should begin with the study of these three basic principles. The following correspondence table is useful for this.

Correspondence Table

Cardinal	Fixed	Mutable
Linear	Quadrangular	Triangular
Red	Blue	Green
Achievement	Pleasure	Sensitivity
Energy	Matter	Thought
Sun	Saturn	Moon
Will	Security	Contact

Once we have established the graphic structure of the aspect pattern, we can look into the individual's basic motivation. As this is a completely new astrological method, we would like to devote a few pages to explaining this topic thoroughly, once again with the aid of example horoscopes. The following statements apply in the interpretation of aspect patterns:

1. **Linear figures** are dynamic in consciousness; will and power are their motivation, the attainment of goals is the driving force.

2. In the **quadrangular** or **polygonal aspect pattern**, consciousness is statically-oriented; security and efficiency are the motivations (with the exception of asymmetrical ones).

3. **Triangular aspect patterns** indicate a changeable or variable consciousness; their motivation is an interest in people and in relationship qualities.

4. **Mixed figures** indicate two or three motivations that are not so easy to reconcile. These people are creative, see many opportunities and act cleverly.

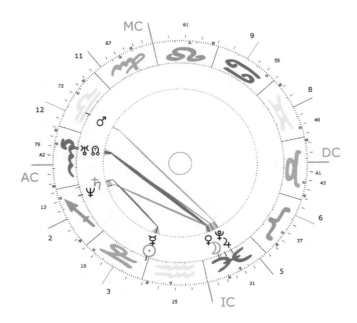

Edgar Allan Poe
19.1.1809, 2.00, Boston/MA (USA)

Linear Figures (Cardinal)

This is a horoscope with a linear aspect pattern. It is interesting that such patterns are relatively rare, triangular and quadrangular patterns being much more common. Edgar Allan Poe was a writer in the 19th century. We can compare the linear type with the cardinal impulse type. They are very capable and are always asking how they can reach their goals. Linear figures look for new opportunities to find a better way to get to the summit. They are restless and dynamic and always running around after something. They are risk-takers, they are strong-willed but endurance and cautiousness are not their strong points. They tend to put all their eggs in one basket and are often gamblers.

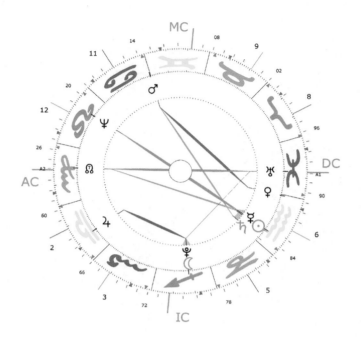

Wolfgang Amadeus Mozart, Composer
27.1.1756, 20.00 LT, Salzburg

With his linear figure, Mozart was unbelievably creative and also very prolific. One goal was not enough for him; he was always trying out several things at once. The motivation to accomplish something special constantly stimulated him; he developed brilliant traits and his creative impulse enabled him to achieve exceptional things. The success was not always necessarily lasting, the impulses were dissipated again, and the interest often disappeared as quickly as it had come. Maintaining the status quo is not a concern; this is the role of the quadrangular type.

Civil Servant
18.11.1918, 10.30, Ettlingen/Germany

Quadrangular Figures (Fixed)

Above, you can see a large red square in the horoscope of a civil servant. Quadrangular or polygonal aspect figures all have an objective. They strive for security, as befits a civil servant, for example. His basic motivation is to achieve a definitive, stable, harmonious, perfect situation and then to maintain it. In some respects we can compare the quadrangular aspect figure with the quality of the fixed cross. Such people are always asking what they should do to achieve the greatest efficiency. They try to protect themselves by perfecting and maintaining the status quo. They take the best from a well-functioning situation and see developments through to the end. They want to see the fruits of their labours and also to harvest them, which is why they never stop tilling the soil, investigating the laws of life so that fruit can grow. These people feel the need to put plans into practice and not just to talk about them. The aspect figures with four or more corners are *tethered* and only come to rest when they have reached the perfect situation and everything is in order. The state of the consciousness is static and the principle corresponds to Saturn.

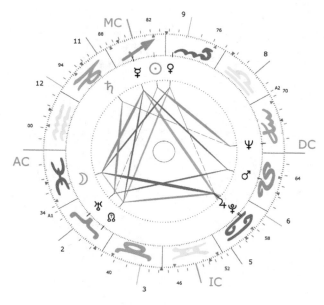

Bruno Huber
29.11.1930, 12.55, Zürich, Switzerland

Triangular Figures (Mutable)

Triangular figures are variable, i.e. changeable and mutable. The above horoscope makes an overall triangular impression. This structure has an affinity with the mutable cross; the motivations are love, contact, communication, learning and research. The consciousness is geared to identifying relationships between things and nature, so as to derive sense and meaning from them. These people are very adaptive, flexible, sensitive and are interested in many things. They always ask "Why is that so, why do I have to do that? Why is that happening to me?" They look and search until they find answers and meaning. Only then can they identify themselves with it. They want to identify the regularity and thus understand and improve interpersonal relations. So they try to relate to everything that exists, to discover the essential, the true, the beautiful and the just. They adapt to situations and people until they have experienced everything about them, then they move on to new things. They are mentally always on the move. Their principle is change.

Mixed Aspect Patterns

The main features mentioned above can be superimposed and modified by other interpretation elements, especially when we find different aspect figures separated from each other. In many horoscopes, there are two or three different geometric shapes, therefore also two or three separate motivations. These parts can each belong to one of the three basic models. Such people are mostly creative and versatile. They find a way out of every difficult situation. Many change their attitude abruptly, jumping from one character to another to adapt to the prevailing circumstances, especially when it is expedient for them.

Carl Gustav Jung
26.7.1875, 19.20, Kesswil/Switzerland

The chart of C. G. Jung contains a triangle, a quadrilateral and a linear figure, thus combining all three motivations. These people are usually all-rounders with a special charisma. They are versatile, can see things they are doing through to the end, and are usually endowed with creativity and productivity. Jung was a creative man. He was dynamic, so that he could sail in and impose his will (linear); but he was also very cautious in his judgments and tenacious in pursuing his goals (quadrangular); and he was personally very attached to his clients (triangular).

4.2. Position, Emphasis, Direction

At the next stage of aspect pattern analysis, we consider the spatial disposition of the horoscope – the position, emphasis and direction of the aspect structure.

The Cross-Hair

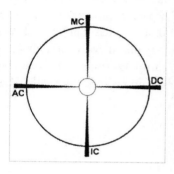

Firstly we divide the horoscope into four using a cross-hair (horizon AC-DC and meridian IC-MC) to find the left, right, top and bottom positions. We know that the themes of the four quadrants are: 1. Impulse (or Drive), 2. Instinct, 3. Thinking, 4. Being. We can see from looking at the aspect structure which area of the horoscope has the greatest concentration of planets.

We can also see the horizontal and vertical line distribution of the aspects. The vertical aspects represent individuation, the horizontal ones relationship to others. If the horoscope consists mainly of vertical lines, then the person is an individualist, wanting to fulfil himself alone. If it contains several horizontal lines, then the main concern is contact with others and the environment. So we can learn a lot from looking at these two line orientations in the aspect structure, we see how the person approaches life.

Horizontal Direction

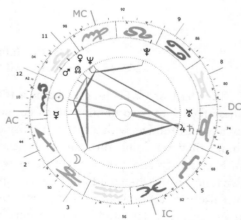

4.11.1940, 08.30, Huttwil/Switzerland

If most aspects run approximately parallel to the horizon line of the horoscope, as in the above example, the consciousness is basically concerned with the ego and the 'you'. Such a person is always oriented towards several other people and has trouble acting alone and independently. He must have someone who is quite devoted to him and gives him reassurance or approval. That also indicates a profession that brings him into contact with other people.

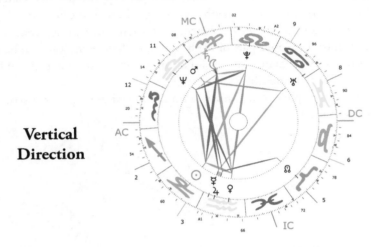

Vertical Direction

9.1.1950, 04.15, St. Gallen/Switzerland

If the aspects are predominantly vertical along the meridian line, the consciousness is markedly individualistic. The person is primarily interested in his own self-development and has trouble getting on with other people on a long-term basis, even if he loves them. These problems arise because independence and freedom are his priorities.

Conversely, someone who is predominantly other-oriented finds it very difficult to live with a person who is predominantly individualistic. These diverging motivations are particularly important in Partner horoscopes. The use of traditional interpretation methods often leads to conflicting conclusions. We then wonder why they sometimes fit and other times do not. It depends on both the aspect direction and on the corresponding life motivations.

Position: Bottom, Top, Left, Right

Whether the aspect pattern lies at the bottom, top, left or right of the horoscope is crucial for understanding basic orientation and goal direction.

A position in the **bottom** part of the horoscope means that the person is mainly interested in belonging to the collective. If the emphasis is on the **left** ('I') side, then all experiences are related to the person's own ego. A **right** ('You') position indicates a tuning in to others and to the environment and a tendency to do what others expect. In the **upper** part of the horoscope, the person wants to be free, his interests are mainly professional and he wants to get ahead and fulfil himself independently.

The example below features a horoscope where the aspect structure lies on the right:

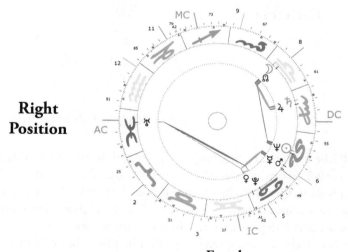

Right Position

Female
8.8.1921, 20.30, Ilanz/Switzerland

Here we can see immediately that the linear figure is predominantly located on the right of the horoscope, emphasising the second quadrant. Only one aspect runs through the 'I' side, to Uranus. This positioning indicates an You-orientation of the consciousness; in this case even a dependency on others for self-worth, so that this person can only feel useful by relating to others. Due to the presence of all three Ego planets (Sun, Moon, Saturn) in this area, we call this a right or 'You' pressure, as ego-validation is expected or even forced from other people. If we combine the right position and the basic motivation of the linear figure, we come to the conclusion that this person directs her energies wilfully and impulsively towards others and acts and reacts dynamically.

Another feature is that the aspect structure is split, the motives are not directed towards the same goal. Because the aspect structure is divided into two parts, the other-oriented impulses are inconsistent and contradictory. They compensate relatively unsuccessfully for egoism. Between the Mars/Mercury conjunction and the Sun/Neptune conjunction there is a gap that indicates a loss of energy and resulting failures. Gaps in the aspect pattern can be seen as open and unprotected places. People usually realise this when their Age Point runs through such a gap (17).

When establishing the emphasis, it is immediately obvious from the above example horoscope that the aspect lines and therefore the energies of the linear aspect structure are targeted at the fifth and sixth houses. This produces a concentration of energies in a small area that in this case activates the second, Instinct quadrant.

Understanding of the concrete circumstances always helps to evaluate correctly, i.e. a knowledge of the reality of the subject's life. In this case it is a woman who constantly took refuge in illnesses (6th house) and controlled and tyrannised the whole family (Cancer) from her sickbed with her overbearing attitude (5th house). The feelings of sympathy and antipathy predominating in the Instinct quadrant were concentrated into reaction patterns that automatically and through no fault of her own became instinctive, i.e. compulsive defensive mechanisms. This explains why she was always ill.

Further clues for interpretation are provided by the evaluation of the positioning.

The Quadrants

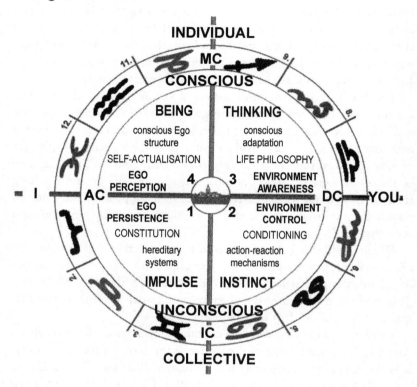

An accumulation of the majority of the planets or aspects in one of the quadrants activates the corresponding areas. Clear guidance is provided by the universally accepted quadrant fields, which are: 1. Impulse quadrant, 2. Instinct quadrant, 3. Thinking quadrant, 4. Being quadrant. You can find more detail in *The Astrological Houses*, "The Quadrants" (16).

Example Horoscope

We now illustrate the significance of this chapter on aspect pattern positioning and direction in more detail with the aid of an example horoscope. First we ascertain how the overall aspect pattern is spread out over the horoscope, evaluate the emphasis of the aspects and planets and the direction in which the pattern is pointing.

Johannes Kepler
6.1.1572, 14.37, Weil der Stadt/Germany

Take a look at the overall aspect picture. What impression does it give? Triangular or quadrangular? Although the triangles in Kepler's horoscope are clearly visible, the overall impression is quadrangular. The figure has six corners, but the whole pattern appears very relaxed. There is wind *blowing* through it causing it to collapse. These are permitted ways of approaching the interpretation.

There are two parts to the figure that are only joined in one place by a stellium conjunction, and their planets mainly lie in the 'You' area. The aspect pattern is clearly pointing towards the seventh and eighth houses. It consists of an active and deliberate You orientation. The great conjunction holds the two or three triangles together. The overall impression that these triangular figures give is quadrangular, which indicates a tendency to self-protection. In addition, they point in different directions; one points towards the seventh house and the other towards the eighth house. This inner antagonism caused feelings of insecurity for Kepler. He felt as though two active forces within him were pulling him in different directions. One possible result of this was that he was constantly looking for a patron to take him under his wing. He was protected by others from a young age, as an astronomer, mathematician and astrologer. He went from one master to another, always one step higher until he himself was the 'astrologer king'. In due course he accomplished great achievements that would make him famous. He was a consultant astrologer for important people who occupied very elevated, secure positions. But he left them behind too and moved on. Triangular figures have the mutable cross as their motivation, which brings constant life changes.

4.3. Coherence

The next stage concerns the coherency or integration of the aspect structure. In other words, we are investigating whether the structure works as a harmonious unit, whether it consists of different figure parts or whether there are detached aspects or unaspected planets.

Closed Aspect Structure

Queen Elizabeth II
21 April 1926, 02.40, London/GB

In this example, the energies of the aspect structure run in a continuum. Wherever we start, if we follow the line we end up back at the same point. The aspect pattern as a self-contained whole is a harmonious, unified consciousness structure, and therefore the consciousness of this individual also functions as a self-contained whole. She thinks in holistic terms and in correct proportions. She looks for the good in what is around her and extends it to cosmic dimensions. She differentiates more subtly than just between opposites, and thinks in three or more dimensions, i.e. universally. There can be ten important details at the start of a thinking process, but then more and more are added until a self-contained whole is reached. A comprehensive thinking method like this is what is needed in modern astrology, so that it can lead to wholeness and synthesis.

Divided Aspect Structure

The aspect pattern depicts the structure of consciousness, representing the interconnection of the contents of our consciousness. This means that, in the case of two unconnected aspect figures, there are two *wiring diagrams* of the consciousness, i.e. the person acts completely differently in two separate areas of life. For example, a thinking process is not a unified process that starts somewhere, goes through everything and then finishes somewhere else, but instead there are breaks, hold-ups and leaps of thought.

In the horoscope below, we see a detached square between the Sun and Moon/Pluto. It hangs like a shield on the You side and defends against influences from this area. However, the Ambivalence Triangle with the opposition on the 3/9 axis and Neptune/Venus in Virgo in the seventh house tells a different story. There are no Ego planets (Saturn, Moon, Sun) in this figure, which is why one can go along quite impersonally with the demands of the You, the partner. But as soon as this person's ego is activated or confused, he switches to the other figure

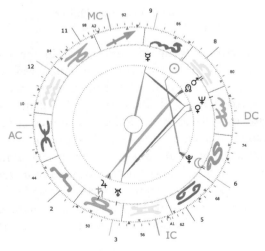

24.10.1940, 15.30, Rafz/Switzerland

and resorts to a defensive attitude, leaving those around him shocked by this change of heart. Then there is a third figure parallel to this one with a quincunx aspect between Jupiter/Saturn and Mars/Moon Node. Such a person can alternate rapidly between three different personality parts. He jumps from one figure to another according to circumstances, which is sometimes difficult to understand and hard to get used to for those around him.

Attached linear aspects

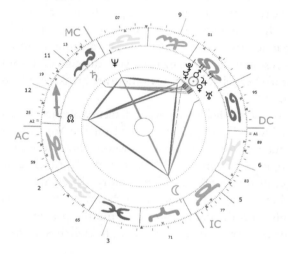

Michael-Alexander Huber
9.8.1955, 17.17, Zürich/Switzerland

Attached linear aspects are quite common, as in the above example from Saturn and Uranus. These connect by square aspect to the large Kite figure. Here they are cardinal red lines, which possess a certain dynamism and strength of will. The release of the talent or matter of the blue Kite figure is activated by the will and then used. The static nature of the Kite can be overcome with the spark of the will.

If the attached aspects are blue lines, then the cardinal will and impulse energies are toned down and can be used more sensitively in a way that increases perceptive abilities and stimulates the alertness of the senses. Such a person can focus his energies on something for as long as necessary. The area of the horoscope that this aspect is pointing at is significant.

If the linear aspect is green, the cardinal energy is consciously directed towards a goal, the person lives for the moment and is very aware of the present. The mutable qualities of the colour green come into play. One special quality of this linear figure is *good timing*, whereby all energies are deployed at the right moment.

One-Way Aspects

As mentioned in the previous chapter, aspects only have a one-sided effect if the Huber orb is not sufficient on one side, in which case the aspect to the planet with the smaller orb is drawn as a dashed line. If it forms part of an aspect figure, this side is not closed and it constitutes a weak point. Many people are not really aware of this figure, it remains latent for a long time. Sometimes energy flares up and it becomes active for a while and then fades again, especially if energy is running low or one is feeling tired. From the developmental point of view, consciously-living people can strengthen this aspect by working on it.

Unaspected Planets

It has been observed that in the case of an unaspected planet, the essential strength that it symbolises is not part of the *consciousness circuit* and therefore causes problems. Here we see Mars in the twelfth house without an aspect. An unaspected Mars often expresses itself sporadically,

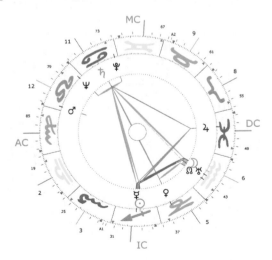

Unaspected Mars
10.12.1915, 23.45, Halberstadt/Germany

sometimes too strongly, sometimes too weakly. It is not reliable because it cannot be consciously implemented. Unaspected planets either work autonomously, i.e. for themselves, or they are delegated by the environment and are then also dependent on environmental influences, other-directed and continually deprived of the conscious supervision of the horoscope owner. It is therefore important to establish whether the planet is close to a house cusp (determined by nurture) or a Low Point (determined by nature) (16).

In an advanced stage of development, however, they do help towards spiritual development. New research shows that unaspected planets in a horoscope can lead to a special talent, and can therefore become positive factors. The planet often gives a clue about the possible career path, so that there are artists' horoscopes with an unaspected Venus, or writers' horoscopes with an unaspected Mercury. Much has already been written in other astrological books about unaspected planets (28).

Tension Ruler

As in Sigmund Freud's horoscope (below) there are aspect patterns in which one single planet lies opposite the main group of planets. We call these planets tension rulers. Empirical evidence shows that this planet dominates all the others; it imposes its influence on them, as it

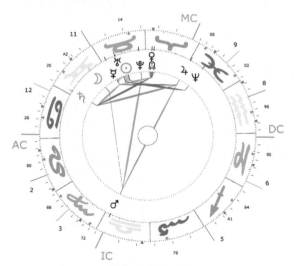

Sigmund Freud
6.5.1856, 9.17, Freiberg (Pribor) former Czechoslovakia

were. In Freud's chart we can see Mars as tension ruler at the bottom in front of the IC in Libra. It is obvious to everyone to what extent this Mars dominated his creativity and work. Mars is the only planet in the unconscious lower area of the horoscope. It is no wonder that he attributed most mental problems to sexuality. Mars and Venus are known to be the two libido planets, Mars being masculine and Venus feminine.

It is always enlightening to discover a tension ruler in an aspect pattern. It is very interesting to compare the influence of this planet with the life of the horoscope owner, as it teaches one a lot about astrology. But one should be able to understand the meaning of the planets that work as tension rulers on all three levels (physical, mental, emotional).

Several Aspect Figures

Most horoscopes contain a number of aspect figures and it is important that each of them is defined accurately. It should be noted if any figure is controlled by one of the three major planets, Sun, Moon and Saturn, because the basic motivations of each one relate to the strength of the ego. For example, two or three different figures, especially if they are not connected to each other, can affect each other – so that someone can be well-adjusted and kind at home and a feared boss at work. Such people can switch relatively easily from one figure to another. In a way they jump from one state of consciousness to another, often so abruptly that they confuse those around them. There are usually two or three completely different reaction types or personality parts. This fact is also influential in the integration or disintegration of a personality. Separate aspect figures can be observed in the horoscope in the case of illness like mental-health problems, schizoid tendencies or schizophrenia.

The question of the coherence of the aspect structure is also important for pyschosynthesis. Divided aspect figures indicate that the consciousness is not working harmoniously. We know from experience that this produces an inner striving for unity. This inner pressure can make an unconsciously-living person ill, but the same inner drive for synthesis and wholeness can make a consciously-living person creative. We would like to illustrate this using the example of the Swiss psychiatrist and depth psychologist C.G. Jung.

Aspect Structure in C.G. Jung's Horoscope

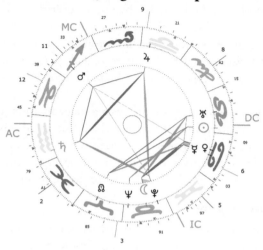

Carl Gustav Jung
26.7.1875, 19.20, Kesswill/Switzerland

The two-part aspect structure in Jung's horoscope stands out: **figure 1** is formed of an extended Model figure with the planets Pluto, Jupiter, Mars and Saturn. The inclination of the Model towards the AC reveals an introverted tendency in Jung's life, which was mainly expressed in his earlier and later years. Pluto, in its conjunction to the Moon, serves as an interface to **figure 2,** a scissors figure formed by the Moon, Uranus, Moon Node, Venus/Mercury and Sun/Neptune square. They indicate a quite different part of Jung's personality, i.e. the cosmopolitan and worldly Leo nature that makes him dependent on the world. Jung himself alludes to the interaction between the two types of personality. The clearly separate aspect figures in Jung's horoscope, with their diverging directions of movement, are responsible for this. He describes how he experienced both parts of his personality consciously in his book *Memories, Dreams and Reflections* (24):

"Play and counterplay between the personality types No 1 and No 2, which run throughout my life, have nothing to do with a "split" in the usual medical sense. On the contrary, everyone experiences this. In particular there are religions that have always spoken to the No 1 side of people, the inner person. In my life, No. 1 has always been predominant and I have always tried to give free rein to my inner voice."

4.4. Aspect Pattern Colouring

As already mentioned in the last chapter, the three colours we use to draw the aspects were chosen according to psychological criteria. Their division into three constitutes a valid analogy to different elements of the horoscope.

Colour Dominance

The colouring tells us a lot about the type of consciousness. In interpretation, we try to establish which colour dominates. If it is red, the person is achievement-orientated or tense; if it is blue, he is an easy-going bon vivant; and if it is green, he is a good thinker but also an irresolute doubter. If all three colours are there and form a harmonious pattern, this indicates an inner balance. This does not necessarily mean that external behaviour is harmonious, but there is an inner knowledge that there are laws of development that rule everything.

Normal Ratio 1-2-3

The golden rule for the distribution of the aspect colours is one green, two red, three blue. This colour ratio of 1:2:3, or multiples thereof, like the most frequently found combination of 2 green, 4 red, 6 blue aspects, is the result of empirical research. This three-coloured aspect ratio produces a character that is well-balanced, possesses a certain harmonious versatility and mobility and can adapt relatively well to the most diverse life circumstances.

Counting the Aspects

We count all the red, blue and green aspects and compare the numbers we arrive at. With planets in a conjunction, we only count the aspect if it has an orb of more than three degrees to the nearest planet. This means that if an aspect from a conjunction of two or three planets meets an opposition, square, sextile, quincunx or trine, only those aspects whose orbs consist of more than three degrees are counted. Those aspects lying within these three degrees only count as one aspect, even if there are several planets in one conjunction. The only case when this rule does not apply is a semi-sextile, because the orb only consists of three degrees for the Sun and the Moon.

Red Dominance

Here the energy is increased, this person enjoys any kind of activity, meaningful or aimless. The important thing is that something is happening. There is a kind of high tension, energy must be transferred or got rid of. He undertakes difficult tasks, is achievement-orientated, willing to take risks and intense. However, in relationships he is almost always insensitive, he overpowers other people. He is full of inner tension and is a kind of live wire; other people shrink from him because he shines too brightly. He therefore gets on badly with others and they avoid him. Who can tolerate such a strong current?

Blue Dominance

Here there is a lot of matter but little energy to transform it. Too much blue causes idleness and indolence, and waiting for things to fall into one's lap. These people don't want to make an effort and are mean with their energy. Because they have so little energy available, they try to get anyone who is willing to help them. Tasks are neatly handed over to those around. Interestingly, high-powered people are happy to help, as both types need each other. The blue type is inwardly content; he knows that he always has everything he needs. Indeed, he has so much matter inside him that he needs nothing more from outside. He is at peace with himself, enjoys the status quo, and doesn't have to try to fight for changes any longer. However, the inner listlessness can lead to lethargy, depression and also to illness.

Green Dominance

Too many green aspects, i.e. more than blue, lead to inner insecurity. Such a person adapts willingly to his surroundings, is easily influenced and led. He cannot take decisions, mainly because he sees too many possibilities. Too many green aspects can lead to an instability of the consciousness and to constantly changing life circumstances. These people are always re-evaluating things and tend not to stick to existing rules. They are perpetually in a state of flux and are very susceptible to external stimuli. This can lead either to extreme sensitivity or to a certain instability. This trait means that such a person rarely achieves his goals. Because he doubts himself and the world, he lacks self-confidence. The development path that this person has to follow can be referred to in the previous chapter on the three steps of the quincunx aspect.

Red-Blue-Green Aspect Patterns

This combination produces a three-dimensional, i.e. constantly evolving awareness. We call the three-coloured aspect figures Learning or Growth figures. They contain a so-called crisis mechanism: the red aspect is conflictive, the green aspect is questioning and the blue aspect finds the solution. People with such an aspect figure strive for all-encompassing understanding. They are not happy if someone only sees one or two sides of a situation, they would rather show as many sides as possible. This feature of their consciousness enables them to recognise more and more subtleties and nuances and also many connections that broaden the picture. The green aspect makes people ask "why?". They get to the roots of things, penetrate the causes of problems and think psychologically.

Single-Coloured Aspect Patterns

Exclusively red, blue or green aspect patterns are almost non-existent; what we often see is one of these colours dominating. But if the overall aspect pattern is **only blue**, then in all likelihood, this person is harmonious, balanced and easy-going, but also lacking in drive. He is certainly not suited to carrying out difficult tasks.

An **exclusively red** aspect pattern is dynamic and hyperactive. One could predict that such a person is unbelievably high-powered, can work without stopping and is much more accomplished than other people. He is also unbalanced and hectic though. Because he cannot ration his energy, he burns himself out and gets on other people's nerves, then feels rejected and often misunderstood.

Exclusively green aspect patterns are very rare. Such a person lacks blue and red and is therefore mostly at the mercy of the environment and dependent on the impulses, help and support of others. These people can prove themselves if they pursue a profession that requires great sensitivity or particular intellectual effort.

Two-Coloured

This comprises red-blue, red-green and blue-green aspect patterns.

Red-Blue Aspect Pattern

29.11.1968, 9.04, Baden/Switzerland

Two-coloured patterns or aspect figures, like the one above, indicate a strong fluctuation in needs between achievement and enjoyment. Activity and passivity alternate according to mood. The red tension is eased by the blue aspect as soon as it has discharged the energies. That causes a bi-polar fluctuation: "Today full of devout optimism, tomorrow full of despondency" reflects this state of mind. This ambivalence makes it difficult to find a middle way, as green, the relativising principle, is lacking. For these people, there are almost always only two possibilities, two sides; there is an either-or consciousness. Something is either true or false; there is no middle way. They are difficult to get on with as they find it hard to understand other points of view. As they only divide human motives into good and evil, they judge very easily, are often wrong and their harsh judgments easily bring them into conflict with those around them.

Ambivalence

The ambivalent state of awareness makes such people absorbed in the conflict between guilt and atonement, punishment and reward, cause and effect, and the friction. Conflict resulting from the experience of these mutually exclusive oppositions makes them suffer until things blow over or the page is turned. This is how harmony is restored, but then they tend not to want to see conflicts that would cause new problems.

In the transformed case, these people transfer their ambivalent tensions into creativity, in which increased motivation helps them carry out creative performances for a good cause. Such people enjoy their achievements and the benefits they bring, they use their energies in a determined and diplomatic way to accomplish a task in order to realise peace and harmony for themselves and others. Initially, they assert themselves confidently and then calmly sit back and enjoy the benefits, according to the motto "Don't mix business with pleasure".

Red-Green Aspect Pattern

Red-Green aspect patterns constitute a so-called stimulation aspect; the blue is missing. The Swiss horoscope looks completely green to the outside world. Green aspects have a particular talent for negotiation; they don't take a position and remain neutral in disputes. That has enabled Switzerland to retain its neutrality during two World Wars.

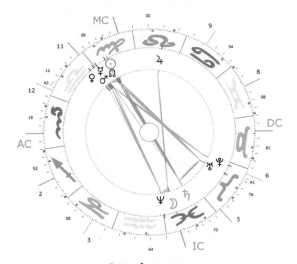

Swiss horoscope
Federal Constitution 12.9.1848, 10.42, Bern/Switzerland

People with mainly red-green influence rarely experience relaxation, rest and pleasure. They are alien to them, and for many even the root of all evil, because they themselves often tend to be addicted to temporary relaxation, in a way in order to compensate for the missing blue. Green (sensitivity, susceptibility to stimuli) is overwhelmed by red (energy, strength). As a result, they often overextend themselves and have the feeling that they are exploited; they often have this effect on other people too but do not notice.

Many are obsessed with work and activity, are perfectionists and criticise everything that still needs improvement, or everyone who does not make enough effort. This means they get on the nerves of those around them, especially if the aspect pattern is oriented horizontally. If it is vertical, they are constantly perfecting their own creations, but are seldom completely happy with their efforts. Their dissatisfaction with themselves and their world sometimes drives them to their best achievements or to rebel against everything (red then becomes aggressive).

Blue-Green Aspect Pattern

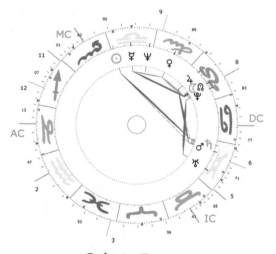

Catherine Deneuve
22.10.1943, 13.35, Paris/France

Blue-green aspect patterns are not very common. There is a certain one-sidedness or instability in the consciousness, because red is missing and both energy and readiness for activity are reduced. These people are sensitive and willingly adapt themselves to the needs of others, as they don't want to assert themselves too much. They can easily become the victims of circumstance because they are unable to defend themselves adequately. There is a devotional aspect to their pronounced attraction to harmony and pleasure. There is no harshness in their consciousness and they are peace-loving to the extent of the *dictatorship of the good*.

Blue-Green aspects produce little motivation for achievement so they are not high-flyers as they are not assertive enough. They cannot therefore be set performance benchmarks; demands are relatively ineffective and make no impression on them. For them, pressure to do well is conflict, for many it is even life-threatening. If they find themselves in this situation, they often take refuge in a fantasy world or in addictive behaviour. Because they do not react or give passive resistance, they are evasive and hard to pin down. With a mainly blue and green aspect pattern, they can still find their place in our achievement orientated society though. They are mostly found in helping and serving or even artistic professions, where sensitivity, patience, devotion and loving care are required. For example, they can look after the terminally ill with patience and care and are happy with small successes. We have observed a special ability in a few of these individuals; they are very good with the deaf and dumb or disabled children and even though they may not see any result from their efforts, they show the patience of a saint.

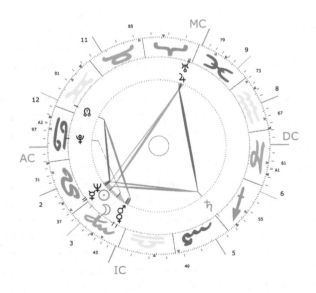

28.8.1927, 01.20, Lucerne/Switzerland

Three-Coloured Aspect Pattern

Three-coloured triangles are **learning** figures with special development potential. A three-coloured triangle indicates a three-stage dynamic with a three-stage crisis mechanism. Briefly, the red aspect brings conflict and disagreement that make the person anxious. He starts to think of seeking help and is given new insights by the green aspect. The blue aspect finally enables the enjoyment of the preceding efforts, i.e. there is resolution. The process then starts again from the beginning and the person is wound up again like a spiral. The crisis phases (red aspect) are important in this learning process. According to the awareness of the person concerned, they present themselves either as an incentive or a problem (desire to learn), or as hardship or conflict (learning through experience). Three-coloured figures contain the impulse to grow, and are therefore a direct expression of the laws of evolution and development.

Missing Colours

It is revealing for interpretation to start with the colours that are lacking in the overall aspect pattern.

Missing Blue means that the person cannot relax; he is always at full throttle and burns himself out. He exudes great agitation.

Missing Green means that it is not possible to argue with this person, he only sees two sides of a problem and his charisma is ambivalent. This either-or philosophy impedes communication and the exchange of thoughts with others.

Missing Red means that the person is sentimental, sensitive and often unstable. He possesses little power and waits passively for things to happen. His charisma is delicate and gentle and appreciated by those around him.

If there are missing colours, the house horoscope should be consulted. It shows the background and related environmental influences. It is the horoscope that most clearly expresses the behaviour and conditioning of the person's family background (influence from the father, mother, siblings and environment). The missing colours are often found in this horoscope, which shows that this person has acquired the appropriate behaviour. He has learned from his social background how to develop and use the qualities of the missing colours in life. For more detail on house horoscopes and their interpretation see our book: *Transformation: Astrology as a Spiritual Path*, Chapter 4 (13).

4.5. Life Motivation

The combination of the points mentioned above produces quite different life motivations. The basic linear, quadrangular and triangular structures correspond to the three basic principles of will, security and love and in a certain way to the three cross qualities: cardinal, fixed and mutable. There is also an analogy with the three basic colours: red, blue and green. The basic motivation is derived from the interaction of these elements.

Although, according to the law of wholeness, everything is connected and interdependent, in the case of partnerships or other close relationships, if the graphic structure of the aspect pattern is quite different, diverging goals do emerge from their basic characters. Such differences can often lead to deep misunderstandings between people. The realisation that one is different from the root, i.e. from the basic motivation, can either lead to greater mutual understanding, tolerance and love or be the cause of separation. The first is the way to wholeness and unity, the second causes conflict and division.

Acceptance

Aspect Pattern Astrology helps us to find out relatively easily what we really want, how our life is motivated and structured. The aspect pattern emits an energy field with active energies of our life motivation. This motivation level of the aspect pattern demands recognition, acceptance and a lively alertness according to the awareness of the person concerned. We should recognise this as the expression of our innermost being, symbolised by the centre circle. This enables us to actualise our spiritual potential and our own freedom to decide. Saying yes or no to ourselves is an excellent way to establish our identity and consciously follow our inner life source.

This helps us to understand and accept other people's individuality, and thus to mature to integrity. We understand that caring for other people is an important part of our wholeness. By understanding that all aspect patterns are naturally different, we accept our fellow men as they are and respect their individuality without trying to change them. It does not even make sense to want them to be like us. On the contrary, once the life motivation is known, one can and should accept it completely and try to live it fully. It would not be possible to re-educate it anyway.

In our courses and consultations, we see time and time again how beneficial it is for people to feel their innermost being addressed by the description of their aspect pattern, and to feel their life motivation identified and acknowledged. It can be the start of a healing integration process. In any case, a correct understanding of the aspect pattern using the presented detailed structure differentiation, gives us a key to understanding our own motivation and that of other people.

5. Basic Aspect Figures

5.1   Interpretation Rules
5.2   Single-coloured Aspect Figures
5.3   Two-coloured Aspect Figures
5.4   Three-coloured Aspect Figures

Introduction

Twentieth century astrology made many attempts to interpret individual aspect patterns. Some authors use terms such as Kite Figure, T-Square, Grand Trine, Mystic Rectangle, Finger of God, Yod Figure. Unfortunately, systematic research and appropriate textbooks were still lacking. In the API Institute, 30 years of research and training have led to the discovery of over 45 aspect figures and the refining and development of their interpretations. This has made horoscope interpretation more psychological, holistic and also more human. Although modern astrological institutes already teach the combination with psychological cognition, they still tend to divide aspects into harmonious and inharmonious, positive and negative. This tendency to judge will persist as long as aspects are interpreted in isolation and not in connection with the whole aspect pattern. It is inevitable that this dualistic black-and-white philosophy will be increasingly replaced by holistic horoscope interpretation methods, and this change is already underway.

Back in the fifties, psychological knowledge was already being used in birth chart interpretation. This psychological approach had the advantage of softening this black or white philosophy. Astrologers moved further and further away from categorical evaluations and judgments. They wanted to use the horoscope to investigate the predispositions and causes of mental-health problems. It was increasingly used as a diagnostic tool in psychological consultations, as were certain additional healing and therapeutic exercises that influenced consultation practice. The work of C.G. Jung on astrological symbols as archetypes and humanistic philosophy were both useful for astrological interpretation. A new form of holistic horoscope interpretation has been gaining ground in the last few years that counterbalances the usual horoscope interpretation with the schematic use of simple interpretation texts and the stringing together of separate statements. There has been no literature available until now on how to interpret the whole aspect pattern, on what we have called aspect pattern astrology, or on the aspect figures it comprises, which are discussed in this book.

In this chapter we write in detail about the combination of overall pattern and aspect figures. New criteria are necessary to bring the various factors together in the right way. A good path to deeper understanding of the individual aspect figures is the logical and analytical investigation of the basics and the wholeness that this makes visible. If we recognise a system of connections that follows natural laws, then we can derive psychological insights from it.

Basic Figures

The separate aspect figures are the building blocks of the aspect pattern, they are almost always just a part of the overall aspect structure. We should not be tempted to divide these into good or bad or to overestimate the importance of certain partial figures. Although the basic figures are of paramount importance as the building blocks of the overall aspect pattern, they are usually connected to other partial figures that modify their effect. We cannot emphasise often enough that we must always consider the aspect pattern as a whole, for it represents our inner motives, our central concerns and our life motivation. Again and again we must go back to this basic motivation and align ourselves with it. On the other hand, the separate aspect figures are indicators of specific contents, abilities and talents. The aspect pattern does not show us the influences of destiny, events or external things, but only connections deep within. These are worked out from the combination of the different aspect figures, the aspect structure, the colours and the three cross qualities. If you can master all these criteria and combine them correctly you will achieve amazingly good results in holistic astrological psychological consultations.

The Importance of Huber Orbs

You will benefit most from the following aspect figure descriptions if you have your horoscopes calculated and charted according to the Huber orbs and Koch houses. See the basics on page 82. These were developed empirically and adapted to reality over long years of research. We use only those aspects that are permanently active, not just sporadically. Everyone can check this on themselves and their family.

Be aware that other schools may use different orbs and may use more than the major 30° aspects. Whether the resulting aspect figures have effects as described here is still a matter for further research.

5.1 Interpretation Rules

Basic Aspect Figures

We begin with the 20 most common aspect figures that are the real building blocks of the aspect structure. In the next chapter we cover another 26 formed from extended constructions of these basic figures.

Aspect Figure Topics

First of all we have to know that every single aspect figure has is own theme or motivation. The figures have been given names that reflect the nature of that particular figure. The subject of each figure can be deduced both from the graphic layout of the aspect (shape), and from its colours. Both shape and colour must definitely be taken into account because they each have a basic psychological significance. The planets contained in the aspect figures initially play only a subordinate role, as do their position in signs and houses. The significance of the colour and shape of the aspect figures is unique and cannot be found in any of the other interpretation elements.

Aspect Figure Classification

Figure Size

1. Large figures either include or encompass the centre and are well spread out in the horoscope.
2. Half figures take up half of the space and go through the centre.
3. Small figures do not touch the centre and often only occupy a quarter of the horoscope (quadrant).

Colour Combinations

1. One-coloured Aspect figures
2. Two-coloured Aspect figures
3. Three-coloured Aspect figures
4. Colour dominance
5. Missing colours

Graphics and Effectiveness

1. Achievement figures
2. Ambivalence figures
3. Talent figures
4. Learning figures
5. Stimulus figures
6. Information figures

Aspect Qualities

1. Conjunction :   Sun/Moon Aspect
2. Sextile :   Venus Aspect
3. Trine :   Jupiter Aspect
4. Square :   Mars Aspect
5. Opposition :   Saturn Aspect
6. Semi-sextile :   Mercury Aspect
7. Quincunx: Saturn Aspect

Interpretation Steps

1. Establish the colours. Which colour dominates? Are all three colours present or is one missing? This is very significant.

2. Split the figures up into large, small or half figures. Large figures are the most important, small or minor figures show extensions and modifications.

3. To which main aspect figure group does the horoscope pattern belong? Linear, triangular, quadrangular or polygonal; incomplete figure?

4. Combination of graphic structures: are there two or three?

5. Which aspect direction predominates, horizontal or vertical?

6. Do the planets in the figure lie on house cusps, Low Points, sign cusps or intercepted signs? These enhance or reduce effectiveness.

7. How many aspect figures make up the overall aspect pattern? Is it closed or split?

8. Which of the Ego planets rule a particular figure? There are figures predominantly ruled by one of Saturn, the Sun or the Moon, or by two of these planets.

9. If there is no Ego planet in a figure, this feature is free from ego motives. It can work free of subjective goals.

Special Cases:

Closed Figures, Partial Figures or Aspects

Aspect patterns very rarely consist of just one aspect figure, usually several different figures are joined together. So the content of one aspect figure is then combined with the content of another and only together do they give a correct picture. In most cases, several topics are linked with each other, which is why interpreting the aspect structure is a special art. Some aspects combine one figure with another one; they are junctions between separate figures and deserve special attention. Some aspects can also project out of the aspect pattern and dangle like loose ends, in which case the energy does not go any further; it just flows back into the aspect pattern again.

One-Way Aspects

Aspects shown with a dashed line on one side have a one-sided effect and are therefore weak. It depends on the orb of the planets concerned. The one with the larger orb forms the aspect to the planet that has a smaller orb (e.g. a spiritual planet). The aspect is drawn as a dashed line to this planet. The best way to understand this effect is to compare it with a telephone that is disconnected on one side. The planet at the end of the dashed line cannot call out, but it can be called by the planet that the line connects it with, and also answer it. This is why it is called the One-Way Aspect.

Many people find that these aspects work when they are feeling well and strong. In situations of weakness, like stress, illness or mental health problems, the aspect doesn't work at all. They also feel that the whole aspect pattern is falling apart. It therefore depends on the consciousness of the person concerned whether a dashed line works or not. One can work on it by actively and consciously cultivating the planets at the end of the solid line, thus enabling contact between these strengthened planets and the other planets.

Gaps in Aspect Structure

Sometimes aspect figures have gaps between two planets, e.g. when a conjunction is not completely formed. Aspect figures overlap each other and either form an intersection or a gap. Gaps usually mean a *leak* through which energy can escape uncontrollably. But on the other hand, gaps are sometimes vulnerable places, especially if the central core is unprotected and external influences can penetrate unhindered. Many figures are open in one corner, which lacks a connection. For example, if two planets lie too far apart at the peak of an Achievement Triangle so that there is no conjunction, there is a gap between them. There is a so-called energy leak, a hole, through which energy is lost. It is hard for this figure to work purposefully and effectively, so that more energy is invested in *trying* than in *achieving*.

Figures in which one corner is closed by a conjunction but whose component planets lie more than three degrees apart are a special case. This conjunction does not, in fact, lead to an energy leak, i.e. scarcely any significant energy is lost, however such a position is hypersensitive to troubling external influences, for example if the Age Point or a transit runs through the middle of both conjunction planets.

Incomplete Aspect Figures

Many figures are not always precise and exact, it can happen that a whole aspect is missing or a one-way aspect is present in the figure. If one side is missing, there is a tendency to make up for the missing aspect, which causes special efforts to be made and sometimes causes disappointments in the case of failure. If, for example, one side is missing from an Achievement Square, the person concerned can try to act as if the whole figure were present, exerting himself to exhaustion in the process and still not satisfying his own high expectations. It would be wiser to recognise that there are actually two intersecting Achievement Triangles and not one incomplete Achievement Square. This then allows the person to work according to his own rhythm.

A similar thing happens if a sextile is missing from a Righteousness Rectangle. This can awaken a highly exaggerated sense of righteousness, with the desperate attempt to form the sextile and to make everything right, so that the ideal world persists and does not collapse in on itself. This figure can also be seen as two Ambivalence Triangles, which does not get rid of the problem but makes it easier to understand and cope with. If you meet someone who makes such exaggerated exertions, take a look at his horoscope – perhaps you will find an aspect figure that is not quite closed.

Stars

It is very interesting if stars are present in an aspect pattern. We distinguish between red, blue and green stars. The intersection of three blue trines forms a star. Two red squares form a red star, two or three long green aspects form a green star. [The normal rule taught to English students by the Hubers is that three intersecting lines are required to form a red or green star, as for blue - Ed.] People with a blue star have a calm place within them which they are constantly drawn back to and where they can recharge their batteries. With a red star they can mobilise their own activity, becoming operational at the push of a button, as it were. With a green star, there is a place for meditation and contemplation, where higher spiritual perceptions and intuitions are also possible. It is a place where the consciousness can be expanded.

The case of two intersecting squares, especially if they are very upright, constitutes a kind of wall opposite the houses that happen to lie behind these intersecting squares. If there is a planet there, experience shows that little will be achieved with it. Some people can be pushed beyond their conscious boundaries and this can cause mental health problems, depending on the planetary qualities involved.

Overall Impression

As mentioned above, the shapes and colours of the aspect pattern provide the perceptive observer with a way to understand people on a deeper level. The overall impression of the aspect pattern allows us to identify the basic structure, the basic tendencies and the essence of a person. It shows which potential is waiting to be developed deep within, what is expected from life and what the basic motivation is. After considering the aspect pattern as a whole, using the aspect figures we can proceed to a more detailed horoscope interpretation and get to know the reality of a person's life. The separate aspect figures conform to this larger structure and serve as aids to deciphering the aspect pattern. They correspond to archetypal qualities that are determined by the planets involved. Here too, we start from an overall impression (first impression), to which all other information is subordinate.

5.2 Single-Coloured Aspect Figures

Red Aspect Figures

These are called 'achievement figures', as the aspects they form are charged with energy. The energetic tension allows people to use it in life, be it to work, to act or to achieve goals. Blue and green are missing from the red figures. Without blue, there is no possibility for relaxation; without green one acts without thinking. Red promotes action, achievement, the attaining of goals and demonstration. These people are very active and many work by the motto "act first, think later", and not the other way around, which means that mistakes can be made very easily.

Achievement Square
[Efficiency Square]

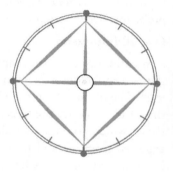

The Achievement Square consists of two oppositions and four squares. Energy is stored and collected in the oppositions like in a battery or an accumulator, according to their character. The energy potential (high tension) created is now discharged along the four sides of the rectangle. Even though in the large rectangle, the power and dynamism of the red aspects are moulded into a fixed form, they can make their presence felt nonetheless. Such people have great potential and almost always achieve their goals. They are able to work very hard and very constantly, with great reliability and rigour, which gives them security.

This single-coloured figure consists of six red lines, which means that the subject knows only the cardinal power of will and action and concepts like control and self-possession. It is hard for him to understand what relaxation or self-satisfaction mean. The diagonal red lines mean a doubling of the energy from the central life source. Consequently, this rectangle has a great deal of available energy from two almost inexhaustible batteries that are constantly recharging each other. This person loves contradictions and knows about the polarity of the world and lives accordingly. He measures his worth by his toughness, his stamina and the responsibility he has, for the right-angled intersection of the diagonals shows the greatest possible stability of all quadrilaterals.

Achievement Square
18.11.1918, 10.30, Ettlingen/Germany

Symmetry

Point symmetry means that, whichever way you turn the square, a red side is always visible, as if we were dealing with a sphere. This means that the subject is very calm, balanced and unflappable. He is not at all vacant, though, but very present, ready to act and can define himself clearly. The effect of this figure is similar to a revolving door or a turntable, hence its ability to change the direction of a force and suddenly to change from one world to another one or to change his mind. As an active and very determined person, he could make a good manager, director or an *eminence grise*, who pulls all the strings. In both mutually dependent opposites lies the wisdom that it ultimately does not matter which opposite we deal with. The person cannot cut himself off at all from his inner truth, even if he does everything for other people or identifies himself with others.

As the figure is only made up of Achievement Triangles, everything becomes possible. If something does not work, it will be attempted again in a different way. Such a person is never at a loss, for he always knows what could still be done. In any case, squares are not very sensitive and sentimental. If the rest of the horoscope contains little blue or green, other people only turn to the horoscope owner if they need help.

Aspect Qualities

The aspect qualities of the squares correspond to Mars (4x) and of the oppositions to Saturn (2x). This indicates an achievement-orientated and practical philosophy and a good memory for work processes, actions and conflicts. The down-to-earth sense of reality can be used very constructively (manual ability), and no one should try to stop him from doing this. The energies can be blocked though, if he cannot live as he wants and if conflicts are not settled immediately. If things are put off, then it is hard to make a second attempt. There is a tendency to repress and to block and decisions are left to be made by fate or other people.

These people often trust their own willpower so much that they don't see other possibilities and advantages and get stuck in habitual work processes. Women in particular with this red square seem to even dislike taking up any position of power of their own, but they are happy to support the power of others with their diligence. They do not want to be leaders but still serve as role models for those around them. They possess the ability to keep others' spirits up.

Endurance

The performance of a person with this figure is unrivalled, because he works with total calm and self-control but can still achieve a great deal. He controls his energy so that he never gets stressed, because he takes all the time he needs to complete his work carefully and conscientiously. We say that he does the work of four people (with four Achievement Triangles). As a stonemason chisels a statue out of stone by chipping away interminably, he can be so tenacious and persistent that once he has started a job he can finish it in one go without a break. He actually hates the work that has to be done, but he is magically attracted to it and forced to deal with it. Problems can arise with work that has to be done by other people. He must learn that not everyone is like him and that he must occupy a special, isolated position in society, and preferably a position where he can serve as many people as possible. For with his will he can turn water into wine, pick apples in the desert or accomplish other almost impossible things.

Fixed Ideas

Sometimes fixed ideas are problematic, especially in human relationships, where these people expect those around them to work and live just as competently and efficiently as they do themselves. This causes them, consciously or unconsciously, to put pressure on their work colleagues and partners. In the best case, they serve as an example for an increase in performance. Other people's value is mostly measured against their own, achievement-oriented benchmark. Often, life demands that expectations are reduced, which can be very painful. According to traditional interpretation, where it is called the 'Karmic Cross', the large red square has a karmic character.

Seriousness

People with a red square take life very seriously, sometimes too seriously. Many are disappointed and embittered if their potential is not recognised by those around them or if they do not achieve their goals. This is often the case if the red square is not quite closed, if one corner is open or one side is formed by a one-sided (partly dashed line) aspect. For them, letting go means losing security, which makes them feel anxious about losing control of their own energies. Losing strength is avoided at all costs, they entrench themselves behind what they already have. Learning new things is often considered to be unnecessary, they are convinced that they are right and refuse to change anything.

The Red Square in the three Crosses

The large red square is naturally located in one of the three crosses (cardinal, fixed or mutable). We can also establish the same thing in the case of Achievement Triangles, which is why the statements of the cross qualities apply for both possibilities. In the case of the zodiac signs, we talk about the genetic inheritance, about the innate energetic motivation that must also be considered in the analysis. The house cross is also effective, with which the inner talent either harmonises or diverges. Here it is a question of the combination of the sign and house (16). So, in interpretation, we must establish in which sign cross and in which house cross this square (or triangle) lies. Only then can we interpret it correctly and accurately.

In the Cardinal Cross

Aries, Cancer, Libra, Capricorn
Houses 1, 4, 7, 10
The aspects that form the Achievement Square with their red energies are expressed to their best advantage in the cardinal cross. But this creates excessive impetus so that the figure can be imagined as a fast revolving

catherine wheel. The expression of free energy from the opposing forces obviously conflicts with the symmetrical rectangular figure. In a way, the energy is fixed in the four corners, thus usually creating an enormous, rapidly functioning potential for achievement.

In the Fixed Cross

Taurus, Leo, Scorpio, Aquarius
Houses 2, 5, 8, 11
In line with analogous thinking, the square has similar qualities to the fixed cross and the same motivation for security. Consequently, this figure appears to be best suited to the fixed cross, so that is can use its power to produce a secure state. These people have the ability to muster all the energies necessary to complete set tasks and to maintain the status quo. However, there is a danger of tension and stiffness, which must constantly be relaxed. The previous example horoscope's Achievement Square belongs to a civil servant whose square lies in the fixed signs and houses, which is an appropriate place for a civil servant. It enables him to carry out his duty carefully and steadily and to climb the career ladder by virtue of his reliability.

In the Mutable Cross

Gemini, Virgo, Sagittarius, Pisces
Houses 3, 6, 9, 12
At first sight at least, this is the cross with which the square figure seems to have the least affinity. The important thing is which house cross it lies in. The fiery energy can encourage the changeability and the need for growth of the mutable cross, from time to time creating uncontrollable situations. The combination with the security-oriented square figure is constantly busy compensating for and fixing their own defects or mistakes. Many break something just to be able to repair it again afterwards.

This figure can also express itself in a constant effort to expand the consciousness. This is the only justification of the traditional name Karmic Cross, as here we are dealing with the transcendence of reality and the implementation of ideas. But humility is required, as otherwise there is a danger of fanaticism or intellectual arrogance. A certain nervous overload is also possible. In the following example of Roberto Assagioli, the founder of psychosynthesis, the red square lies in the mutable signs, combined with a blue Righteousness Rectangle. (You can find a fuller description of the aspect pattern in chapter 7, page 238.)

Roberto Assagioli
27.2.1888, 12.03, Venice/Italy

The same is true for the house arrangement, where it is very rare to see one single cross arrangement; sometimes one axis of the figure lies in one cross and the other in the neighbouring house cross, as in the above example. This should always be accurately investigated.

Achievement Triangle
[Efficiency Triangle]

The aspects of this triangle consist of two squares that are joined by an opposition. This red triangle is the classic achievement figure. In the Achievement Triangle (or T-square), the purposeful, cardinal impetus (red) finds its clearest expression. The apex of the triangle and the planet that lies there indicate where

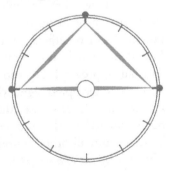

the achievement is directed and which planetary principle is used. While in the case of the red square work is carried out continuously and progressively, in the case of the Achievement Triangle, the energy is paralysed again and again. A person with a red Achievement Triangle should complete his work quickly and successfully, so that he can rest again afterwards. After a short or long break, he can go back to work with renewed vigour. A person with an Achievement Triangle produces a greater output per measurable unit of time than someone with a square. The latter's performance is regular and constant and hence takes up more time. The dynamic of these two red figures is therefore very different.

Of course, the square seeks security, constancy and symmetry, while the triangle's motivation is more flexible and more dynamic. Such a person would like to reach his goal as fast as possible. Someone with an Achievement Triangle can work like mad and when he is ready, he moves onto the next job assertively and highly dynamically. Energy is stored and bottled up in the opposition. The energy tension produced by the opposing pressures is discharged along both squares and in fact from two sides towards one point. In this way the apex of the Achievement Triangle (where the squares come together) forms the power point at which achievement is produced and transferred into work by the discharge of tension. An unsuccessful energy transfer leads to rigid states of awareness; one cannot change and the same mistakes are made again and again.

House Position

The house position is important in the evaluation of the type of action. The successful application of the potential that is waiting to be used in the Achievement Triangle also depends whether the planets lie on the house cusps or on the Low Points. With planets on the cusps, the potential can be efficiently utilised in the environment, while on the Low Points much more time is needed until one gets the chance to act and gain approval. It can also happen that the triangle and its opposition lie in an intercepted sign, which also delays the reaching of goals for a long time. In any case, the dynamics of the intensity curve should be considered in the evaluation of the efficiency of an Achievement Triangle, and all other figures. You can read more on this in the book: *The Astrological Houses* (16).

Planets in the Achievement Triangle

The planets that form the figures must also be considered. It is different if the red triangle is formed by the *hard planets* (Sun, Mars, Saturn, Uranus, Pluto, and to some extent Jupiter) or by the *soft planets* (Moon, Mercury, Venus, Neptune, Jupiter, and to an extent Saturn, according to its sign and house position). You can read in more detail about this in the previous chapter or in *Lifeclock* (17). With the Sun, Mars and Saturn, the potential within this figure can be optimally realised, especially if they lie at the achievement apex. In the case of the soft planets, the motivation and the principle of the red figure contradict each other. Adequate functioning is usually only barely possible, leading to psychological pressures and problems. Such a figure can find success in the helping and healing professions, where the intensity leads to the danger of helper syndrome.

Achievement Triangle in the Crosses

It is also revealing to relate the effect of the Achievement Triangle to the cross qualities. The triangle is part of a whole square and therefore always lies in a certain cross. The signs also have a motivating role here and houses indicate the way in which things are done.

In the cardinal cross, this triangle is endowed with strong willpower and energies are focussed. In the fixed cross, security is the motivation, the achievement motivation is oriented to the maintenance of the status quo, the protection of assets and the elimination of problems. In the mutable cross, love and contact are the motivation, which is why the achievement can take place in the field of relationships and communication. This Achievement Triangle is well suited for work in the helping professions.

There must then be integration in the houses, whether the cross agrees with the cross in the signs or not. You can read more about the sign/house combination in our book *Transformation* (13).

In Galileo's horoscope (next page), the red Achievement Triangle lies in mutable signs Pisces, Gemini and Sagittarius. It is situated on the You-side and combines the Sun as an ego planet with the two spiritual planets Neptune and Uranus. The Sun and Uranus indicate a creative spirit, but Neptune makes him sentimental, sensitive and indulgent. It is no wonder that for his part, Galileo could not assert himself effectively; this aspect pattern does not allow resistance to external pressure. The detached aspects can also be said to weaken the strength. The detached semi-sextile of the Moon to the Pluto-Venus conjunction points to the eighth house, so that there is an adaptation to the demands of the environment. One side of the small green aspect is attached to Mercury, which transmits information to the Sun. This small attached green figure with the Moon position works like a sensitive antenna, with which the

Galileo Galilei
15.2.1564, 16.00 LT, Pisa/Italy

truth can be perceived and intuitively absorbed. The Moon in Aries in the ninth house (both fire elements) strengthens the intuitive character. But this position is not suited to assertion. There is also the detached sextile of Jupiter/Saturn in the twelfth to Mars in the tenth house. This blue partial figure does not facilitate assertion either.

The Achievement Triangle is still connected with a three-coloured learning triangle to the Moon Node. The Moon Node in the fifth house as an ascending point makes one love to experiment and be creative too (18). It enriches the Achievement Triangle, thus enabling remarkable insights. One can therefore sum up by saying that the Achievement Triangle in Galileo's horoscope helped him to have basic scientific insights. The eighth house components made him very dependent on the structure of society, of which he would also turn out to be a victim.

Blue Aspect Figures

Talent Figures

The second single-coloured figure group is formed of blue talent triangles. There is a large and a small talent triangle; the large one consists of three trines, the small one of two sextiles and one trine. People with such figures have a lot of reserves. Talent triangles indicate an abundance of available abilities, competence, expressiveness, skilfulness and striving for harmony. It depends on the quality of the planets that form the talent triangle, whether it can be implemented or whether it remains unused due to idleness, complacency or indifference. Both talent figures consist of blue aspects that form triangles. These correspond to the mutable cross, making the blue aspects more versatile and animated than their lethargic nature would indicate. Especially when the motivation is love, they react with much understanding and kindness.

Large Talent Triangle

A large blue triangle in the horoscope represents a special talent. It reveals an accomplished ability, indicating varied experiences and pervading and forming the personality. The abundance and perfection of the energy is linked with three trine aspects in three signs of the same element. The planets and element enable one to deduce what kind of talent 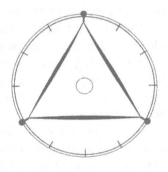 is present. The cross qualities of cardinal, fixed and mutable are united in the trine. The person with such a trine therefore has three possible alternative actions and drives, as well as the behaviour appropriate to the element. If the talent triangle is in the fire signs, the nature of the talent is enthusiastic and intuitive, while in the earth element it relates to the observable reality. Air lets the intellectual level shine and water has an affinity with the spiritual, empathic nature. The Large Talent Triangle corresponds to the tree that is bearing fully ripened fruit and waiting for them to be picked. If left unpicked, the fruits fall unused to the ground or rot on the tree.

Complacency

It so happens that the blue, material aspect figure containing latent energy gives people a tendency to complacency. They let themselves go and think that they do not need to make an effort in life, as they manage anyway and don't need to learn anything new. A Large Talent Triangle is firmly set in its ways, and has great trouble changing, as it is already perfect. This gives a certain rigidity, an unteachability when learning is required. Such people can use what they have to offer to adapt to the changing demands of life. They usually get through easily and therefore see no need to develop new features and methods, but they do tend to rely too often on the talent that they already possess. Additional squares (or oppositions) are desirable here, as latent strengths can develop through their demands for achievement.

Pride and Self-assurance

People with such a triangle can be unpleasantly proud and look down on other people, without being able to say exactly what they are proud of. They even get angry if they are told the effect they have on others. However, that doesn't mean that everyone with such a triangle must be so proud. Being able to do many things easily gives self-certainty and a heightened self-confidence. With this figure, an accomplished manner appropriate to the element is adopted, and displayed with typical self-assurance.

The quality of the trine in its relationship with Jupiter, and the fact that the figure fits symmetrically around the centre of the horoscope, indicate the need to address the question of purpose. This is to find out what should be done with the given talent and how a suitable challenge and form of expression could be found. One of the challenges of this figure is to develop an appropriate creative will. With a suitable Jupiter orientation, the right balance can be struck between perfectionism, pleasure-seeking and obsessive behaviour.

The horoscope of Swiss novelist Walter Diggelmann contains a Large Talent Triangle mainly consisting of intelligence planets (23): Saturn in Sagittarius in the second house, Uranus and Jupiter in Aries in the sixth house and Mercury in Leo above the MC. It is therefore a fiery talent triangle with writing ability. Mercury on the MC does indicate a masterly association with words and writing. The Moon opposes the planets Jupiter and Uranus on the sixth house cusp. As a blue trine can work mainly in an outward direction on a red aspect, his subject would

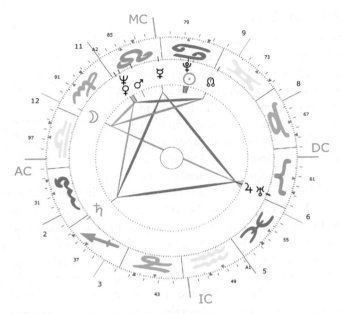

Walter M. Diggelmann
5.7.1927, 13.50, Bischofszell/Switzerland

be the social-critical field of his subject matter. Diggelman's intelligence featured abundant knowledge and the required intuition. He had the ability to encourage and convince other people (fire). The other parts of the whole aspect pattern appeared in his case in the personality department. In his horoscope, most of the planets are in the upper space; they form a separate figure and work on a different level. The talent triangle did not really help him to solve his own problems. As he himself wrote, he suffered throughout his whole life in personal relationships and in love. One side of this problem is shown by the Moon's position in the twelfth house in Virgo, which indicates a repressive childhood. In fact he was in service as a boy. The other side of the ego problem is indicated by his unaspected Sun/Pluto conjunction in the ninth house in Cancer. For even his flexible, wide-ranging intelligence was not enough to help him grow out of these ego problems. On the transition of the Age Point over the Sun/Pluto conjunction, he died relatively young from cancer.

Small Talent Triangle

The Small Talent Triangle also consists of blue aspects; it is formed of a trine facing the core and two sextiles. This figure has a similar motivation and mode of action to the Large Talent Triangle, but as an asymmetrical figure it is more dynamic. It shows a still developing talent, as opposed to one already developed. The sextiles with their Venus quality assimilate the 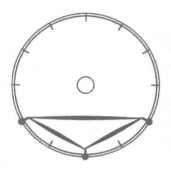 signs and houses that they are stretched across. The small blue triangle takes up a third of the signs of the zodiac, and usually one quadrant of the houses. In this part of the personality, growth is achieved by adapting, as far as possible without stress, to enjoy the subject of this life area as befits their element. The appropriate properties are developed gradually into a distinctive and specialised talent and are formed during the course of the life. Usually knowledge and skills are constantly accumulated by calmly absorbing experiences into the consciousness, not through active exertion and hard work.

Venus Quality

Both sextiles correspond to the Venus quality, symbolic of the blossoming stage of a plant, and are keen to keep on growing and absorbing matter, and to enjoy what is facilitated by the triangle. The richness of the inner attitude (trine) is harmoniously implemented with available opportunities and as far as possible expressed without friction and conflict. These are happy people who enjoy life without over-extending themselves. They plan their energies, are careful and selective in their goal setting. Once they have decided on something and it has captured all their interest, all goes smoothly. They deploy their energies with relative ease and can be active around the clock without flagging.

In the horoscope of Edgar Cayce, the 'sleeping prophet', we can see quite clearly the importance of the Small Talent Triangle that points at the large Saturn/Venus/Mercury/Moon Node conjunction in the seventh house. The apex of the triangle is always a kind of goal direction. The positioning in the sign of Pisces and in the seventh house is typical of a doctor's chart. His potential was his charisma, his effect on his environment and on those people who sought healing from him. This talent triangle enables him to put this ability to optimal use, people

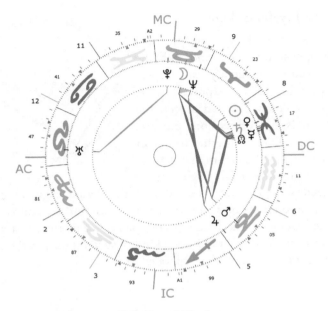

Edgar Cayce, Healer
18.3.1877, 15.00, Hopkinsville, Kentucky/ USA

benefited from his healing talent. The blue talent triangle stands on its own, has no red aspect and is therefore passive and must be activated by the environment, from outside.

5.3 Two-Coloured Aspect Figures

Red-Blue Aspect Figures

A large group of aspect figures are formed by a combination of the aspect colours red and blue. These people have an ambivalent attitude, a dualistic world outlook and a tendency to think in black and white terms. Their sometimes absolutist either/or attitude can get them involved in arguments.

Single Ambivalence Figure

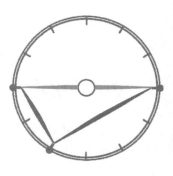

The Single Ambivalence figure formed by one opposition, one trine and one sextile occurs frequently in aspect patterns. Ambivalence is expressed in the two aspect colours. The red aspect, the opposition, is full of tension, pressure and conflict. Directly connected with this is a relaxed, pleasure-oriented pole, which forms the apex of this right-angled blue-legged triangle. The blue sides of this figure suggest an ideal world, where one sees only beauty and goodness and tension is swiftly despatched along it. The blue aspected planet forms the third pole to the opposition planets; it indicates a kind of switch point in the correct management of the ambivalent energies.

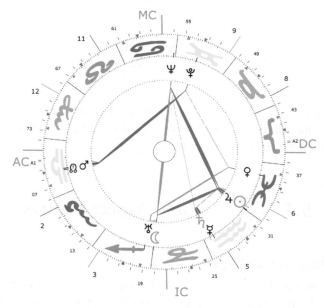

Anaïs Nin, French writer
21.2.1903, 20.30, Paris/France

Anaïs Nin was famous for her novels and stories in which she dealt with the problems women have in relating to other people, because she herself had the same problems. For a long time, she tried to fulfil her role in life as a woman, but without much success. If relationships got into a rut, she finished them. In astrological terms, she reverted to the planets on the blue peak, i.e. the Sun/Jupiter conjunction, which lies at the start of Pisces in the fifth house. This blue Sun position made her unable to deal with conflict. She wanted to enjoy life and if problems arose, she ran away. She often asked herself why she had to experience hard reactions in spite of her own softness. It was relatively easy for her to diffuse the opposition tension along the blue aspects, but the Moon/Neptune opposition always caught up with her. Next to the single ambivalence figure, we recognise another linear figure that ends at Uranus. This means a strong inner restlessness that would suddenly take over and embroil her in problems again. On the other hand, we know that the planet at the blue apex can enable a freer view of things, thus making the opposition more bearable. For her this meant the chance to bring both opposing elements to the Sun/Jupiter conjunction, which being in Pisces deals with the subject of transformation, into synthesis. This was expressed in her books.

Double Ambivalence Figure

As it is quadrangular, this figure shows a need for security as well as a tendency to structure life according to personal ideas. People with this figure try to fulfil themselves in life in different ways with the red side and the blue side. Here it depends mainly on which side of the horoscope the two different triangles lie. If the blue triangle lies on the I-side, the relaxing moments are acted out there. If it is on the You-side, one has a relaxing effect on the environment instead. However, the red triangle acts according to the position in the horoscope of the relevant houses.

Internal ambivalence is the reason for the pugnacious attitude often shown by this individual, as well as for the striving for harmony. Both sides are skilfully deployed for self-advancement. As it is a large figure, encompassing the central core, this person cannot be untrue to himself. Whatever he does he does out of inner conviction. Since there is never any insecurity, except in the present, where he must sometimes decide: "Should I go for it or should I hold back?"

Depending on the accuracy of the angles and the orbs of the planets, there may be a quincunx aspect (150 degree angle) between the apexes of the red and blue triangles. This large figure is more strongly character building than the Single Ambivalence figure. The tendency to repression is not as strong in the large figure as in the red-blue triangle, because the consciousness has more room for involvement and the oscillation between red and blue is longer and fluctuates more.

Fluctuating States

People with a Double Ambivalence figure almost always fluctuate from one state to another. In the red figure they are active and conscientious; in the blue figure they let themselves go. If too long is devoted to rest or pleasure they feel slightly guilty. There is an ambivalence between achievement and pleasure. To be able to adopt and maintain an enjoyable and experienced attitude in one area of life (blue apex), targeted effort is needed (red apex). Conversely, one must also question the point of this effort. It is a question of cultivating the correct use of work relative to the desired attitude and ability to enjoy. At best, their motto is "don't mix business and pleasure", which enables them to advocate and live with this dual nature. A constant effort motivated by duty without phases of meaningful relaxation is just as impossible as the opposite: the escape into wild, unbridled hedonism, without the active management of the basic tension produced by the opposition. The resulting quadrangular figure reveals the inherent motivation of stability; but its asymmetrical shape betrays its dynamic character, and expresses the oscillation between the two ambivalent attitudes.

Polarities

A polar system can also be understood as parallel thoughts or actions. Such people understand one side of an issue or thing, but on the other hand do something completely different, without contradicting themselves. This could be called a conscious and opportunistic switching and can be very successful. An interesting comparison is with the Janus head, with its two faces. The face looking forwards is white and open, and the backward looking one has a black and impenetrable expression. But those around them only know one of the two extremely different sides of this individual, unless they also have two extremes inside them. The Double Ambivalence figure understands very well, for not only does it see the polarities in this world, it lives with them and finds it completely normal that we humans live in dualities. So if anything it seems well-adjusted, conservative and correct. What many people do not know though, is the inner pain linked with guilty feelings that time and again drive the Double Ambivalence figure to achieve still more intense experiences or better performances. This person is not only hard on himself, but always demands more from himself and really drives himself. If the opposition lies on house cusps, this can often mean that he puts pressure on those around him too.

Strong Will

People with a Double Ambivalence figure usually have a strong will with which to realise their ideas. They have a spirit that outshines many people and often leads to great achievements. On the other hand, they have a deep understanding of culture, luxury and well-being. With this rather introspective side, they observe and like to enjoy, collect experiences and have a harmonising effect on other people. They prefer active and hard-working people, with whom they can build something. This means they like to be with influential people who support them and whose willpower encourages them to great things. This quadrilateral allows the owner to be quite influential himself, to lead others and to control them like a manager. Many even become politically active or are concerned with improving the world, so that improvements can be carried out and things changed a little. If this person has a clear goal, it is just a question of time until they reach it. With their ability to motivate passive people, their plans always have enough support.

The Double Ambivalence figure is very common, but in more than half of all cases, the green diagonal is missing, because the quincunx has a small tolerance value (orb). The differences between such figures with or without the long green aspect are noticeable and can be exactly understood, which incidentally is evidence in favour of the Huber Orb Table.

With Quincunx

If the green line is present, one can see that actions are deliberately coordinated and run according to an internal plan. This often makes people feel that the person is somehow manipulative or that they have covered their backs e.g. with the boss or some other authority figure, who stays in the background. With the green line one also knows that without contacts things don't quite work, for the green aspect cultivates relationships and communication. Something is either good, worthwhile and profitable or it is ignored. The green diagonal indicates willpower and consciousness, which is linked to the planets in the red-green corner. This person knows he can achieve everything if he is fully aware of his goal, has thought out all eventualities and has informed himself through appropriate communication. Many have a penchant for whimsical, worthless or at least antique objects that they collect or like to deal with.

Without Quincunx

If the green line is missing, the person is more natural, and more interested in the present. He doesn't make people feel he is manipulating them. He goes more often from one extreme to another, thinks in terms of black and white, vacillates between blind optimism and despondency and is also impressionable. Without the green line, the Double Ambivalence figure becomes a red-blue polar figure. With the clear separation of the blue and red sides, this person splits his environment into two halves. In the houses lying behind the blue triangle he gathers experiences and enjoys life. In the red half, he acts energetically in those houses and asserts himself wilfully. On the one hand he is affable and on the other as hard as nails. The so-called ambivalent behaviour indicates the ability to switch immediately, according to the situation, from one state to another. People with this disposition act according to the tenets of our society: "Money makes the world go around", "No pain, no gain", "Business before pleasure", etc.

Asymmetry

In spite of the asymmetry, the Double Ambivalence figure is somehow impregnable, perhaps due to the respect that its size commands. The large amount of space it takes up is a kind of showing off that keeps people at a distance. In any case, it certainly stands out and people with this figure can hardly be ignored. They always exercise a certain power and dominance, according to their level of consciousness and inner maturity. They do need a certain developmental period until the whole of a demand can be evaluated. Many are unhappy with themselves and notice that there are always still things that they cannot achieve. That is a somewhat unpleasant guarantee for their further development.

Red-Blue Planets

The two planets forming the opposition have a red-blue influence and are pressurised by the polar black and white attitude. The other two are inwardly green and receive from outside, like a gable, red and blue lines at right-angles. One is controlled harmony, the other controlled achievement. However, as the green line joins these two planets directly, the controlling green energy of both extremes is the same. That means that this person achieves what he consciously wants, with the alternate activation of both planets. If we observe his consciousness more closely, we notice that he is always moving back and forth between two conflicting attitudes, perceptions or activities.

The Single Ambivalence triangle bestows great potential and strong willpower. The Double Ambivalence quadrilateral weakens both, due to its unstable starting position. Although the achievement often receives stronger energies through the red triangle, the strong powers of self-assertion are constantly being reduced and turned off by the blue aspect. The Large Learning Triangle in this quadrilateral prevents this standstill. This person is always learning new things, pursuing their goals and consistently living what they have learnt to be right. They can rarely be told anything and rarely take advice from others; they always want to be true to their inner development.

Aspect Qualities

Here too, interesting clues can be obtained by comparing the planet distribution and the aspects. The two Mars and two Saturn aspects mean

22,12,1930, 12.00, Belz/Poland

that people with the Double Ambivalence figure tend to be creative, enterprising or productive. The Mars quality finds a double expression in the planet that lies at the red corner. If the planet there is sensitive (Moon, Jupiter, Mercury, Neptune), the potential is of a sensitive nature, which can sometimes cause nervous disorders. With the combination of Saturn and Venus aspects, such people are concerned with health issues, and in the end, Mars (square aspect) and Venus (sextile aspect) are also interested in erotic, sensual experiences and in the difference between men and women.

The green aspect inside the figure, between Venus and the Moon Node in the above example, indicates doubt and insecurity that are not shown outwardly. Behind complete composure there are hidden anxieties that could be missed (Venus 8th house cusp). However, such crises are a chance for these people to broaden their ideas and expectations and to entertain new points of view. These learning processes are often very painful and radical. They require a deep change of motive through a constant psychological demand of the eighth house. The related crises mean that this person gives his absolute composure, his standards and ideas to his relationships, in order to be able to align himself to reality again. This can lead to overcompensation. If the tension from the opposition is experienced as incompetence or a guilt complex, one stops enjoying life and gets depressed easily. But then the active phase comes round again to lift one out of the depression. One pulls oneself together, activates the red aspect and works diligently and efficiently again. There is also the chance to resolve the conflict creatively, where the potential hidden in the talent (blue aspect) is converted into achievement (red aspect).

Righteousness Rectangle

There are three more blue-red aspect figures, the Righteousness Rectangle, the Kite and the Cradle. In all three, the first thing to be considered should be the elements in which the figure lies. Their structure means that they can either lie in active signs (fire and air) or in passive signs (water and earth). So the figure's features are expressed passively or

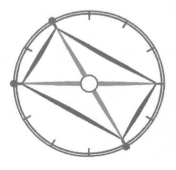

actively depending on the case, which is significant in the analysis of the personality and the basic attitude.

Envelope

In the Righteousness Rectangle, four blue aspects form a rectangle. This indicates a rich supply of talent, which is kept on solid ground by the fixed principle. The Righteousness Rectangle looks like an envelope in which the inside, charged with the tension of the two oppositions, is protected. The two red aspects are well wrapped up and are not visible from outside. The blue aspects show the need for harmony, good behaviour and give an impression of security, so that no-one notices the inner tension. Just as one cannot see the contents of a closed envelope, people who have this figure in their horoscope seem inscrutable. They are outwardly calm, balanced, *righteous* and only rarely betray their internal tensions and problems. They are often not aware of the effect they give, as they are too preoccupied with their internal problems. Many are busy trying to keep up a good outward appearance. They don't accept that anyone can have problems, because they don't want to have any themselves. This attitude is more common in superficial people. On the other hand, people who try to identify their inner problems (oppositions) and solve them tend to suggest the most perfect possible solutions to those around them.

Motivation

The motivation of this rectangle is clear: the person wants to spread harmony and acquire security. That is not always easy in a world full of contradictions and polar energies, but it is reasonable. It is not that people with this rectangle must stop always looking for meaning; rather they just always recognise the meaning and value of things but have trouble letting go. If their sensuality is aroused, this person reacts very devotedly, for he is able to feel pleasure and knows the value of relaxation; however for him, that can be too much, like a wet sponge. Then he finds a private retreat and broods.

If this person suffers, no-one notices, for externally he only shows his blue balanced side. He can be very affectionate, but still hold back. He can have a harmonising effect on those around him though. When he settles disputes, he instinctively makes sure that everyone agrees with him. His great sensitivity enables him to be very considerate, responsive and to provide constructive energies, he possesses a natural therapeutic gift. The two red diagonals mean that everything is controlled centrally and all life processes are ultimately subject to the will.

Aspect Qualities

The aspect qualities in this rectangle are evenly distributed between Venus (2x), Jupiter (2x) and Saturn (2x). Saturn and Jupiter represent sensorial intelligence and are practically orientated. Practical thinking and clear standards combine in the search for meaning. Venus and Saturn, being receptive and accepting, show the special gift of storing sensations and feelings. Finally, the Venus-Jupiter combination has an artistic side; it shows aesthetic sensibility and a feeling for art and beauty.

People with this rectangle have a depressive prevailing mood, because life can be so difficult and yet so beautiful. They are perfectionists, who want to please everybody and also possess a deep understanding of human nature. Such people are popular and their passive presence is appreciated by those around them. Sometimes they can be controversial, to relax other people and to be able to reveal more depth. They can quickly get someone back onto their feet from the depths of despair. They aim to show that life has meaning, thereby helping to keep the person on track.

Ambivalence

As a blue-red rectangle, the Righteousness Rectangle is one of the ambivalent figures that only knows two states or extremes: strong-weak, harmonious-tense, black-white, good-bad, and so on. The will (red) combines with the substance (blue) and collected experiences can be adapted to circumstances. Due to its four-fold symmetry, the Righteousness Rectangle is practically unassailable. These people can ride out any storm, mental pressure or emotional discharge, even when they had previously suffered from it. Their blue cushioning enables them to weather every blow and return to their familiar form after an adaptation phase. They seem to have something unchangeable and constant in their lives and therefore behave quite conservatively.

This symmetrical rectangle consists of four ambivalence triangles. The ability to settle conflicts and differences is therefore 'multiplied' by four. Indeed this person knows no other way; insight, logic or knowledge are not very helpful by themselves. He either does something and thereby gains valuable experience or he forgets it. The four triangles work like a windmill, giving the impression that this person is stuck in a perpetual loop. He rarely has to really make an effort to take a decision; the wheel of life revolves again and brings him the experience anyway.

Position

In the horizontal position, the blue rectangle looks like an envelope with a seal in the middle. In the vertical position, it looks like a lift door or a window that is reinforced with two crossbars. One could even identify a goalkeeper with outstretched arms and legs. What is he guarding with his impenetrable all-round vision? Secrets, old and forgotten knowledge or something about you? The fascination of people with this rectangle grows in accordance with their increased   spiritual learning. Many possess a mystical disposition.

In contrast to the other ambivalence figures, this figure boasts two oppositions, which gives it a high energy potential with which the conflict between inside and outside can be expressed creatively. The internal pressure caused by the oppositions can sometimes lead to a breakdown. If the internal tension is not diffused, substance is lost. Sometimes, the bottled up internal pressure leads to mental confusion, there is a conversion, a transformation from Saul to Paul. That leads to a wholesale abandonment of everything that was important before, thus enabling a spiritual rebirth. This figure is therefore also called a Mystic

Georges Braque, French artist
9.5.1882, 2.30, Argenteuil/Paris/France

Rectangle. Something of higher inner value is then present that can be given to the world along the blue aspect.

In George Braque's horoscope, the four corners of the Righteousness Rectangle lie on different zodiac cusps, which enhances his versatile talent. It can be said that his blue rectangle is influenced by eight signs, not four. His development of Cubism made him one of the founders of modern art and his original sculptures also brought him fame. It should be noted that his inspired works of art are also expressed in the prominent trine of Saturn to Uranus, towards the You-point in the horoscope. He was highly original and a shining example for other artists as both a painter and a sculptor.

Kite

The Kite figure is composed of a Small Talent Triangle on top of a large one that together form a large quadrangular figure. So both talent triangles are joined in a fixed structure with the intrinsic motive of security. In the Kite, there are five blue aspects surrounding one red one. While the Righteousness Rectangle has the ratio of four blue to two red aspects, the ratio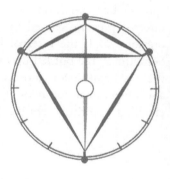
in the Kite is five to one, i.e. there is an excess of blue substance aspects. These are influenced by the pleasure and harmony principles.

Red-Blue Ambivalence

In this figure there is an ambivalent striving (red and blue colours) for further development. The right angles created in the centre say that only that which is long-standing and brings proven knowledge is acceptable. This must be tested constantly and be able to be verified by personal experience. This person wants to know the meaning of everything and if something has become meaningless, it is rejected. He often goes from one extreme to another (red-blue) in order to know the best and worst alternatives, and then finds his own middle way.

The Opposition Planets

The planet at the Kite's tail works like a tension ruler, and lies opposite the small Learning triangle in the other half of the horoscope, which indicates the talent to be developed by the opposition. We call the planet at the Kite's head the peak planet, to which everything in the figure is oriented. The other three planets must work towards the development of the peak planet. Both uniquely blue influenced planets have a lot of available substance according to the house and sign quality; they can make the correct choices without much effort and channel misdirected energies into positive development.

Either-Or Attitude

As two ambivalence triangles are facing each other, the two different sides of the horoscope produce an either-or behaviour. This person is either totally preoccupied with an issue or he avoids it; he either uses his Large Talent Triangle for his own development or he adapts himself with his Small Talent Triangle to someone else. In the small triangle there is more capacity for devotion and also often an artistic gift. Together with the large triangle, this makes such a person a hedonist who finds many things easy and whose needs are met by what is around him. But only with humility can he also use these advantages for others and do good with them. To the right and left of the opposition run two equidistant blue lines that are connected by a line that gives meaning (trine = Jupiter = clear personal standards), where conflicts, tensions or crises are settled almost scientifically by accurate reasoning based on observation and experience and the cross-comparison of all available knowledge. It could be said about them that "Every question has an answer and for every problem there is a solution, one must just know the direction in which to develop."

Aspect Qualities

The qualities of the blue aspects (Venus aspects 2x, Jupiter aspects 3x) and the red Saturn aspects (opposition) show that the vigour, the sensory awareness and the optimistic enjoyment of life of Jupiter are represented just as strongly as the passive, conservative Saturn and that of the perfectionist Venus. The ability to concentrate and to identify the sense and use of things (Saturn, Jupiter), are stronger than the sense of little things, beauty, and enjoyment. This person gets the greatest pleasure from meaningful activity or by making others happy and content through sense recognition, aesthetics and harmony.

External Peace

External peace and harmonious charisma make these people good partners. The person with a Kite enjoys contact with others, is sensual and well-balanced, but requires a lot of peace and quiet to enable him to develop his talents and make his own way. An abundance of blue facilitates a relaxed and enjoyable life, but the opposition aspect works like a thorn in his side. Things could be so ideal and harmonious if the red line were not there. The desire to help comes from the deep inner pain he must constantly balance or repress, since no one else can help him and he can only be supported by his own soul. Outsiders do not see his pain. They perceive inner stability and self-loyalty, making it hard to help such a person, and the exemplary role he increasingly plays as a result of his talents leaves him feeling more and more isolated.

The familiar Kite figure resembles a toy blown around by the wind. That emphasises the ability to remain calm in stormy times and to use available energy correctly. However, in this image, stability is provided by an outside person who holds the string. In reality, this figure provides the person with his own strong inner stability that others like to lean on.

Striving for Perfection

Such people strive for perfection, not because they want to reach a fixed state though, but to be true to themselves, i.e. in all situations to act in line with their innermost convictions and their heart of hearts. This is the only way for this person to develop. He feels the urge to provide growing life with the best opportunities for development possibilities. He is always checking what people really need and whether a certain need is valid or not. He quickly recognises possible obstacles and suitable opportunities or necessary steps for further development.

People with the Kite figure need the inner tension provided by the opposition aspect in order to work on self-improvement. The planets that form the opposition indicate the topic. Initially, with the blue aspects, they build the image of an ideal world and see the world as they would like it to be. They see it in their own way from the central core outwards, through which the opposition passes. They are so used to the constant pressure or pain of the opposition that they even believe that everyone else thinks in the same way. They can repress or deny the inner tension relatively easily. The tension pressure is toned down and harmonised by the blue aspects. They live mostly successfully with the environment above both sextiles and in a conflict-free, harmonious, aesthetically-pleasing way. But even the Kite figure is not immune to crisis. One day even these people need to open up to new people and develop themselves. The opposition as an inner red aspect indicates the axis topic of the signs and houses it occupies, where the crisis must take place.

Charisma

Due to their own harmonious perception and make-up, these people radiate a certain superiority and self-awareness that often astounds those around them. From outside, nothing can be seen of the inner conflict taking place, in secret as it were, on the opposition axis. The blue aspects of their Kite figure have a magnetic attraction for what is good for them. They avoid unpleasant things and people and conflicts and withdraw from potentially dangerous situations. When one has contact with such people, one often borrows their positive quality of life, even their suggested image of an ideal world. They have the ability to pass on their philosophy to others and to lead by their own example. This attitude can lead to a pronounced self-satisfaction. Many develop a narcissistic feeling of the personality, which suffers greatly when hurt.

Initiation Figure

From an esoteric point of view, we talk about an Initiation Figure, in which the final state of a certain stage of development has been reached. It is common knowledge that at each end of an evolutionary stage there is an initiation that reaches closure after a development. This results in the stabilising of a state of awareness as symbolised by the Kite. But not everyone with a Kite has already reached this stage.

The development task consists of having a good look at the theme of the planets that lie at the peak or the kite tail and form the opposition. In the following horoscope, the Moon is in Aries in the third house. The opposition to Neptune extends the Moon problem into the dimension of universal love, into advocating a philosophy of unity and forgiveness. Here the polarity of inside and outside, of the inner tension of conflict and the outwardly displayed harmonious attitude find direct expression. That is why the planets at the apex of the Kite must be accurately defined and understood. The kite tail can point downwards, upwards, to the left or to the right. If these people live with and learn to deal with this topic, they will not see the world so naively, as is the case of less-developed awareness. They can experience their conflict on the two apexes with more awareness than on the two corners, which are only blue.

However, the energy pole of the red aspect meets a substance pole (blue aspect) on both ends of the opposition. This orientation enables a better control of life and allows the discovery of the richness of substance

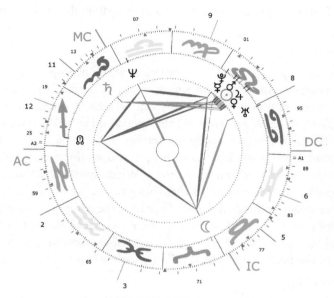

Michael-A. Huber
9.8.1955, 17.17, Zürich/Switzerland

contained in this figure. Then the other special name for this figure, the initiation figure, as mentioned above, comes into its own. This means the initiation in one's own abilities, the meaningful substance of the trine aspect. So a person becomes more and more able to radiate a transcendent peace and harmony, and to meet and transform karmic duties.

Cradle

The Cradle also consists of five blue aspects and one red one, which are connected in a stable shape (quadrilateral) like the Kite. The great difference lies in the visibility of the red aspect, which lies along the border of the two horoscope halves, like an energy-charged barrier. The other half remains unexplored, unknown territory. The Cradle derives great stability from 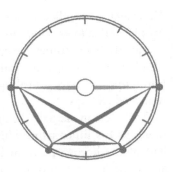 its symmetry. If something unpleasant approaches, this person can just switch over and is suddenly protected by an invisible wall from any criticism or attack. It reflects others' opinions or intentions like a mirror and appears untouched by them.

The Baby in the Cradle

A cradle reminds us of birth and babies. The baby in the cradle has entered our material world from the spiritual one and reflects perfect purity. The interface between life and death can be seen as a mirror, and life reflects what lies in the soul. This figure means that sooner or later one takes an interest in sleep, dreams and death, in order to learn about the transition from one dimension to another. People with a Cradle retain their childhood faith for a long time, they believe in good and are harmless. They would like to have the security and protection of a stable life situation and actively pursue this. In other words, they try to avoid falling out of the cradle. They cling to it and like to be clung to. But it is just those people with a Cradle in their horoscope who have the development task of leaving the security of the Cradle and going out into the world, which can be likened to going in to the empty space of the horoscope, in order to become independent.

Relaxation and Harmony

On the one hand, in this figure there is the ability to imitate others or to reflect their mood; on the other hand he can harmonise with, and even heal, other people from the depths of his soul. The person collects or soaks up like a sponge the feelings, needs and pain of other people without being burdened by them. He makes almost everything harmonious. If something is too tough he cuts himself off from it completely and it then just ceases to exist and effectively disappears.

Nevertheless, conflicts occur over and over again, for he provokes other people and allows them to push against his "glass wall". After this energy discharge comes the opposite: relaxation and harmony. With this simple way of resolving conflicts, the individual with the Cradle in his horoscope can have a healing effect and help others to deal with their repressed feelings.

This person actually seems talented and balanced, but he often represses his inner pain, which is activated by the other, unoccupied half of the horoscope from his environment. This leads to retreat, to an escape inwards in order to maintain harmony (5 x blue to 1 x red). He must passively reflect on the meaning of life, at which point he is very vulnerable. By learning to accept this withdrawal as a process of self-purification, he allows his harmony to radiate brighter and more intensely.

Inner Harmony

The five-fold blue does not just mean harmonious energy, but also the collection of much substance and experience. This person possesses sympathy and an open heart, as he views the world in a very positive light. There is an inner harmony, as well as the ability to live in harmony with the environment thanks to the three sextiles. They can adapt themselves and deal with the demands of their environment. Because the motive of security dominates, these people are mostly anxiously concerned about protecting what they have achieved against intruders. They have difficulty letting themselves go, and prefer to remain in the familiar security of their cradle.

Other people can see the afflicted red side, and they therefore treat it with consideration. For his inner harmony means that he sees everyone as being basically good, and is therefore sometimes too gullible. The inevitable disappointments make him strong and wise when it comes to understanding human feelings and idiosyncrasies. Although he can only participate superficially, he is always striving for deeper contact. In this quadrilateral, there are two only-blue-influenced planets. They possess great receptiveness, devotion, ability to enjoy and have flair. They have great control over their personality, as experiences are so thoroughly processed and integrated that failure is almost impossible (perfectionist).

Two talent triangles form a semi-circular dish that oscillates in two directions between its polarities. Conversely though, there are two possible middle paths or ways out of this conflict. So there is a double talent that can transform the conflicts of our life and give them new meaning and new opportunities. The person is invulnerable, because he always keeps an escape route open into his own personal creativity, where there are no more conflicts to deal with.

Aspect Qualities

The aspect qualities of Venus (3x), Jupiter (2x) and Saturn (1x) show a dominance of the feminine-passive side, supported by Jupiter's sensory awareness, which doesn't want to miss any opportunity. With its Venus quality, this mirror quadrilateral possesses good taste in all artistic matters. This person could also be an artist himself; however this area is not so clearly recognisable The Saturn quality teaches him to limit himself and concentrate on one thing. Otherwise he would just live his life in the pursuit of sensual pleasures. The Cradle figure is controlled in the middle by two trines, from which two small talent triangles project. The axis topic of the opposition aspect provides the basis for the pleasure-seeking inherent in the blue aspects.

The interpretation of the Cradle depends greatly on the area of the horoscope where it is situated. The positions are described separately below.

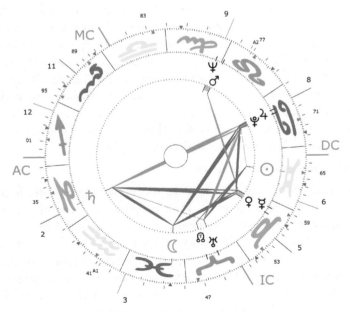

8.6.1931, 21.00, Basel/Switzerland

Cradle in the Collective Space

The classic Cradle feels most secure in the bottom half of the horoscope, where the fixed quadrangular quality is expressed most strongly. It feels less comfortable in other spaces because it tends to feel that it is falling out of the security of the cradle and being thrown out unprotected into the world.

In the case of the Cradle, many talents are gathered in one half of the horoscope. In this lower space we find the practical person for whom everything is effortless and easy, who is happy with this and creates a harmonious environment for himself (as in the case of the Kite). The person takes life as it comes, works contentedly and needs no theoretical background knowledge. What lies above the barrier makes him anxious and threatens his harmony. He protects himself from this space, attacking anyone who represents it either openly or covertly. What he denies from the outset must not be looked at.

Cradle in the You-Space

If the Cradle lies in the You-space, the person is afraid of being alone, and makes every effort to maintain existing partnerships; which can sometimes lead to a loss of identity. He wants to feel cared for and seeks a partner who is stronger than him who will give him stability. Many need motivation and validation from outside, from the You. In such a case, the partner or the task to be mastered can bring the talent triangle to life. But in the case of conflict, most react badly, i.e. ambivalently. There are actually two ambivalence triangles in this figure. They either allow themselves be wrapped up in cotton wool again and play the conforming child, or they refuse to continue the relationship. Due to the blue-red aspects, they can be forced into an either-or attitude, where they have to go back on possible decisions again.

Cradle in the Individual Space

If the cradle lies at the top, it looks more like a parachute. It is not grounded and there are no roots. These people are often ambitious, strive for unattainable goals and are constantly experiencing defeats and the thwarting of their plans. In reality they are too security- and stability-minded to really come to terms with the individual space, for the top of the horoscope demands moral courage, independence, acceptance of responsibility and self-awareness. A Cradle finds it very hard to display these qualities all the time; it prefers to be left in peace.

In the Cradle there is also a highly developed aptitude that is called on to overcome a fear of certain tasks. In the upper area there is often a certain value system that people with a Cradle cling onto. Whether it is valid or not is not as important if it can resist attacks and provide security. From a positive point of view, a Cradle can also be productive; after all it does contain two talent triangles. Evident creativity can bring greater confidence with which to confront the empty hemisphere. Producing something that can be presented to others increases the feeling of self-worth and inner security. In the case of the Cradle too, drastic crises are needed to be prepared for the confrontation of anxieties and the implementation of one's own abilities.

Cradle in the I-Space

A cradle on the I side of the horoscope is a sign of introversion. Such a person is very self-sufficient and closed and avoids deep encounters with others. He protects himself from the outside, is preoccupied with himself and only lets invited guests inside. The inner space, the intimate sphere is kept shut and only opened to those who know the password, as it were. Such a person finds it very unpleasant if someone enters without being invited and if he is talked about or judged. He wants to live undisturbed in the protection of his inner space and only open up when he is sure that those who are knocking to come in are true friends. If a stranger intrudes, the opposition immediately becomes an impenetrable barrier; he would rather remain alone and is happy in his own world. This can often lead to real problems in relating to others.

In the case of aspects of Age Points located in this figure, the feelings of security are frequently shaken, thus making the consciousness aware of a change in internal or external conditions. The person should not stay in his *cradle*, instead one day he should be thrown out of the nest in order to participate in the growth process of life.

Red-Green Aspect Figures

Figures with a combination of red and green aspects are called *stimulus* or *irritation* figures due to the lack of blue aspects. There is constant inner tension, and rest and relaxation are almost impossible. The energy almost never comes to a halt and is constantly recharging itself. Red-green aspects can either take the form of an Irritation Triangle or an Irritation Rectangle.

Missing Blue

Red and green aspects are both stimulating, but in different ways. The green aspects are stimulated by the red aspects and are always thinking up new possibilities. But blue, the third dimension, is lacking, which means that they cannot be realised. That does not make much difference to this triangle; there are other people who can do it. When red and green come together, it is difficult to take a break as they whip each other up. Green makes one always want to know more and red makes one want to achieve something and reach goals. People with a marked red-green aspect pattern or a stimulus figure in their horoscope can be very nervous. This is due to the high energy potential present in the red aspects. This energy is kept constantly on-call by the green thinking aspects, leading to a permanent state of tension and being constantly on the go, which can overtax the nerves, especially when the opportunity for resolution and relaxation is lacking.

This is just where the need for the third colour in the aspect pattern becomes obvious. The blue aspect is missing, i.e. the possibility of slowly and thoughtfully preparing a structure in which energy (red) and intelligence (green) can appear. In the case of these irritation figures, the other figures must be accurately defined, as they could possibly reduce some of the tension.

Exploitation

When one is motivated, one draws on one's own energies, which can sometimes lead to breakdowns. The stored energies of the opposition and the permanent, sensitive receptivity of the whole perception system understandably make the person very uneasy and nervous. The slightest resistance or inconsistency challenges their conflictive spirit. Their pronounced philosophy of achievement leads them to undertake all-out efforts and to be constantly planning new things. This makes them push and exploit themselves and others. However, it seldom leads to the desired results, or if it does, they don't last. As the principle of form is alien to them, efforts are often fruitless. Despite their wealth of ideas, such people need others to help them carry out their plans.

Irritation Triangle
[Stimulus Triangle]

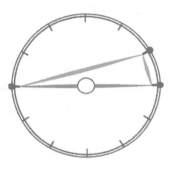

As an Irritation Triangle, this figure needs constant movement and stimulating activity. Triangles have a mutable motivation, which is why there are shorter or longer periods of hectic overexertion. The Irritation Triangle is formed by one opposition (red), one semi-sextile and a quincunx (both green). The subject of the figure is once again to be derived from the opposition. The energies stored in it are looking for a way to resolve the state of the opposing pressures, the blockage of energy flow and the rigid attitude they produce. Because of the quincunx, people with this triangle are painfully aware of the liberation of tension as a desperate longing. However, their endeavours are only sufficient for a permanent communication process (semi-sextile) that manifests itself predominantly in the areas and topics (house position) in which the green corner of this figure lies.

Fits of Anger

Sudden bursts of anger can arise as a reaction to external pressures. This defensive behaviour does not last long, though, it is over quickly and forgotten again. The ability for flexibility and adaptation enables these people to be evasive and to quickly make up for damage caused or hurt feelings (triangle).

The opposition of the red-green triangle is found in the horoscope of Henry Rousseau on the 4/10 axis, which implies an individuation process. The opposition is resolved by the green aspect to the Moon and Venus, which is where the solution can be found. Rousseau was a self-taught painter and co-founder of the Naïve Art school. With the Moon and Venus in the fifth house, it is not surprising as they indicate artistic ability. He could transfer his Irritation Triangle creatively and even learnt under the patronage of Picasso. The talent triangle present in the horoscope and the other blue aspects all point to this. However,

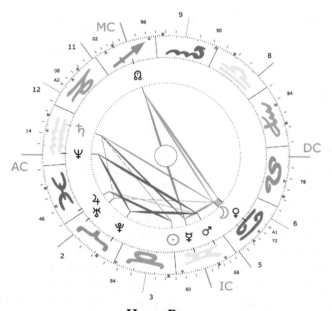

Henry Rousseau
21.5.1844, 01.00 LT, Laval/France

he himself had to overcome many obstacles; there are no gifts with an Irritation Triangle.

Irritation Rectangle
[Stimulus Rectangle]

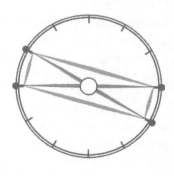

This symmetrical, green rectangle indicates a great stability of consciousness, and the person is constantly striving for mental continuity and to expand awareness. However, that can lead to stagnation if he sticks fanatically to his decisions, and his mental rigidity can lead to dualistic conflict. This figure offers a large target, due to its length, and the person learns early on to defend himself verbally against attack, which makes real contact with him difficult. Being a rectangle, this figure tends to resist movement, unlike the triangle. It bows little to outside pressures. The stimulus quality of red and green is kept under control by the rectangle. Only the green is visible from the outside, which indicates uncertainty and in many cases also a compulsion to learn, in order to alleviate the inner tension by constant further study and searching. The Irritation Rectangle has a less aggressive effect than the triangle.

There are attempts to carry out certain ideas, but this leads to pressure being unintentionally put on others. This figure sometimes even provokes fanatical characteristics.

Alert Information Seeking

From outside, the green aspects of the Irritation Triangle make it appear to be adaptable. This person perceives all the activity around him alertly and deliberately, and in checking it identifies many connections. The four-fold green makes this rectangle act insecurely and makes him dependent on love, all the while constantly looking for information. He has twice as many green lines as red ones and no blue. It can look as though this person is mentally running away from his inner suffering, because no harmonisation is possible. Life can only be managed with willpower and lucidity, and what matters is to recognise the challenges and confront the painful experiences they involve. The thin green rectangle is like a barrier, but it could also be a bridge. As a barrier, it guards certain knowledge that no-one else is allowed look at unless they ask the right questions. Or, alternatively, he builds a bridge of understanding with information and knowledge. In both cases, his increased perception helps him avoid misunderstandings and misinterpretations.

The four Irritation Triangles that make up the Irritation Rectangle should not be interpreted as an over stimulation, for the more a quality is repeated, the more atypical it becomes. The sensitive reaction to the environment goes around in a regular cycle (like a radar antenna). That is why these people are very controlled and resilient, even if their alert eyes are flashing and their ears are pricking up.

Adjacent Aspects

Irritation figures are hard to deal with, and even the people concerned have problems with them. Adjacent aspects, especially blue ones, are therefore very important as potential aids. In most cases, this role is taken by Jupiter and its trine. On the other hand, these people are used to *high voltage* situations, and they don't mind dealing with conflicts or coping with setbacks. For example, they have an ability to handle situations where communication is tense. Given their creative personalities and level of intelligence, they can establish a forum of constructive communication, be it socially, in a relationship or at work.

Aspect Qualities

The aspect qualities correspond to Mercury (2x) and Saturn (4x) giving an academic combination in which the memory is stronger than the intellect (*elephant memory*). This person becomes a know-all in his field. Saturn makes its presence clearly felt as reserve, inner distance or strength. However, the Mercury aspect makes him very communicative and almost overzealously eager to really understand others or to communicate everything he knows. Mercury absorbs information from other peoples' experiences, which resonate in his green Saturn lines and are reproduced in the red lines.

Information Flow

A person with this rectangle is aware that many things need not happen and many more would be possible if one only had the right knowledge. He therefore feels responsible for getting information to the right place. He is aware of the power of truth and handles his information carefully and is interested in open and straightforward debate. Secrecy irritates him and he hates it if information is not passed on. He therefore learns to filter out the truth from the smallest piece of information and knows things that no-one else does. Information flows to him just as water flows unceasingly into a pool. Sometimes he feels almost crushed by this knowledge, though, and takes flight as he wants to forget those thoughts and cut them out.

Many people react as though they don't notice what is happening around them, they are imperturbable. In reality, they take everything in and prepare themselves inwardly for how they want to react. People with an Irritation Rectangle are almost continuously occupied with planning for the future. They think out their own reactions so as to be prepared for the right moment. Many possess an enormous diversity of creative plans and activities. Again and again they come with great new ideas and old ones are thrown out. They are usually not put into practice though, because the blue, the form-creating principle, is missing. It becomes a bottomless pit, a big investment of energy remains fruitless or nothing lasting comes of it. It is obvious that these people demand more than they receive from the environment. There are many instances of exploitative behaviour, which is why this aspect figure is called the Exploitation Figure.

The Problem

The Irritation Rectangle requires that inner tension be used as the impetus for personal development, not that other people are overloaded by forcing one's knowledge on them. This figure wants to transfer the pressure of the red aspects to the breadth, tolerance and flexibility of the green aspects, which is a hard task with this figure.

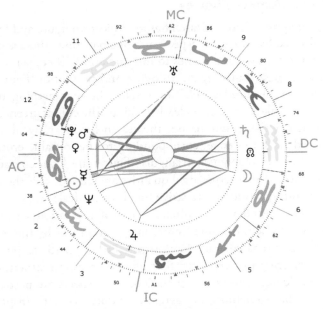

Norman Schwarzkopf, US-General
22.8.1934, 4.45 EST, Trenton, N.J./ USA

In the horoscope of US General Schwarzkopf, who commanded the Allied Forces in the 1991 Gulf War, the strong ordering principle of the rectangle is visually striking. The motivation of this aspect pattern is therefore evident, i.e. to find a secure state, an enduring form of communication. He seeks information from everywhere via the four outside green aspects and is open to all environmental stimuli. Particular attention should be paid to the house axis in which this long, narrow figure falls. It is the I-You, the encounter axis, on which the information search and communication (semi-sextile) are continuously stimulated. Both oppositions show a rather compulsive relationship and a rigid attitude towards the outside world. However, strong inner desires and ideas try to loosen things up. The Irritation Rectangle can be interpreted as a channel between the I and the You. There is an almost unbroken flow of information across the small green aspect, which could not necessarily be perceived or accepted by the oppositional topics on the I side. This can lead to congestion or blockages.

Blue-Green Aspect Figures

All three blue-green figures (Search figure, Projection figure and Eye) are triangles formed by two green aspects and one blue one. There is no red, which is important when it comes to interpretation. There is no active, dynamic awareness, but they are thinking and perception figures that enable sensitive communication. The need to achieve something, to have conflicts or to make decisions is clearly lacking. The colour green, as well as the triangular shape, emphasises the search for meaning, flexibility and the need for knowledge, corresponding to the mutable cross. The motivations of the blue-green triangular figures are love, contact and communication. The interpersonal qualities are refined, as is the ability to live in a fantasy world and to strive for abstract ideals.

Blue-green aspect figures are often a source of inspiration, with which plans can be hatched, our intellectual imagination can be trained and projects can be prepared. But they provide little impetus to put them into practice. They are very often part of a larger aspect structure that must be considered during interpretation. Red aspects are particularly necessary so that something can actually be done with the inspiration and intellectual capacity of these figures. Otherwise the person will float above the clouds building castles in the air and avoiding hard work.

Escapist Tendency

People with a predominantly blue-green aspect pattern tend to avoid conflicts, tension and stress; they look for the path of least resistance and often escape from reality. They are very inquisitive and interested and have a wonderful, often excessive, imagination. But when it comes to making a special effort to attain a certain result or to make an important decision, they then evade the issue and their instability shows itself, hence the name Evasive or Escapist aspect. As already mentioned above, the missing red aspect (the square) often makes itself felt by a lack of motivation and efficiency. According to the situation, though, this can be offset by this person's remarkable ability to create relaxed, sensitive, aesthetically pleasing and subtle contact situations and to introduce imaginative points of view and reasoning.

Search Figure

This green-blue figure consists of one long and one small green aspect that are connected across a trine to form a triangle. It is only effective in one half of the horoscope and cannot condition the whole character to the same extent as an aspect figure that goes through the centre. The description of this figure can only deal with a partial facet of the owner

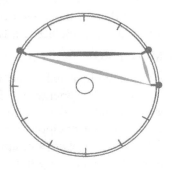

of the horoscope, and will probably be superimposed by other figures. The figure is usually part of a larger structure.

Aspect Qualities

The aspect qualities are conditioned by a long green Saturn aspect, a small green Mercury aspect and a trine Jupiter aspect, i.e. a combination of Jupiter, Mercury and Saturn. They are intelligence planets with an academic character (23). These people have a strong inner motivation to serve the truth and to make wise decisions. They are suited to working on long-term projects and can wait patiently until success comes of its own accord. They work continuously with the same dedication as at the start and know that everything takes time.

The green aspects and the triangular shape mean that the Search figure typifies the mutable qualities almost perfectly. The planets from which it is formed make it adaptable, gentle, searching and shy. The trine brings a talent for seeking wisdom or meaning. People with this figure always look for an abstract goal or ideal, and they are often gripped by a yearning for a better world. They have the feeling "If only I could achieve the goal of my longing, then my life would be complete". This can be expressed as the search for a beloved person, for music or art or also for a guru to emulate.

States of Awareness

This figure leads many people to experiment with different states of awareness, sometimes by means of drugs. The Search figure embodies the longing for another dimension of awareness. One can also be slightly addicted to a type of being that promises luck and happiness.

An incoherent, divided aspect pattern complicates boundaries, and the Search figure gives a tendency to addiction or escaping reality. The Search figure gives a lack of protection in its area, as intense drives cannot defend themselves or be disassociated from. The stronger an aspect pattern, the better it is able to cope with such figures.

Missing Red

Because cardinal red is missing from the Search figure, it is yet to be tested whether energy can flow in from adjacent red aspects. If red is completely missing from the aspect pattern, then these people are absolutely not equipped for such impulses. If someone has a violent, demanding or aggressive approach, they can either succumb to it, or take the only other option, which is flight. This is also noticeable if the figure is alone in a horoscope or determined by the contact space (DC).

In this horoscope, the Search figure runs from the lower area of the horoscope up to the eleventh house. It is combined with other figure parts. The aspect pattern is mainly vertical and indicates an individual aspiration. On close inspection, we notice the dashed trine of Mars and Venus to Pluto. The Search figure is therefore not completely closed. One-way aspects are not so strong and mostly have a one-sided effect;

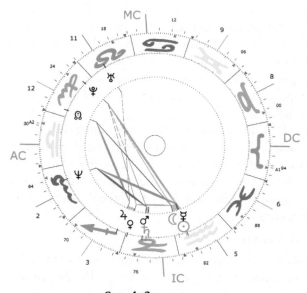

Search figure
27.1.1960, 23.35, Zürich, Switzerland

although they can be developed. Pluto in the eleventh house, to which the triangle points, implies a longing for a better world, for the perfect person, but also for an ideal, role model or guru. The base of the Search Triangle lies in the third and fourth houses. General collective structures determine life for a long time, until they are questioned by new discoveries or shocks (Pluto in 11th house). After one has experienced the shortcomings of the previous state in the fourth house, where the Sun/Moon and Mercury lie, one tries to liberate oneself from them. Although the Ego Planets in the fourth house possess inner strengths, at the start of life the person adapts to the house environment and lives according to family tradition.

However, the Search figure causes a mounting dissatisfaction with the status quo. The person initially starts by imaging a better, freer world, but liberation does not come immediately. All three intellectual planets lie in the upper part of the horoscope and represent an over-idealistic world view with high demands that are hard to put into practice. So this person spends a long time thinking out all the possible perspectives and alternatives but he cannot free himself, he stays in the nest for a long time. But there is a way to bring high ideals and principles into the collective, i.e. to work from top to bottom instead of from bottom to top. Many times we have observed an inversion in the interpretation of the intellectual planets.

The Search figure implies a constant striving for the extension and completion of the topic provided by the trine. The green aspects destabilise the apparent calm with new information and ideas. A Search figure in the horoscope means that one is interested in refining sensibilities, the growth of knowledge and increasing opportunities for pleasure and communication; although without being prepared to make a big personal effort, unless there are corresponding abilities in other parts of the whole aspect pattern that can correct this one-sidedness.

Projection Figure

The Projection figure is the only one of the three blue-green figures that encompasses the centre, the core personality of the individual, and as such is the biggest of the three. Both quincunx aspects surround the inner core and, as a sensitive aspect, pick up the information and energy of the core like an antenna. The core provides the figure with the motivation to awareness that mainly favours the planets that form the apex of the triangle. This gives the figure its creativity.

The Projection figure is also important for spiritual development. It is not for nothing that it is called the Finger of God. We will deal with this in more detail later. The two long green aspects are on the one hand thinking aspects, but also Saturn aspects (see also chapter 2 on Aspect Theory), which is why this figure is lived either consciously or unconsciously. Because both quincunxes are awareness-forming aspects, awareness training is beneficial. That is why we will also deal with this figure more thoroughly later on.

Dual Channel System

The planet at the apex of the triangle sends its qualities down the two long green aspects to the sextile aspect and the energy radiates back from there; thus making it a dual channel system. To illustrate this better, many people compare the Projection figure with a slide projector or a cinematograph. A projection source, the meeting point of the two quincunxes, projects the sextile onto a screen, which receives and makes visible the imagined images. You should take into account whether these projections are made consciously or unconsciously. For example, people with a developed awareness can find that this figure indicates an ability to foresee the future. People with a less-developed awareness experience this figure as a spontaneous, unconscious process, in which personal needs, deficiencies and images are relayed to the environment. C.G. Jung said "projection is the transfer of a subjective process into an object" (24). The person's awareness determines the meaning given to this figure in the horoscope. It should be added that everyone runs projections continuously, even if they have no Projection figure in their horoscope. But with this figure, *projecting awareness* can be trained as a mental ability and used creatively.

Position

The position in the horoscope is revealing in terms of the interpretation of this figure. If the Projection triangle lies on I-You axis, one projects one's own ideas onto other people. In the direction from the DC to the AC, one tends to give too much importance to others' opinions. Projection processes are then the transfer of idealised or negative images onto a romantic partner, who is either put on a pedestal and seen through rose-coloured glasses, or as the enemy.

9.5.1932, 18.30, Bernburg/Germany

If the projection runs from the lower space to the upper space in the horoscope and includes two Ego Planets, as in the above example, then this figure becomes an essential element in the character of the horoscope owner. Below, at the apex of the triangle we see Saturn and on the ninth cusp Moon/Venus there is a dashed sextile to Neptune. This is the horoscope of a woman. She tends to project an ideal image of herself as an individual into the upper space. Although she tried to develop her individuality, initially she made her partner responsible for assuming this role. The Sun in Taurus in the seventh house naturally reinforces this claim. In the case of a Projection figure that runs from bottom to top, either one has a very individualistic father, or one is looking for a partner who fulfils this role. While this projection is lived out on the emotional level, one does not really experience the topic itself. With the Projection figure, processes run slowly as two long thinking steps are required that take time and often last a lifetime. But this is exactly why they are also development aspects.

If it runs from the MC to the IC, i.e. in the opposite direction, the person might try to impose their strongly held ideals of collective thinking and feeling patterns, whereas the real issue would be for him to change these strongly-held ideals, which would allow the basic needs of both himself and others to be met.

Levels and Stages

Particularly in the case of this figure, it is not just the position in the house system that should be considered, but also the levels on which it works. This determines whether the projection is into the physical, emotional or mental world. As already described in Chapter 2, all the components of the horoscope can be laid out in three or four dimensions. The horoscope owner must find out for himself on which level his consciousness is mainly active.

A developmental event can certainly be observed too. According to the laws of evolution, our initial awareness is on the physical level. Then comes the second stage, at which we consciously experience all types of emotions in polarised and conflictive situations, i.e. in our encounter with the world. The third stage is the thinking or mental level, where the consciousness can be expanded intellectually. We learn to study, meditate, reflect and intuit by systematically contributing to large-scale projects. This is why on this level we talk about a 'Project figure'. The mind is broadened here. Project figures on the mental level have produced many great thinkers in the past. They have used their brains to reach further than other people and also brought along creative ideas and thoughts. Below, we try to explain in greater detail the effects of the Projection figure on the three human levels.

First Level: Unconscious Living

The Projection figure acts largely unconsciously on the physical level. Images from the unconscious are projected outwards, which include undealt with psychological factors. The person drifts along for a long time in the belief that he has no problems, blaming those around for any mistakes. Whether he fails, has failed to reach his goals or has not fulfilled his duties, it is always the fault of the environment or of other people. Many areas represented by the principles of the planets that lie at the green apex of the aspect figure are triggers for this transfer of guilt. Such people tend not to attribute the topic to these corresponding planetary functions, instead only see them reflected on their projection screen, i.e. in blue in the sextile. If there are still one or more additional planets within the sextile aspect, which often happens, then they concentrate the unconscious topics on them.

Second Level: Emotional Perception
The emotional or feeling level is one of the most natural projection surfaces for this triangle, but also the most eventful. The emotional level is best suited to project wishes or feelings onto objects or people. This level corresponds to our quite exaggerated illusory world, as communicated by the television, for example. There, people with such triangles are required because they possess a wealth of ideas, imaginative vision and a remarkable talent for presenting things so that they can be communicated to others. According to the planet involved, in this figure there is often a suggestive, magical power with which others can be impressed or influenced. For example, if Pluto is at the green apex, the magical powers are stimulated. Such a person can project his inner images onto others, influence them or mentally confuse them, if he uses thought as an instrument of power.

Third Level: Intellectual Results
The third stage is particularly interesting for this figure because it shows the two long thinking steps off to their best advantage on the thinking level. The projection activity for each person is different in principle, but on the mental or thinking level it forms awareness and leads to creative intellectual processes. With continual work on awareness and willpower, it is possible to control this normally unconscious process. On this level, people with this figure are both inspired and access a higher level of awareness regarding many things in life. That is why the Project triangle enables these people not only to project their ideas to the outside world, but also enables an ongoing expansion of awareness. The awareness can be extended to draw in more and more intellectual dimensions. Like a searchlight, people with this Project triangle on the thinking level scan

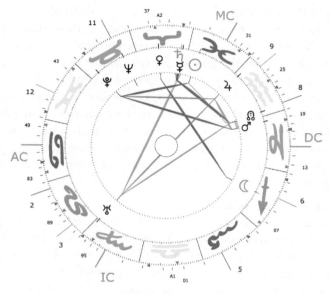

Albert Einstein
14.3.1879, 11.30, Ulm/Germany

the surrounding area for knowledge, seeking the evolutionary plan in a visionary way so as to implement a small piece of it.

A classic example is found in the horoscope of Albert Einstein, whose Theory of Relativity changed both our way of thinking and our idea of the world. His Projection triangle has another opposition on the Thinking axis 3/9 from Uranus to Jupiter. The red aspect combines perfectly with the Projection figure and also represents a Uranus-Jupiter-aspected intuition. If the small green semi-sextile aspect of Jupiter to Mercury/Saturn were not missing, it would be a Striving figure, which would have made him excessively ambitious – which Einstein was not. Here we see that incomplete figures can still be exceptional.

Yod Figure

One must go through many changes in life before reaching the last stage. A person with this figure is very often confronted with far-reaching decisions. As already mentioned in Chapter 2, the long green aspect is also called the Decision Aspect. On this level, this figure deserves the name that has already been used for years in America, where it is called the Yod, or Finger of God. It was discovered that the Yod figure points very clearly towards the personal spiritual destiny like a finger. If the Age Point runs across the target planets that lie at the green apex, for example, there is almost always a big inner transformation. In Einstein's case, the Age Point passed Uranus, at the apex of the triangle, when he was 14. Even at this age he was interested in science, especially physics. In his autobiography, he says that this was the age when he first laid his hands on books on physics and science. He himself found great pleasure in solving simple algebraic and geometric equations. This would lay the foundation stone for his later research. His inner vocation was thus decided.

Development Process

It is obvious from the above that the Projection figure involves substantial development processes, not just small changes. We have to answer the question: "What is it that actually motivates us, which part of us is used in conscious projection?" It is the power of imagination, a kind of mental migration or wandering of our thoughts that develops abilities which actually enable us to move our awareness to where we want to go. These can be both terrestrial and spiritual goals. It starts off as just imagination or the idea that we have of our goal, until one day our awareness is so well trained that it produces tangible results.

Contact with the Age Point

When they come into contact with the Age Point, many people are beset by an inner restlessness that they cannot explain. They have a nagging doubt as to whether everything they have done up to now is right. Although they are convinced that a change is due, they usually don't know what is right for them or where they should be going. They reach decision crises that go right to the roots of their existence. The insecurity of not knowing where to go but still having to make a decision is a crisis filled with doubt and discontent. Many are seized by an incomprehensible longing to give up everything and drop out. Although they often have no security and don't know what will happen next, they cast everything aside.

From a spiritual point of view, the Projection figure is concerned with inner conversion, with transformations and changes of awareness. The positive side of acute crises is that they force one to take stock of one's life and ask oneself "What has my life been about so far?" If one discovers that one is passing essential things by, then a quick decision must be made to alter one's way of life as soon as possible.

The House Position

The other question is: "How does a person with a Projection figure get to the third stage, and how does he access his intuitions?" He develops a plan based on wishes and longings in order to reach a specific aim. This aim is formulated according to the houses in which the triangle is situated and where it is pointing. To a large extent, this reconnects with the theme of the planets that both quincunxes point to. The projections are thus cancelled out and an increasing sense of reality is restored; in other words: the projection is reversed or transformed. What was previously projected outwards is now reflected back to the emitter. That is the process on the emotional level, if the person gets as far as cancelling his projections with spiritual values like understanding and forgiveness. That is one theme of the three spiritual planets if one of them lies either at the green apex or at another corner of the triangle. Such a person is familiar with the way of transformation, can free himself from his projections, and similarly free his partner of them too. Otherwise there is the danger that one's own wishes and mental processes, like anxieties, aversions and feelings of danger, are mistaken for reality and that one remains trapped in one's problems.

The Zodiac Signs

In the deeper evaluation of such a triangle, one should also consider the quality of the zodiac signs involved. As the Projection Triangle has three corners, it always lies in the three cross qualities cardinal, fixed and mutable, so that three of the elements are also involved. This is also a clue as to the significance of this triangle. For such awareness is far-reaching, universal and highly differentiated. Just one element is missing here, and one should find out oneself the importance this has for interpretation. It is worthwhile researching this triangle further.

Overstepping Boundaries

All blue-green figures, especially the Eye and the Projection Triangle, have the same characteristic, that due to their sensitivity they sometimes lose the boundary between inside and outside. So they take all processes and events personally or project inner themes outwards, and can then be overwhelmed by the abundance of what they perceive. That is why emotional realisation, discernment and strengthening of the core personality are needed, so that false ideas can eventually be eliminated from projections. This figure then brings consciously planned, creative thinking, innovations and brilliant inspiration.

Project Triangle

As mentioned above, on the mental level where thinking and the will are active, the Projection Triangle becomes a Project Triangle, because the person has made up their mind and is able to incorporate their mental images into scientific knowledge. There is a decision-making factor involved (the third level of the quincunx aspect). A developed intellectual capacity allows for the planning and targeting of important projects that could benefit a large number of people. At this stage, the correct decisions are made, i.e. "to make a creative contribution to evolution". With the help of a developed will, the person is in a position to mobilise the necessary strength to introduce changes on earth that help to carry out God's plan.

Eye or Information Figure

This figure consists of two green Mercury aspects and one blue sextile aspect, thus forming a small blue-green triangle that we call the Eye. The Eye's flexibility, inquisitiveness and alertness produce a state of concentrated attention. It is open to all sides and assimilates more than other figures. In the area of this aspect figure, information is sought and found, everything is observed in detail, nothing escapes the *eagle eye*. The Eye can also be compared with a radar screen, which rotates to take in all sides, scans the surroundings and records everything it comes across.

Small Spheres of Interest

The Eye is the smallest of all aspect figures, and encompasses only two or three houses, thus giving it a small sphere of interest in which it is very active and expresses the mutable qualities in concentrated form. According to the size of the houses, the Eye can only extend over one house, where it is highly specialised, be it in work or in relationships. If it covers two or more houses, the effect is more diffuse. Due to the prevailing Mercurial ability (2 semi-sextiles), this figure works in a very impersonal and unselective way. That is why it often cannot separate the wheat from the chaff. Many things are lumped together. That is why it is often difficult to know which information is important, what belongs together and what doesn't. This inability to discriminate produces disappointments, misjudgements and naivety.

As mentioned, both semi-sextiles have a Mercurial quality, i.e. the continual intake of information from the area of the corresponding houses. That takes place at the periphery of the horoscope, and often unconsciously and automatically. Facts and data are gathered in the outside world and this figure absorbs everything that comes into reach. Absorbing too much leads to over-stimulation that can become intolerable. Many become so sensitised that they have a sixth sense. That is why dissociation from adjacent aspects is necessary.

Radar Screen

This aspect figure can [in some cases] also pick things up that are not visible as if it were a rotating radar screen, producing parapsychological abilities like clairvoyance, clairaudience or clairsentience, especially if the spiritual planets are involved. A few of these people possess a sixth sense and can scent danger or protect others. A deeper insight into motivations and life patterns can also be gained, which is why they often have a special aptitude for teaching and counselling. Several sides of all issues are taken in mainly unconsciously so that they see more than normal perception allows; it is something like an instinctive intuition. Most people find it difficult to make out where the sudden knowledge is coming from, which is why they often seem untrustworthy. People with a Little Eye should therefore always aim to be mentally discriminating and look for provable facts.

Sextile Aspects

The blue aspect is helpful. The information can be taken in by the Venus sextile aspect and processed and assimilated, to be stored for future use. That is why this figure can accumulate a great deal of information. However, if the planets at either end of the sextile aspect are not up to the task of assimilating and storing everything, it can lead to a nervous breakdown. So it should be noted whether these planets are hard, soft or personality planets and whether other figures apart from the blue-green Eye are involved. Blue helps with storage and red enables positive use to be made of the information acquired.

The whole aspect structure of the following horoscope is situated in the thinking quadrant, which means that the Eye receives all necessary information about the You. In the You-space, such a person must constantly adapt and learn to master new situations. A strong active impulse is associated with the constant effort of gathering and assimilating information and broadening one's own point of view. This is understandable, as the more one moves around, the more one comes across different places and people and the more one experiences, lives and learns. Here it depends on the rest of the aspect pattern as to what the personality concerned does with the information and how the perspective is focused (house position of the Eye). According to the level of awareness, the person concerned can be merely inquisitive, or someone who also transfers information, like a writer or a journalist.

Perception Figure

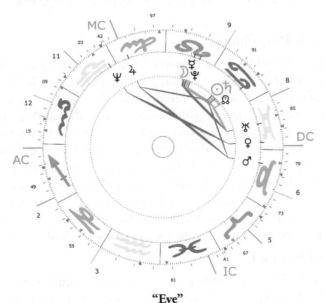

"Eye"
11.7.1945, 16.45, Winterthur/Switzerland

This Perception figure actively faces all sides, both within the horoscope and outside in the surroundings. Looking at its planets we see Moon, Mercury and Pluto in conjunction, Uranus at the other corner, and the Saturn/Sun conjunction at the peak. It is important to determine the planets at the apex, because the figure points towards them. In this example they are Sun and Saturn, two personality planets which are vital for the person's ego. Such people take themselves very seriously, are self-involved and react sensitively to the judgments of those around them, for example personal criticism. Their interest is mainly in their own development, so that they most easily absorb knowledge that is useful for the growth of their own personality.

For spiritually-oriented people, the perceptive abilities can be very pronounced with this figure, so that they perceive things that others hide. Others have a new experience of nature and a higher, holistic inspiration or vision that is echoed in the ecology movement.

5.4 Three-Coloured Aspect Figures

Red-Green-Blue Figures

The three-coloured figures are typical learning or development figures, in which the third colour (i.e. green) plays an important role. The green aspects, which have an affinity with the mutable cross (or contact cross) are added to the red aspects, which correspond to the cardinal cross (or impulse cross) and the blue aspects which are associated with the fixed cross (or substance cross). This therefore brings a third point of view into the equation, which, for better or worse supersedes the polarised thinking of the red and blue aspects with a third pole. Green aspects allow an escape from black-or-white thinking and a search for causes, possible solutions and meaning. We are already familiar with the small green aspect (semi-sextile) and the long green aspect (quincunx).

Semi-Sextile Aspect

The semi-sextile is the smallest aspect after the conjunction. It is the small thinking step, which gathers the information necessary for us to think objectively and neutrally. With the semi-sextile one thinks in small steps, adding one piece of information to another until the collected perceptions make sense. The green semi-sextile aspect works by providing information, communicating and reacting to external stimuli. It is easily influenced and often changes its opinion.

Quincunx Aspect

With the quincunx, the information provided by the small green aspect is classified and integrated with the greater whole until the connections are understood. As a big thinking step, it develops a micro-macrocosmic way of thinking based on the hermetic principle *as above, so below.* The person questions the meaning of existence, searches for causes and motivations and has a better understanding of different kinds of human behaviour. This mind-expanding aspect encourages psychological thinking, the understanding of connections and facilitates the discovery of the meaning or purpose of things.

Learning and Development Triangles

When interpreting Learning triangles we make distinctions between four triangles of differing sizes and one trapeze figure. In the three-coloured aspect figures there is a procedure that conditions growth by an ongoing crisis mechanism, opening up great opportunities for development.

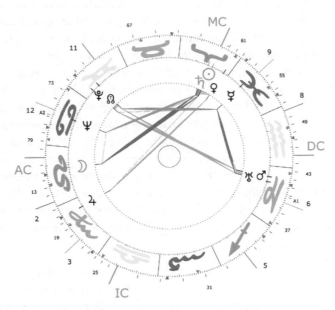

Two Learning triangles, small and large
31.3.1909, 12.00, Belfast/Northern Ireland

Crisis Mechanism

There are three phases to the crisis mechanism: red-green-blue in line with the aspect sequence. The dynamic process starts with the red aspect (square). The point of conflict is where the red and blue aspects touch each other. The calm and balanced, pleasure-seeking state of the blue aspect is disturbed or irritated, causing tension or conflict and some kind of decision or effort must be made. The old state is no longer tenable, a problem has arisen that must be solved.

There is a development spiral that aims to achieve another point of view with every completed transition. Every passage through the three phases and each one of these crises contains the possibility of finding solutions that previously did not exist, i.e. breaking new ground. Whether that is successful or not depends on the attitude of the person concerned towards this crisis process. If one inwardly recognises the opportunities, then development is likely. If one treats the crises as mere disruptions, the development process will be blocked. Communication and the provision of information usually lead to new experiences (green aspect). The person is always ready to experiment, and the newly acquired discoveries lead them to try to establish a new, harmonious state in a still unsure and unstable position (green-blue contact point in the aspect figure), which meets the requirements of the initial problem.

So this process would seem to be complete. But only until a new problem comes along and the crisis mechanism gets going again: conflict – striving for solution – harmonisation. The Learning triangle is more directly involved than any other aspect figure in this development spiral. If there is more than one Learning triangle in a horoscope, the person concerned can find himself undergoing different processes at the same time, which complicates the overview and the understanding. If there is only one Learning triangle in a horoscope, a clear theme takes shape that can be defined very precisely by the three planets. The basic attitude and motivation towards the development process and its theme can be deduced from the aspect situated nearest to the central core.

Rotation Direction

If we look closely at the Learning triangle, we notice that the colour sequence red-green-blue can run both to the right and to the left. If we start at the blue-green corner and go along the red line, we find two different rotation directions. The learning process takes much longer in a clockwise direction than in an anticlockwise direction. According to our experience, this is not so significant in the case of the Small Learning triangle as it is with the large Dominant triangles in which the central core is enclosed. The direct or retrograde rotation direction means a faster or slower cognition process. We will go into this in more detail later.

Small Learning Triangle

In the small Learning triangle, the largest aspect, the square and the smallest, the semi-sextile, are connected by a blue sextile. The aspect facing the centre is the tension aspect, the square. The harmonious aspect, the sextile, is facing outwards. The inner tension produces dissatisfaction with the external situation. The centre stresses the inner need for growth so that the individual decides (=conflict), not to let himself be satisfied with reality.

Repetitions

With the small Learning triangle, this process is repeated many times. There are certain life themes that come to maturity with the figure and crop up again and again. Over the semi-sextile (green aspect) there is a search for new information in the environment with which to be able to resolve the tension of the square and to be able to live in harmony with the environment again. Often, people with this aspect figure are motivated by an inner unrest and dissatisfaction that those around them cannot really explain; when questioned about it their answers seem evasive. If the blunt point of this triangle (green-blue) is facing the outside, then that is the object of their dissatisfaction. It therefore depends on where the blue-green apex is pointing as to where the dissatisfaction strikes. This aspect figure occupies only a quarter of the horoscope and therefore only affects part of the character.

The main preoccupation of people with this Learning triangle is the processing of their experiences in the fields of life concerned. They are not so interested in an analysis of the contents of the area; what they want is to experience themselves via a permanent communication process in this area. This small Learning triangle is the next smallest aspect after the Eye, and is therefore strongly oriented towards the environment.

Medium Learning Triangle

The biggest aspect in the medium Learning triangle is a trine. There is also a semi-sextile aspect and an outwards facing square. The starting situation is an internally latent state, since the trine is turned towards the inner core. The Jupiter aspect confers, on the one hand, a particular ability to enjoy and perfectionism and, on the other, a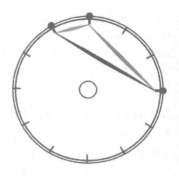
tendency to complacency and carelessness. Both states are shaken by conflicts and problems in the environment. External circumstances, daily responsibilities, social rules, reminders, prohibitions, etc disturb one's peaceful existence. Suddenly, from the rich inner reserves, there are decisions to be made and services to be performed. Experiences and the fruits of labours gone by, collected in the trine, are constantly called into question by different circumstances (square). New efforts must be made to cope with these demands. For many people, their own perspective (trine) makes them want to improve their environment, to be active in it and to fight it if needs be (square). This is achieved by entering into relationships with others, communicating and sequencing pieces of information (green aspect) so that the activity moves in the right direction and the lost inner peace derived from accomplished actions is regained. This person appears outwardly rather nervous, irritable and constantly in a rush, as the blunt point of the triangle that faces the environment has a red-green aspect (square).

Large Learning Triangle

The biggest aspect of the large Learning triangle is the 150 degree quincunx. It is the nearest to the inner centre and picks up its influence like an antenna. The basic motivation is the expansion of consciousness, learning and development. Though large, this figure does not encompass the horoscope core, which means that interest in growth is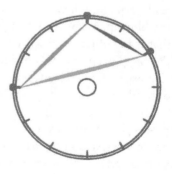
restricted to the area covered by the house and quadrants in which the figure is situated.

Aspect Qualities

The red-blue peak of the pyramid is facing the outside world. The Mars square and the Venus sextile convey an ambivalent attitude to the environment and the tendency to want to solve problems using an either-or attitude. The harmonious situation and its inherent tendency to adapt (sextile) are just the starting point and are abandoned if a real incentive to grow is provided. Tension is sought out and conflicts are not avoided (red aspect) as conflict tension leads to the challenge and stimulation of adopting an appropriate searching attitude and striving for a solution to the conflict (green aspect).

The danger of this figure is to offer solutions that are too simplistic (sextile), thereby continuing to live in a state of inner doubt (quincunx) because personal desires for harmony and longing have been given in to too soon and the pressures of reality (square) have only been coped with for a short time.

Dominant Triangle

The Dominant triangle is fundamentally different from the three other Learning triangles in that it encompasses the centre of the horoscope that symbolises the core personality. This means that the whole personality is affected by problems of growth. This does not just affect one partial area, as in the case of the other Learning triangles, but influences all

areas of life. The small figures are much more flexible than the large ones. They are the expression of processes that run over and over again at a relatively fast rate, so that experiencing events and processes is more important than the actual nature of these events, which seem to be interchangeable. It is different for the larger figures that encompass the centre. In the case of the Dominant triangle, the processes are often slower and therefore more profound and radical, but still relating to growth and transformation. The question of freedom is much more important here than for the smaller Learning triangles, which are in closer communication with, and therefore more dependent upon, the environment.

Creativity

There is a pronounced creative quality to the Dominant triangle, thus, in the case of successful problem-solving, producing a personality with a stronger influence and dominance over the environment. But there is a long way to go, during which the individual must delve into the source of his ego, before he can resolve problems successfully. Resolution, liberation and objectives can only be achieved through the growth of his own core personality. Whereas the small Learning triangle was mainly concerned with procedural experience and the growth of the personality, because of constantly recurring crises in one area of life, the basic problems of the Dominant triangle are the form and content of self-expression and the formation of the personality. The ego aligns itself to the trine, which possesses experiences, cognition and perspective. The theme of the square usually contradicts this and indicates the direction in which a transformation should take place and where efforts should be made.

Change and Transformation

The cognitive abilities are often put to the test here and a qualitative change in the active, achievement-oriented self-expression is called for. Changes of motive and transformations are the order of the day for long periods. A recurrent experience of extreme conflict (square) occasioned by feelings of personal inadequacy vis à vis a certain problem makes one decide to deal with it. Now begins the process of the great search (quincunx), which often entails a revision of one's self image.

Rotation Direction of the Dominant Triangle

The direction in which the Dominant triangle rotates, from red to green to blue, is an important feature in its evaluation. We start at the red-blue corner then go along the red line, come to the green line and finally to the third point which is the green-blue corner.

Cognition Triangle (Direct)

An anti-clockwise rotation direction, i.e. in the order of the zodiac, follows the cosmic sequence in which discoveries can be made rapidly. As a direct Cognition triangle it provides the necessary insight when crises appear. The task to be learned is understood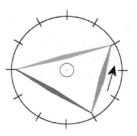

and intelligence is used to find a solution. With time, one learns how to control and accelerate the process. An active, positive attitude towards the theme makes it easier to resolve.

Experience Triangle (Retrograde)

If the rotation direction is clockwise, i.e. in the same direction as the earth and in the opposite direction to the zodiac, it is a retrograde Experience triangle. Here the appropriate experience must be processed many more times than in the other direction. The person does not adapt as easily as in the case of the Cognition 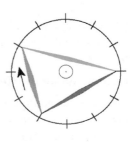 triangle and experiences the same theme for as long as it takes to learn the lesson. Many take half a lifetime to deal with a deep-seated problem.

Trapeze Figure

The Trapeze figure is transversely symmetrical and has the largest surface area of all quadrilaterals, which is why it is also often called the Dominant quadrilateral. It has very symmetrical angles, so that it almost looks like an impregnable sphere or like a knight with two shields. It also acts as a stable base of a high tower, i.e. a person who has 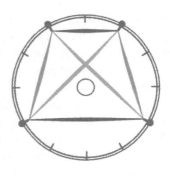 worked on the foundations of his personality and has therefore become a model of self-actualisation. If he creates enough personal freedom, he can also become creative and show deep wisdom.

Three Colours

All four corners of the Trapeze figure have three-coloured aspects; this person learns fast and is constantly evolving. The two green diagonal aspects intersect each other at a particularly stable right-angle, which indicates that their inner attitude cannot be changed or influenced. Alternatively, they are seen as a pivot through which one red line crosses over rapidly to the other one. This person can therefore either repress any tension that occurs or redouble and bring it out into the open.

So, according to the colours involved, there are two large Learning triangles, which turn in both directions. They clearly show that this person can learn something from and develop in all possible circumstances of life. On each line, a Dominant and Learning triangle always run in opposing directions. Every small learning process brings personal development, and every experience has an explanation. These processes are strongly connected to each other, and they can hardly be separated. All of life becomes an ongoing learning and developing process.

Encompassing the Centre

This large aspect figure encompasses the centre of the horoscope, which means that the person must be true to himself and not go against his inner convictions, though this rule is not as crucial in the case of the three-coloured Trapeze as for similarly large aspect patterns. The person can switch around easily, move from one side to the other and therefore adapt quickly to changing circumstances. As the green lines are contained within the figure, their high level of sensitivity is directed, not outwards to the environment but inwards, towards the core personality, principally manifesting as personal insecurity and a need to find peace once and for all. This insecurity is not outwardly visible, as the person is either active, working intensively and tenaciously to carry out plans, or passive, hedonistic and lazy. Sometimes this polarity is so strongly expressed that the person goes from one extreme to the other, adapting to modern society without becoming internally dependent. As a human artist, he or she takes life exactly as it comes. The efficiency lines (squares) enable small successes or pleasures to become sources of greater fulfilment or meaning (trines). Small things worked upon can turn into bigger and better achievements, while all disturbing influences are blocked out (by the red lines).

The Green Cross of the Diagonals

This person conceives that the answer to everything lies in thinking and that every problem can be solved by communication and logical reflection. A clearly thought-out idea is sufficient to guide the personality, behaviour and actions. The person could be an actor, or even a planner or a constructor who likes designing structures for people. The person's basic need to create or work on forms and structures is fine tuned with artistic sensitivity and holistic intercommunication. The lesser and the greater pleasures (sextile and trine) are connected to each other by developing better forms, or converted into one another. Everything must be useful or tangible.

These larger-than-life personalities can sometimes double their impact. When discussing a topic of current interest to them, they concentrate their full attention and enthusiasm on the conversation. This usually makes them dominant in a group, where they serve as a role model and must accept the responsibility that goes with it. They act rather conservatively, mostly diligently and steadily. They possess abilities and experience and can also be tough. If they do trample on someone, they realise and usually come back to them. This is when they show how big-hearted they really are.

Repetition

A person with a Trapeze figure always goes over everything twice, he learns by repetition. If he only partly gives his opinion, it is because he is aware that he still has a lot more to say. In the next conversation, he takes up the thread again, repeats what he said before and gives more away. So he returns rhythmically to the same statements until everything has been understood. Perhaps he has had the experience early on that other people are weaker and slower than him and has therefore learnt to be considerate and happy with partial successes. He should never do everything in one go, for his inner self is too big. He should instead discover his own rhythmic, repetitive way of doing things.

This effect can best be described as the fast exchange of feelings or dimensions. The person himself, however, perceives it as simultaneity, as if he had two different parts or levels inside him that are interconnected by conscious will impulses. One part contains personal and the other part external experiences, or even conscious and unconscious issues. He stimulates the conscious connection between the two opposing areas by simultaneously intensifying both sides.

Crisis Mechanism

As explained above, in the three-coloured aspect figures there is a process that conditions growth by a continual crisis mechanism that presents great opportunities for development. The Trapeze figure contains two, possibly four, three-coloured Learning triangles. As the Learning triangles are incorporated into a larger figure, here in the Trapeze, they easily lose their individual quality. They must integrate and become part of a greater whole. So as the planets and the separate aspects integrate into an aspect figure, the smaller aspect figure integrates into the larger one. The flexibility of the Learning triangles is reduced; they are stabilised by a four-sided frame that needs a stable life situation. The quadrangular structure gives this figure a static character with a theme of security, as with all such figures.

On the other hand, the three-coloured character makes this figure eager to create and maintain a dynamic state in which constant growth is possible. The Trapeze's learning and crisis mechanism is hard to understand, as here there is no clear starting point as in the case of the Learning triangle. To find this figure's objective, look at the axis of symmetry of the Trapeze. This lies at right-angles between the two unequal frame aspects, the sextile and the trine, and cuts through the intersection of both internal quincunxes. The dynamic growth process runs in both directions along the axis of symmetry.

Learning Process

In this learning Trapeze, both blue aspects (sextile and trine) represent two thematic levels which are harmonious but whose mutual outward connection is interrupted by conflictive tension. These are expressed via both squares. This means firstly that both harmonious themes are in diverging opposition to each other and are keen to establish their autonomy and independence from each other. On the other hand, though, the personality must be aware and take care that between the latent levels there is an essential connection (quincunxes); the task there is to bring the two levels together with great awareness and unflagging effort.

It is then possible to implement the dynamics of the four Learning triangles, consisting of two Experience triangles and two Cognition triangles, namely in the form of two Dominant triangles and two large Learning triangles. The Learning triangles can help to soften any inner armour and liberate the soft centre. By consciously connecting with the centre of the horoscope, both quincunxes can become a controlling information pathway, along which the creative structuring process of the polarised frame aspect and the opposition of energy (red aspects) and form (blue aspects) can be channelled. People with a consciously managed and lived Trapeze figure can help to implement ideas, ideals and concepts. They can create the form that most accurately expresses the initial concept.

In Louise Huber's horoscope, a green diagonal present in the normal Trapeze figure is missing. It is replaced by a quincunx aspect of Mars to Pluto, but this is not directly connected to the Trapeze. This makes the figure more unstable, and gives it increased flexibility. It is this creative

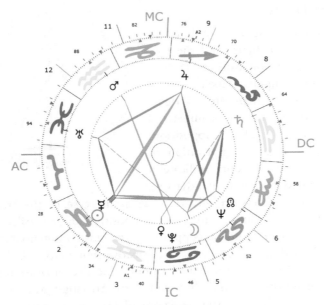

Louise Huber
10.5.1924, 3.15, Bamberg/Germany

dynamic that gives this figure its nickname "Constructor figure". It enabled the subject of the horoscope to create something active and enduring from her understanding of the processes of life. The creative power and the will to achieve the best are constantly active. The planets that form the Trapeze indicate the type of subject matter that the horoscope owner deals with. They are Mercury/Sun, Uranus, Jupiter and Neptune. These planets are very good at dealing with fringe subjects like astrology and esotericism. She was a specialist in these fields. She preferred to use her Trapeze to improve all the texts of her numerous books and her capacities at various levels until a certain degree of perfection was reached. She spared no efforts to take the necessary steps to allow life in the API School to flourish and grow in peace. This motivation never allowed her to rest; she made sure things were always fun, in true red-green-blue fashion breathing new life into them.

A person's level of development corresponds to the format of the task that is set for him. This cannot be evaluated solely from the horoscope pattern.

Striving Figure

This figure consists of a combination of the Projection figure and the Eye, bisected by an opposition. It is a quadrangular figure, albeit a very dynamic one, as there are no right-angles and it is only symmetrical around the plane of the opposition. The graphic reveals a motivation of security and the colours indicate a three-coloured developmental dynamic.

The frame aspects are all green, as in the case of the Irritation Rectangle, but the internal aspects, an opposition and a sextile, are red and blue. As there is only one opposition, the tension potential is lower than in the Irritation Rectangle. The sensitive frame aspect indicates a great receptivity to environmental stimuli. The Eye provides intuitive interpersonal skills, and the blunt end of the Striving figure forms the base and also the anchor. The sextile provides receptivity and a unifying force, which means that the information obtained by the Eye can be assimilated and used for long-term objectives.

Long Term Objectives

These objectives get their energy and intrinsic tension from the opposition. The field of activity is denoted by the axis topic of the opposition (determined by signs and houses). The objective topic is also strongly stimulated by the combination of the green aspects with the red aspects. People with this figure try to reach the apex with much effort and dynamism, and to function brilliantly with the planets in the surrounding area (house positions). Often the claims made are beyond their actual ability. There are also too few blue aspects available to provide the necessary substance, hence the real danger of not attaining the set objective. People with this figure are not usually tough or persistent enough to reach their goals. Many act as though they could do everything and show off their self-assurance like an actor, even though they do not really possess any; they come a cropper sooner or later.

Sensitivity

The great sensitivity of the green aspects tends to weaken the backbone, so that such people have to sail too close to the wind and can become opportunists. There is often a tendency to use others to further one's own ends. This attitude makes them unpopular, reduces other peoples' trust in them and brings them into dead ends. For such a figure, salvation lies in using their sensitivity and intelligence to strengthen their backbone and to develop the qualities needed to achieve their goals. Although this way is more long-winded and tiresome than pretending to be something one is not, it often means renouncing too easily achieved successes. The green aspects mean that this person is always receptive to the needs of others though. It is clear that this requires real self-scrutiny, but also the conversion of possible deep-seated feelings of inferiority into true humility and unselfishness. This is certainly no easy task, but perhaps the highest goal that we can inwardly aspire to.

The Striving figure is composed of two Irritation triangles whose apexes meet and whose blunt ends are joined by a sextile. Even in the blue breathing space, in which it is nevertheless very receptive and accepting, the strain of being alert at the apex is alternately absorbed from one or other Irritation triangles. The small Eye watches from a distance and nothing escapes it that could be of interest for its project. The long triangle provides the tenacity to reach objectives or to find the root or crux of the desired truth.

Thinking Aspects

The long green aspects facilitate thinking. Such people possess the special ability to get to the heart of complex matters and to face facts. They can sometimes take on the negative characteristics of a whole group and can therefore easily be made scapegoats; or else they are pilloried for their exemplary conduct. This is hard for them to cope with when they are young and they easily become outsiders. In this role they can develop their own inner ritual to explain their situation in peace. The inner urge to get to the bottom of everything is better pursued when they are alone.

In people with a Striving figure, just one single fact is enough from which to build a great theory. This can be a (still lacking) clue for a theory that can now be established. If the objective is clear, this person attacks once the occasion or opportunity presents itself. He is always one of the first to react to new things. He picks up on changes at the speed of light and adapts to them. His natural talent is to react to information, knowledge and truths like a teacher who seems to have a better knowledge of many things. He is sociable and communicative, but can charge forwards alone like an ace striker. There is no doubting his flexibility, for he bounces back again and again to have another go.

The combination of red and green means energy and awareness, nervous strength and alertness of will. With a sextile aspect, the person unceasingly collects substance through cognition and knowledge. This has an unsettling effect as everything is unsure. The green dominance leaves him open on all sides, and he gathers knowledge even if it cannot be utilised.

Symmetry

The Striving figure is symmetrical around the vertical axis, like a rocket. If placed horizontally, it could easily drill into something. The arrow-shaped figure indicates that a person with this figure can easily shoot outwards and would then think that all knowledge and experience came from others. He also believes that he knows what is best for other people and is too quick to interfere with his opinion, which many people find offensive. He will suffer painful setbacks until he has learnt to really listen to his inner voice.

Aspect Qualities

The aspect qualities of Mercury (2x), Venus (1x) and Saturn (3x), show that the power of memory and the ability to concentrate are a good basis for intelligence. Saturn-Mercury combinations indicate realistic logic, form-creating expression and practical thinking. Due to the almost academic disposition, the aesthetic and artistic sides of the Venus quality are expressed more as perfectionism and the urge to collect things. Just visible, but much-needed, is the small pleasure aspect that makes this person open to spontaneous contact.

This horoscope of Franz Josef Strauss shows a Striving figure that contains all three personality planets at the bottom next to the Eye, which is anchored in the collective space. His main objective was therefore the successful actualisation of his own personality in the context of a specific collective environment. The opposition on the Individual axis gives rise to a tense inner aspiration, and the highly perceptive green aspects cover all sides. The figure is dynamic and its flexibility is nevertheless assured, almost unassailably, by its stability. Even a walk through the briar patch leaves this individual untouched, exemplifying his ability to find a way through even the most inhospitable terrain. The right-angled blue-red cross provides material stability, courage and experience and instinctive knowledge as to how to take the path of least resistance. However, this

Franz Josef Strauss
6.9.1915, 22.15, Eichstätt/Germany

ability is not noticeable from outside, especially when a person is quiet. Only when such people speak do they reveal their mental stability and dynamic aspiration for knowledge that lead to interesting and intense discussions.

The internal linear figure of Pluto square Mercury meant that Strauss was often involved in arguments. As it was hard for him to find stability, he often had to excuse his behaviour (Pluto square Mercury: Demagogue aspect), but the two intersecting blue sextile aspects ensured that he always managed to get away with it. He thus managed to attain most of his difficult objectives, but he never found stability. People with this Striving figure often talk about their projects and goals without ever attaining them. Uranus on the MC with red-green influence is not a planet that can carry off a lasting victory. Falling from a great height is the feature of this configuration.

6. Variants

Chapter 5 has described the basic aspect figures. These are now supplemented by several groupings of more complex or less commonly found figures:

6.1	Ten New Aspect Figures
6.2	Aspect Quadrilaterals
6.3	Seven Opposition Quadrilaterals
6.4	Four Talented Trapezoids
6.5	Five Rare Quadrilaterals
6.6	Small Aspect Patterns

6.1 Ten New Aspect Figures

Pandora's Box

This figure is a pentagon, but not a pentagram, as it is asymmetrical. The blue triangle could be removed, leaving the quadrangular box that is covered by a blue lid. The lid seals the box and keeps inside what is said to be all the evil in the world. But the figure is not so black and white, as it is dominated by green aspects.

The Pandora's Box consists of two red, four green and three blue aspects, and is therefore one of the three-coloured development figures. But as a pentagon it offers even more security than a quadrilateral and is very reluctant to change the status quo. A person with this inwardly exclusively green and outwardly red and blue figure initially appears to those around him to be red and blue, i.e. ambivalent. He is liable to vacillate and shows contrasts and contradictions in his behaviour and verbal expression, but he does not usually realise that other people see him in this way. He himself feels fine, secure and stable, although the green aspects do provoke internal insecurities and vacillations.

Greek mythology has given us many archetypes and symbols that are basically black and white. At that time there was no concept for what is inside the box, i.e. for what we now understand that the green aspects represent, which is latent or awakened awareness and the ability for differentiated thinking. Ptolemy had already mentioned the green aspects but was not yet able to define them, and until the 20th century the green aspects were ignored. More on this can be found in chapters 2 and 3.

A person with Pandora's Box in his horoscope gives out contradictory messages about himself which make him stand out. He acts as though he were quite sure of himself, but usually the opposite is the case, which leads to external and internal problems. His internal functioning differs from how he expresses himself outwardly. The green aspects enable him to consciously process everything in a highly sophisticated way, but it is hard for him to show this on the outside. Outwardly, he wants to or is only able to function dualistically, perhaps also because those around him expect that. This person must accept that he is inwardly broad-minded, tolerant and sophisticated, but cannot express these qualities outwardly. Very often he has to "do in Rome as the Romans do", although he doesn't want to at all. The discrepancy between inside and outside can sometimes become a problem.

The "evil in the box" is according to the traditional view the differentiated awareness that cannot just be divided into good and bad. Dominant colours, especially if they are enclosed like the green aspects in this figure, are always difficult. If the box is opened a little, there are always a couple of people who react, mostly negatively, and at best inquisitively, but then they expect something shocking. A person with this structure should already have learnt as a child that what he says can be taken the wrong way. This teaches him to keep everything to himself. This can mean that as an adult, he has forgotten what a treasure he has inside him, and he then needs to work on himself to rediscover it.

Bathtub

The Bathtub consists of three green, two blue and one red aspect. People for whom green predominates are always very sensitive but find it hard to cope with life. They easily become chaotic, which those around them have to constantly adapt to. The Bathtub shows the constructive attempt not to *let the tide go out*. In

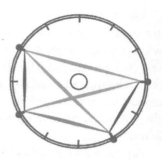

psychological terms, people with a Bathtub in their horoscope aspire to keep what they have at any price. They cleverly avoid losses, want to keep everything together and make every effort not to dissipate their energies. A stable, energy-charged bottom with two high walls forms the frame for the green *bubble bath*.

It is a large figure, in which the central core lies inside the figure and therefore determines the person's profile, even if there are other aspects present. As there is a certain sleepy credulity inherent in this figure, this person can often get himself into trouble if he thinks too simplistically. If he has put his world in order to some extent, he is at peace. However, the world can have a very disruptive effect on this peace, as the bath has a large opening: it is closed on the longest side by a green aspect and on the opposite side by a square aspect. Red-green combinations produce Irritation aspects, which can have a significant unsettling effect.

The two internal green aspects give the person a tendency to subjectivity and sensitivity when it comes to evaluating perceptions. Because of their own naivety, they tend to see things too positively, too rosily; they are too trusting. Yet another tendency is dependent on the planets involved: if the green side of the Bath is pointing towards the DC, it can indicate a strong dependency on the immediate environment, i.e. on what is happening around the person. Like a cupping bell, this figure has the tendency to draw and suck everything towards itself, so that the person often feels exhausted and without energy.

The learning in this figure is characterised by long and hard experience, as well as a certain reluctance to learn. The protection philosophy is to sort out the simple things in life quickly. As long as something is happening the sensitivity is stimulated and something can be learnt, if only passively.

Butterfly

This is a blue-green dynamic linear figure, where movement runs back on itself like in a figure of eight, perpetually circulating. As they tend to get caught up in the circuit, nothing new is produced despite the constant movement; its reflex reactions even make it meaningless. Because the active red colour is missing,

it cannot go anywhere. The movement impulse is important because the figure only has two colours in ratio of 2:2. The nature of its movement is rather transient and the person does not like to settle. Intense or targeted movements are lacking as there are no red aspects.

This motion can be compared to a dance. Because of the length of the figure, there is a certain channelling or directing effect. Energy flows in one of two possible directions at the axis of symmetry. People with such a figure collect (blue) with their dancing movement a lot of information (green) and carry it with them, often without knowing what to do with it.

This figure is quite interesting and entertaining, as what the person can take in depends on environmental stimulation. The experience of stimulation is felt very personally (the green aspects are on the inside of the figure). The blue aspects act like shields that keep everything out. That also means that these people can be impenetrable when they want to be, unless they are caught on the open edges, i.e. on their vulnerable spots. This figure can have a very useful effect if it is part of a larger aspect group.

This figure is mainly a sensual (blue) information gatherer (green), a greenhorn with a neutral attitude. The type of pleasure is determined by the pinning planets; for example intellectual planets indicate a talkative person.

There are other types of Butterfly figures. According to the combination, two squares with trines can also form a Butterfly. [See Runner, page 203.] In principle the energy is always circulating, which means they contain a kind of perpetual motion.

Trawler

In the Trawler, the blue aspects form stable side walls. The square closes off the wide end of the figure. If it is on its side, this figure forms a massive basket with a narrow sensitive opening above a big container. If the red side is facing upwards, the figure works like a vacuum cleaner that points towards people and

sucks them in if they come near. They then find it hard to get away, not because they are tied down but because they can't find their way out. In a vertical basket, the figure acts like a catchment tank. Not much can come through the narrow opening though, which leads to isolation for many people (solitary qualities).

As the green diagonals intersect inside the figure, this person has a great ability to process absorbed information and to evaluate it consciously. He has a good selective learning ability. This figure has extremely different forms: from the exploiter to the creative. However, being mainly blue-green, there is a tendency to be complacent. The danger with this figure is that this complacency causes wisdom to be neglected.

Trampoline

Two blue loosely connected bars stand on a red base and are held together like a mainspring by small green aspects. The trampoline works as a whole as if there were a green rubber sheet stretched over it. One thing standing out is that the quadrangular figure has three green sides and one red one. Such people act

red-green outwardly, i.e. they react directly, are hypersensitive and easily irritated, highly perceptive, always wide awake and incapable of rigid thinking. Inwardly, they often have an idealistic approach (blue), are highly sensitive and their opinions are formed according to their inner ideals. The main priorities for such people are learning to adapt constantly to changing circumstances and getting on with new people. Their inner standards empower them. People with a Trampoline do not exactly have much time for those around them, as they are never focused

Mikhail Gorbachev

2.3.1931, 08.00, Privolnoje/Stavropol, Soviet Union

on the outside. Like a trampoline, they are hard to pin down and they just jump away.

This figure is also an inveterate collector of knowledge, i.e. would like to experience as much of the world as possible. This takes place on the intellectual level if the intelligence planets are present there. The small square is not sufficient for the energetic transfer of knowledge into action, other elements in the horoscope have also to participate in that. (Dominant element in Mikhael Gorbachev's chart).

Runner (Jumper)
[Dancing Figure]

Strength is required to be able to run, and in this figure it is provided by the two squares (in contrast to the Butterfly). Red aspects release energy that can be used to create and to encourage others to do the same. Many pressurise others but are themselves very pressure-sensitive. This

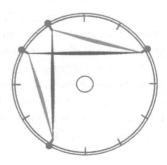

figure reacts very strongly to external pressure with movement, initially by running or jumping. In the figure there is a flight mechanism or reflex and it is certainly not in their nature to fight. The internal blue aspects make the person feel himself to be a harmonious being who needs peace and quiet.

Reflex mechanisms were learnt back in childhood that could develop into addictions to certain actions and activities. This figure just needs to be nudged at one corner and it springs into life. Unlike the Butterfly, this one is always getting into conflicts (red-blue polarised thinking). Perhaps one projects something into the world (blue) that does not suit it. Many people react to this by taking refuge in their work (workaholics), or depending on the pinning planets, in sport or sex.

Once this figure is activated, the mechanism runs by itself and can only be controlled if it is understood. If this figure is part of a larger figure, it works better. Receptiveness to the colour green from other figures in the aspect pattern brings sensitivity.

Tele-Microscope

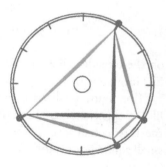

This figure has two possibilities: as a telescope looking into the distance, or as a microscope looking at what is close at hand. The orientation determines how it is used. If the long green side is facing upwards we have a telescope, and if it is facing downwards a microscope. The diagonals of the figure are blue, the sides red and the base and top green. This means that the figure is permeable on the symmetrical axis. This figure, with its colour ratio of 2:2:2, is predominantly sensitive. Although all three colours are present, there is a certain ambivalence; the green can sometimes cause trouble and unsettle people. Too many ideas cause confusion and disorientation.

The person is curious and wants to know, but is not defensive. Instead he dares to use and test the possibilities of the green. But this gives rise to the so-called magnifying glass effect, allowing things to get out of proportion. The best possible applications are obtained by very accurate observation. The figure can be used in both ways in any location, but a certain self-awareness is required. One must know that one possesses this ability and should have learnt how to handle it.

The semi-sextile enables meticulous differentiation and the quincunx allows the wider context to be seen. If the awareness is adequate, from the small, the great can be understood. Otherwise everything is just seen in its great interconnectedness and the small things are avoided (telescope position), or one always sees the little things and is not interested in the big picture (microscope position). These are one-sided attitudes that form the basic predispositions of this figure. Everything is seen too narrowly (one side of the figure is narrow) and does not accept the other point of view. Being quadrangular, the figure tends to have an attitude of security. It is important that the red sides give the strength for long-term observation. The blue diagonals enable absorption and processing.

Irrespective of the planets involved, this figure is characterised by a very good memory. This can be observed in all figures with blue diagonals (as blue collects and retains). The figure can be considered as a kind of bucket, albeit with a loose bottom, i.e. no firm point of view. The red aspect provides the strength, structured and varied by the corner planets, to endure difficult life situations.

It is important to see this figure as a kind of outlet mechanism, in which the green aspects are lenses (to condense the unseen), membranes (to condense the unheard) or sensors (to condense the intangible).

Buffer

This two-coloured linear figure contains a kind of protection mechanism and is a perfect 'energy mechanism'. A trine and a sextile run parallel to each other and are joined by two intersecting squares. There is a kind of springiness between blue and red, where the transition is very rapid and there is a kind of constantly moving rhythmic conversion. The motivation of 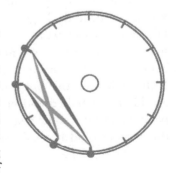 a linear figure is fundamentally different from that of a quadrangular figure; it expects knocks within the movement. As a two-coloured figure it actually goes looking for the blows itself. Alternatively, the Buffer can also beat itself up.

The dual coloured nature causes a complementary backwards and forwards movement, an elastic reaction to external opportunities. At best, there is an antagonism, similar to the way the joints work in our arms. Flexors and extensors move in rhythm and allow a great deal of manipulation.

Psychologically, the weak and vulnerable points of this figure are the two open sides. In the Buffer, the blows suffered are transferred into matter, sometimes even beaten off, but over the long term it cannot protect itself effectively. There is a danger that energies and experiences are constantly being lost through the open sides. Then the movement starts again from scratch.

Shield

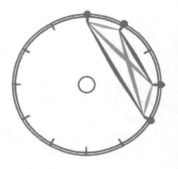

The Shield figure is similar to the Buffer but has two green semi-sextile aspects and is a quadrangular figure. As the orb of a semi-sextile is very small, the Shield is relatively rare. People with a Shield figure avoid energy loss by using the Shield as a defence to keep others at a distance. That is often expressed as a threatening gesture or also by them complaining or accusing others. A Shield has something rigid about it. One holds it in front of oneself, but does not fight with it. One tries to deter or even to absorb the enemy's incoming strength. The absorption power of this figure is very high due to the large surface area of the external blue aspect. It can take hard knocks, which are then transferred into matter. In fact this figure is much more resilient than people expect. On top of that, they complain loudly (sensitivity of the semi-sextile).

It can happen that only one semi-sextile is present, in which case the Shield is destabilised and becomes more and more one-sided. This is painful and reduces the defensive strength. Those around quickly notice this weakness and attack the sensitive place, so one must learn to protect oneself better there.

Diamond

This is the largest possible aspect figure that can be made with the ten planets and the Moon Node. It has (theoretically) 55 aspects: 20 blue, 15 red and 20 green. However, this requires that each planet stand alone and at 30 degree intervals from the next. We can say that the Diamond figure has about eight corners. According to the normal ratio of 1:2:3 (see chapter 4), there should be 31 blue, 16 red and only 8 green aspects. A Diamond therefore has too many green aspects. This green predominance indicates heightened communicativeness. A large amount of information is gathered that cannot be utilised. There is great curiosity and excessive kindness prevents the formation of necessary boundaries. This over-stimulation means that experiences cannot be sufficiently processed, which provokes inner insecurity combined with constant decision-making problems.

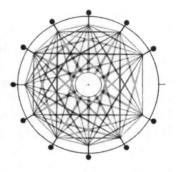

Austrian Treaty
15.5.1955, 11.31, Vienna

The national horoscope of Austria has this figure. The great variety of the Austrian landscape and its people is surely due to this complex aspect pattern. It is interesting that the planet Mercury is only connected to the large figure by a long green quincunx aspect to Saturn, thus making it almost detached, which has a special importance. It creates special characteristics in the soul of the people. It is known that in Austria interpersonal relationships are considered very important. The Austrian language or dialect, as well as the joy of singing and talking, are particular national characteristics. They like to learn, to talk to each other and exchange thoughts. The prominent Saturn in the fourth house wants to establish security, which requires a lot of effort. But just like the Sun in Taurus in the tenth house, he can pull all the strings and ensure a slow economic upswing.

Observations have shown that everyone who has a Diamond in their horoscope has one thing in common. At some point, usually in the middle of their lives, they drop out of their jobs, leave their families and go into the "desert", to return as an artist. It is typical that this person tries to escape from the possibly over-structured nature of this figure. Initially they seem very structured, because every aspect that connects with the centre goes outwards and links with the environment. Indeed, this person looks for connection, but there are so many aspects that he sometimes feels as though he is in a straitjacket. People with this Diamond figure start off as good citizens, but make mistakes again and again until they eventually drop out of normal life.

It is almost impossible though, to cope with so many aspects and bring them into a life function network without losing control. Because of the number of aspects, this person must inevitably be a late starter; he needs a much longer walk if he is to find his way through the jungle. Artistic creativity is the best activity for him to find himself. Through such creativity, these people can come to terms with their complicated structure, not with words or intellectual work.

6.2 Aspect Quadrilaterals

By Michael Alexander Huber

Interpreting quadrilaterals means learning to read aspect patterns.
Reading aspect patterns means understanding what makes us individual.
The better we are able to read the aspect pattern, the more we are astonished
at the diversity of individuality.

Using our seven 30° aspects, you can form twelve different triangles and
a total of 29 different quadrilaterals. If we also count the mirror images
of the 14 asymmetrical quadrilaterals, with the same lines and triangles
but in different positions, there are as many as 43 possible quadrilaterals.
There is a remarkable cosmic system behind the 29 quadrilaterals.
Taking the symmetrical quadrilateral as a special case, there are 2 x 7
symmetrical and 2 x 7 (altogether 4 x 7) asymmetrical quadrilaterals.

So far we have covered thirteen mainly the symmetrical and
exemplary quadrilaterals. We now present the remaining sixteen, mainly
asymmetrical, quadrilaterals.

The interpretation method is based on analytical-systematic
experiences gained from the previously known quadrilaterals, as well as
from the basic interpretation of the shapes, colours and aspect qualities.
The 16 new names come from a kind of stress meditation in which all
information, impressions and experiences were compressed.

In 1976, the author used his knowledge of geometry to draw all
the possible quadrangular forms and research the natural laws. The
experiences encountered since then have been complemented by
observation and intensive questioning during consultation and on
courses.

Definitions and Differences

A quadrilateral is composed of 4 triangles and has 6 aspects that connect four planets together.

If we astrologers want to find clear definitions and names for the aspect quadrilaterals or to check existing knowledge, we should initially see how they look in reality. The same quadrilateral can appear quite different for different individuals, according to whether it is **extrovert or introvert,** whether it is an important **component** or just a small part of the horoscope. Extrovert means that the planets lie on house cusps and introvert that the planets lie on the Low Points of the houses.

Psychological starting points

Concrete evidence and effects can only be recognised for an **extrovert** quadrilateral if at least two of the planets lie close to house cusps. We can then also ask the person concerned for more detail. It has also been shown that the fewer other figures there are in the horoscope, the more clearly the function of the quadrilateral can be defined.

If the average of the four planets is **introvert** (i.e. close to a Low Point), we need to observe the person for longer and ask more searching questions in order to learn about the way the figure works. Vivid and emotional wording are important for this process.

Astrological Features

1. Exemplary Quadrilateral

An exemplary quadrilateral consists of six strong lines, a maximum of one of which can be one-way. The figure works most effectively if all aspects are exact. Of the four planets that form the quadrilateral, only one must be a spiritual planet (Uranus, Neptune, Pluto) or the Moon Node. If several planets are involved, they must be carefully defined and close attention paid to the orbs.

Depending on how near to the cusp the corner planets are situated, this person's psychological quality is expressed as personal stability, which is clearly recognised and appreciated by those around them. The person has more or less conscious control of these abilities, and can talk about them and give concrete examples.

2. Latent Quadrilateral

A latent quadrilateral is irregular and contains gaps or is spread out.

a) 2-3 of the 6 lines
are dashed

b) one diagonal is missing
(only 2 triangles)

c) one corner is spread over
a conjunction

d) a double, intersecting
unclosed side.

The fixed, reassuring quality of the quadrilateral only appears in certain situations and more time is needed to develop it. Sometimes, the results appear to be stable, but sooner or later they collapse again or are consigned to oblivion. The motivation to achieve something everlasting is eclipsed by the urge to continue to evolve and to abandon the old. Compensation mechanisms arise because other fixed elements in the horoscope try to prevent this. The research of useful findings and experiences by the horoscope owner are rare, or only possible in the second half of life.

3. Pseudo-Quadrilateral and Pulsar

As combinations with fixed motivation, pseudo-quadrilaterals and pulsars form the transition to cardinal or mutable motives. They are still made up of a combination of four planets, but are no longer really quadrilaterals as we understand them. However, there are typical similarities: rhythmic and regular processes, sense of utility and a certain system and a constructive attitude with the desire to be useful.

a) Pseudo-Quadrilateral

These figures are formed of two triangles that share one line. They are one line short of a quadrilateral, so we should check whether the missing connection would be a valid goodwill aspect. If so, this figure counts as a latent quadrilateral. If not, the figure shows a dynamic and adaptable rhythm, a habit for change or the creative ability to always do things in different ways. It is as though it swings from one triangle to the other on the same base line. The motivation is mutable, but still has some fixed energy.

b) Pulsar

The Pulsar lacks two facing sides, leaving a figure of eight composed of four lines. See for example the Runner on page 203.

The "eternal" eight causes a familiar motion sequence or typical thought patterns in all areas. This characteristic leaves no lasting traces and appears only to be useful to the individual concerned. But it does give something to others, in the shape of stimulating impetus. As this figure is hard to control consciously, compensation mechanisms, even nervous tics, can arise. On the one hand it has cardinal motivation, for it gives off impulses, and on the other hand its fixed energy is constant.

6.3 Seven Opposition Quadrilaterals

Megaphone – Animated – Provocative – Arena – Streamer – Decorative – Bijou

Megaphone

Examples: John Lennon, Jacques Cousteau,
J. W. v. Goethe, Françoise Sagan

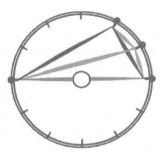

We speak quietly into the narrow end and our voice suddenly fills the room. The other way around it works like the old-fashioned ear trumpet, as used in the past by the hard-of-hearing. But it could also be a bag to catch whispered words to keep them secret.

Graphic Analysis

The Megaphone is limited to one half of the horoscope by an opposition and therefore belongs to the group of *half quadrilaterals* (five in total, four of which are mentioned in this chapter). When interpreting this figure, it is important to accurately define in which half of the horoscope it lies. The Megaphone should be very sensitive in this surrounding area and appear rather gentle and artistic (blue-green). This person is also a thinker who extracts a lot of information from communication, which he can then check for value and truth.

The extremely pointed shape, resembling a paper dart or a wedge, stands out. It makes the figure very dynamic and lightning fast, while still giving off a sense of calm, steady security. It never settles for long and takes what it needs with it. At one end there is a planet that can direct its abilities towards an objective in a three-coloured, i.e. intelligent, way, for example to manipulate others or to get them to do what he thinks is correct and important. The planet at the apex of the Eye has three green aspects, which means that control over all the figure's mental activities is exerted from here; but targeted information from the environment can also have a manipulative effect and create dependency.

Animated Figure

Examples: Sammy Davis, Alfred Fankhauser, Maurice Utrillo, Vincent van Gogh, Neil F. Michelsen.

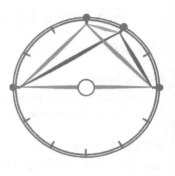

Hidden in this term is the profession of the animator. In cartoons he produces, he shows all the movements of a character precisely in frames; which requires imagination, patience and a lot of hard work. A more general definition for the animator is that he brings inanimate things to life. This can be interpreted on both a physical or a mental level. Repressed emotions are reactivated and made conscious and thoughts or memories are evoked.

Graphic Analysis

This figure is one of the *half quadrilaterals*. The ends of the opposition show a strong either-or attitude. For example, a person with such a figure can rapidly switch from approval to disapproval. He is achievement-oriented and attaches more importance to the acquisition of material possessions and the creation of forms than to communication. One side of this figure is an inwardly blue skilfully handled "drillbit" that is outwardly red. On the other, smaller side (blue-green) there is harmonious listening. This combination wins a certain respect from those around, making it easy for him to dominate.

The motivations are a thirst for action and utilitarian thinking with energy and skill, or even "no gain without pain". There is a constructive orientation towards adapting and modifying the status quo, and a desire to know what is what. Seen from the red apex, this figure is stable, balanced and seems like a dome-shaped vault under which people can feel safe.

The blue-green influenced planet forms the opposite pole to the red triangle. It is very sensitive to tense or conflictive situations. New things are constantly learnt from the oscillation between achievement and pleasure, between giving and taking and between work and private life, so that what is possible is immediately put into practice.

Provocative Figure

Example: Telly Savalas

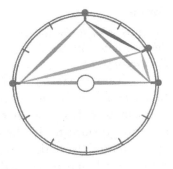

In general linguistic usage, a provocation is a one-sided challenge. But it is actually only half-active, for it depends very much on who or what is being provoked. There is more intensity in the perception and in the ability to recognise other people's sore points. If the horoscope owner himself provokes others, he will even feel responsible and act as a lawyer. In this way, this figure can easily dominate or make itself indispensable. "Pro" means to be in favour of something, in this case to assert oneself in favour of a particular thing against existing resistance. What is special is that this person authorises himself and has the courage to bring things into the open that would otherwise remain hidden.

Graphic Analysis

This quadrilateral wants to accomplish achievements provoked by thoughts (Efficiency Triangle). With the blue sextile, matter can be gathered in the form of knowledge or personal experience, but probably only insofar as it is useful for progress. Otherwise, the red-green combination is really nervous; a person who often scorns pleasure and whose inner restlessness always finds something that is not right. He focuses on a specific task with exclusive concentration, but at the same time should not forget to question his ignorance and take off his blinkers from time to time.

The motivation is planned will, which is why it might be difficult to evade what this figure wants. As a listener, this person likes to interrupt with a question or to make a conjecture. Due to his inner insecurity (quincunx), this can easily become too intrusive, even manipulative, always according to the motto "attack is the best form of defence". All in all this person seems to be keen on difficult tasks, in which he makes too much of the apparently irrelevant and takes many things too seriously or turns them into problems, probably as a way of kickstarting the learning process.

Arena

Examples: Abbé Pierre, Roberto Assagioli, Johannes Rau, Alan Leo, Norman Schwarzkopf.

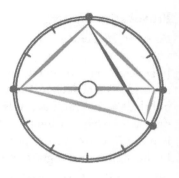

In a duel fought in an arena, there can normally be only one winner. However, in this quadrilateral there is the opportunity to let both parties win: one with strength and power and the other with shrewdness and knowledge. For this reason, the person always puts himself in hot water or in the middle between two conflicting parties, so that he can develop his ability to understand two conflicting opinions. He creates suitable relationships for both opponents and helps them to get over the conflict. He does not require much to enjoy life, for "business is the salt of life", "practice makes perfect" or "only dead fish go with the flow" are the mottos he likes to live by. That is why he tries persistently to change fixed structures.

Graphic Analysis

The blue connecting trine enables this figure to unite the contrasts between the red and green triangles. There are two very different sides to this person. He knows two different social groups, ways of life or standpoints and keeps them separate. To get to the centre, the opposition, requires the overcoming of opposites, and the blue-red motivation states: harmony through conflict.

The red-green influenced planets of the opposition tend to blame all conflicts on the environment. It takes a long time for these people to realise their own contradictions and adapt to find their own destiny. The Dominant Triangle shows that it is mainly a question of personal development, for which the long Learning Triangle is used. The Efficiency Triangle puts pressure on the Irritation Triangle; it makes a noise to wake people from their sleep or to draw attention to itself.

Streamer

Example: Joan Baez

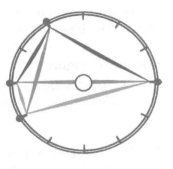

The Streamer is familiar with all kinds of streaming. It can flow in either direction in a river without losing balance. It is also a cable layer who can deal with currents and high voltages. Or he can be a policeman who controls and directs the traffic. In any case, this figure likes to control powerful forces; he wants to direct or even generate currents, e.g. trends in fashion and art, current trends or other peoples' mental preferences. This is nevertheless perceived as manipulation or interference in the private sphere and provokes emotional reactions. This person is probably a loner who has few long-standing friends.

Graphic Analysis

As all three colours are balanced in this figure, it can be equally and deliberately active in all three areas. It has substance and an awareness of values, it is motivated and tough but also intellectual and communicative. It moves between two worlds, one harmonious (blue), in which everything is ordered, and one intellectual (green), in which there is constant questioning and discussion. Once the person realises that the conflicts lie within himself, he can be very creative.

With its two red diagonals this person aspires to power and possesses great self-control. He can achieve anything with his will and always sets himself difficult goals. The apex of this quadrilateral looks sharp (pointed and red), although it is externally blue and green, so that it gently but deftly separates the wheat from the chaff and can immediately spot other people's sore points. All this enables him to get many things going, which not everyone is ready for.

This personality gathers knowledge and experience equally in both directions (the opposition points are three-coloured). What is learned is processed by the senses and the intellect. This person learns quickly, and can develop his character just as quickly. It goes without saying that the will, knowledge and skills are combined, so he wants to develop many abilities, learn a lot, always search deeper, and commit himself. However, he still does not know clearly where life is taking him. This person ultimately wants to challenge fate itself and experience life for himself. This is one of two quadrilaterals that possess all six aspect types!

Decorative Figure

Examples: Telly Savalas, Roberto Assagioli, Whitney Houston, Marlon Brando, Karsten Rohweder

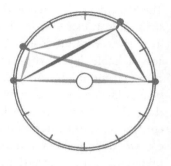

No one can pass a good decoration without noticing it. This figure aspires to perfection and uniqueness. It can convert tension into harmony, unite the ugly and the beautiful and break hard truths gently. The perfectionism of this figure leads the person to find mistakes easily and to rectify them as soon as possible.

This figure can be understood as a *decoder*; it has the ability to convert coded messages into plain language. It makes the person receptive to quite specific channels, so that he is well-informed about things that others don't know about. For example, he knows from where and from whom attitude or mood come. He has good filtering ability from which to develop a diplomatic aptitude.

Graphic Analysis

As the majority of the figure's outside is red, the Decorative figure may appear closed and secretive. The square leaning at a slight angle towards the opposition makes this figure look like a battering ram, like a narrowing cone or a vacuum cleaner. A person with such a figure is tough and gives intensely. The inside is wrapped up and is visible as accumulated intellectual strength in the small green line. This person also has a harmonious, open and artistic side. The long blue-green diagonals indicate a long processing time (meditative, remembering roots). He follows through personal plans tenaciously, and single-mindedly picks up a great deal of knowledge with its own classification system. This person moves forwards unstoppably like a bulldozer. He clears intellectual obstacles out of the way with the narrow end, and with the wider red end he acquires a place in the world for himself and others, without a fight! He just expands slowly, and leaves what he has acquired behind for other people.

The contradiction (opposition) is either harmonised by experience or explained by knowledge (blue and green triangle), although both are insufficient: "an eternal solution seeker".

Bijou or Bi-Sho

Examples: Joan Baez, Jiddhu Krishnamurti,
Antoine de Saint-Exupéry,

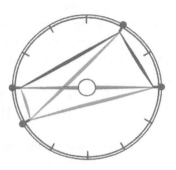

"Bi" means double or two-sided. This figure has two matching sides that have a harmonious and graceful influence, so that these people could possibly be called "Bijou" (Jewel). This makes them very popular in the long run, and so they occupy a position where they are just irreplaceable. However, they often feel misunderstood.

The "Bio Sheep" is harmless, willing to make sacrifices and has dedicated himself to the care of nature and people and values authentic and living things. Or the "Bio Shop", which sells only natural, unadulterated food and makes this its philosophy. Another meaning that could be given to this quadrilateral is "Bishop", a person who protects beliefs/ values and possesses a mystical power of persuasion that makes him almost untouchable. This person only rarely makes mistakes, as he is a perfectionist in behaviour, thinking and actions. Superiority and their solitude lie at the root of these people's pain.

Graphic Analysis

In the blue half of the figure there is substance and harmony. The green side is very sensitive, alert and never seems to stop thinking. It lives on a substance that comes from the spiritual area. It also has the ability to settle disputes with good reasoning and the most neutral wisdom possible. It always tries to balance things out, to mediate and to guide others positively.

Blue-green predominates, as the only red line present is hidden. There is no power available, except in relation to the search for inner meaning that can only be achieved by exertion. This person's strengths lie in dealing with thoughts, ideas and concepts. Too circumspect to engage in gossip or argumentative communication, he likes to study and always classifies his experience into spheres of knowledge. With the long diagonal, he thinks on a grand scale and looks for salvation in what is far away. He is driven on and on by an inner longing that stops him living in the here and now.

The **Bijou** is a light, dynamic and soft quadrilateral that looks like a large, wedge-shaped cushion. Other people would like to rest on it or see it as a source of zest for life, optimism or sensuality. However, after some time, a putative saturation or an emerging dependency overtakes the owner, for he possesses little strength for daily activities.

6.4 Four Talented Trapezoids

From the two single-coloured symmetrical Talent Triangles are formed the two original symmetrical quadrilaterals the Kite and the Cradle and four asymmetrical quadrilaterals. The small Talent Triangle has three possible ways of connecting with a fourth point in an asymmetrical quadrilateral, whereas in the large Talent Triangle there is only one possible way. In all four asymmetrical figures, the fourth corner has a red-green influence that can be interpreted as self-critical ability. The obvious blue triangle is deliberately spotlighted, focused and activated. All these figures have the same colour ratio: 1 red – 2 green – 3 blue aspects.

This predominantly blue-green quadrangular type is very sensitive, alert and adaptable, but can become apathetic if it runs out of energy.

Detective

Examples: Kemal Atatürk, Oskar Lafontaine, Slobodan Milosevic

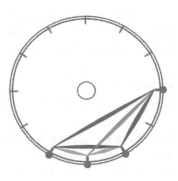

A detective can discover the smallest clue, insignificant information and slight alterations and incorporate them into a large jigsaw puzzle. He sticks to a trail, has a wide-awake character that nearly nothing escapes, likes to uncover the truth and can detect every lie.

A detector is a tool that can also record oscillations, gases or radiation. With this figure in the horoscope, the person can adapt themselves meticulously to things and eliminate disruptive influences, resulting in an ability to purge or even to eradicate, and a feeling for mental-spiritual health.

Graphic Analysis

This dynamic quadrilateral is really compact and portable like camping furniture. That means that it can quickly be set up, but then disappear again equally suddenly.

The Detective figure lies on the border of the horoscope, and is more likely to obey the environment than work on personal development, which can be neglected. The large, 240° open side contains an exposure, a kind of vulnerability or an over-devotional nature. Being mostly blue and green, it is mainly perceived as harmonious and healing. It aspires to independence. Its neutrality and real objectivity make it very sensitive and it likes to communicate.

However, inside there is a red-blue polarity of will and experience, criticism and contentment, as well as a polarity between the sexes. The motivation to make the unpleasant pleasant or to smooth out disagreements is caused by a tendency to repression. The red-green apex is an irritable, almost grouchy side that somehow does not suit this quiet and contented character. It is, however, the ability to find the mistakes, the lies, the unsavouriness of something, or to cause chaos, no matter how coherent and ordered its environment may be.

Along with the small Talent Triangle and the Eye there are two Learning triangles. What the pricked up ears or the great sensitivity pick up in the way of information is incorporated with exceptional speed and talent into its place in a puzzle. So learning is ongoing and takes two different forms: the first is observation and the search for truth and the second is the gathering and assimilation of knowledge.

Recorder

Examples: Sean Connery, Olivia Newton-John

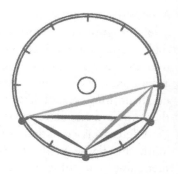

This figure acts like a recorder that stores, among other things, feelings, situations and destinies, and can replay them in such a way that one imagines they are there. This person loves the truth, but does allow for diplomatic alterations. He can also dramatise to get to the heart of something or to gain more respect for his views. He is sometimes vindictive, as he has a very sensitive side. If he does put up a fight, it is always for a just cause.

Graphic Analysis

The Recorder figure can also be seen as a thick wedge that cannot be pushed around, or as a record player, in which the red needle is precisely (green) suspended over the blue record. The red-green influenced planet is a critical observer that spots and immediately tries to fill every gap in logic or experience.

The blue-green outer frame conceals inner conflict and tension, which is why this person behaves harmlessly and consistently. He is always alert and always ready to go though. If he has set his heart on something, nothing will escape him and he waits patiently for the right time to come. Due to the rather static form, he likes to sit on things for a while, but to move on when he has learnt enough. Much care, security and nurture are required for this figure to function correctly and not just to drift around aimlessly.

The centre is touched by a quincunx. As this person is usually concerned with his environment, this reminds him of his own destiny. The red-blue motivation wants to control matter, give power to justice or give life to human structures. The small Talent triangle is harmoniously complemented by the Search triangle, so that the person looks where he thinks something is hidden. With the large Learning triangle that points to the centre, he can ask exactly the right questions or get right to the heart of the matter. The small Learning triangle enables him to learn by communicating or from books, so that with the small Talent triangle all results can be quickly sorted, integrated and stored.

Model

Examples: Yasser Arafat, Isaac Newton

A model is like a prototype that is produced to enable a better understanding of a finished product. A model can also be made of something that already exists. Artistic design talent is expressed in the verb "to model". "To remodel" is another word with an interesting meaning: to give a thing another meaning, to change its original form, for example like what happens in the modern recycling methods.

This figure is an example of the old hermetic rule: "As in the great, so in the small" and vice versa. It provides a greater context in which experiences can be perceived and generalised. Conversely, one can conform better to general rules, agree with people or even help others to reintegrate into society.

Graphic Analysis

This dynamic quadrilateral looks almost symmetrical, like a pyramid on wheels! Externally it is predominantly blue-green, i.e. receptive, sensitive and harmonious. But in the nearly right-angled section that is bordered by the red line, it can be hard and uncompromising. In this environment it can get very intense, be very demanding and successfully tolerate the concomitant stress.

The red-green influenced planet is alert, nervous and certainly conspicuous. If it is the tension ruler in the horoscope, it is permanently opposed by the other three self-satisfied planets in the blue corner. This can give rise to the danger that their talents are not developed, because the stimulation of the red-green planets, to always be jumping headlong into experiences is too great.

The inner motivation is extremely stable, because it intersects the blue-green diagonals almost at right-angles. This person aspires to an ideal world and hardly ever lets pessimistic people bring him down, and in fact his centred persistence can give courage and hope to other people.

The Talent triangle points towards and appears to become the overlaying, single-minded Projection triangle. Out of this a Dominant triangle and a large Learning triangle are formed, and are given critical impetus by the environment, i.e. a perception matures and becomes a goal and eventually leads to a dominant personality.

Representative

Examples: Karl Jaspers, Marilyn Monroe,
Mao Tse-tung.

A representative defends an idea, a philosophy or a political trend with their whole being. He can feel under obligation to a community or else represent something on his own initiative with his versatile, sometimes fantastic powers of persuasion. He can also regain what has been lost.

The word comes from the latin "repraesentare: to imagine, to visualise". In the context of this figure it means that these people and their invariably genuine opinions strike others as harmonious in a holistic or cathartic way, so that it can be said of them: "What you see is what you get". The name Representative also conveys a sense of presence: alert and wide-awake, taking everything in, at peace with itself but always ready. The willingness to be open to other people at all times enables such a person to a step outside the box, though this may result in his being initially misunderstood or not taken seriously. However, he is patient and can wait until the time is right for an idea, a new way of life or a whole philosophy. He is then a steady, reliable point of reference.

Graphic Analysis

Two thirds of the people around him see a devoted and harmonious person who seems very stable and invulnerable. The Achilles Heel is the red-green influenced planet. His innate critical sensitivity is honed by painful experiences, making him become more self-critical and self-aware. The single red line means that this person sometimes seems rather lazy or even inflexible. He only fights if his integrity is questioned or if someone tries to impose their will on him.

This figure has an important function as a role model, as it covers a large area and is adaptable (asymmetrical) and possesses a lot of substance in the three blue lines. He can gain the trust of a person or become the representative of a whole group, only to turn away, since inner freedom and development are more important to him. The small green line stands out in comparison to the five long lines around it: expressing something in words always means reproducing part of one's experience in a changed form. This gives rise to a new understanding that is immediately integrated into one's own substance.

A Search triangle and a medium Learning triangle form a wedge between the large Talent and the Dominant triangles. Intelligent searching for the right answers leads to personal development, which is a holistic process that is stored for ever in the blue triangle.

6.5 Five Rare Quadrilaterals

Stage, Magic Cap, UFO, Surfer, Oscillo

These quadrilaterals are less common because they have a preponderance of green aspects, which have the smallest tolerance limits and are therefore rarer. But there are seven more equally rare and mainly green quadrilaterals that have already been described: Irritation Rectangle, Striving figure, Bathtub, Trampoline, Trawler, Bijou and Megaphone.

Perhaps we should use the term *the greens* for these figures, to highlight the strong qualities of the mutable cross. They are loving types and need real human contact, sincere attention and non-obligatory, spontaneous communication. These things are in short supply in our society, though, which is why free, unhindered development is often not ensured for *the greens*, so things are not easy for them. They often fall by the wayside because they are so often misunderstood. But if they liberate themselves from daily routine and can reorient themselves, they can blossom. Despite their fixed quadrangular form, they need constant change in their lives.

Of particular interest in these figures (except the Oscillo) are the single-coloured diagonals, indicators of a coherent inner motivation, prototypical of one of the three basic motivations cardinal, fixed or mutable. However, all of them aspire towards security in the sense of self control, building on firm values and gathering experiences.

Stage

Examples: Umberto Eco, Antoine de Saint Exupéry

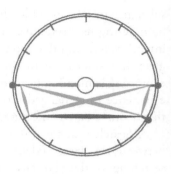

This is similar to the vertical Striving figure, with the same number of aspects, including two Irritation triangles. In the Stage figure, the Irritation triangles are reversed and joined together. Both figures have four green lines, similar to the Cradle and the Kite which, composed of three Ambivalence Figures and with five blue aspects, are the prototypes of the blue figures.

A stage is a place where a group of people perform a play. Literary stories, human destiny, emotions, love, and critical ideas are revealed to the public. The Stage figure knows many roles and bit parts, and gets to know new ones with every meeting. In its search for new people with as yet undiscovered qualities, it is inquisitive, careful and foresighted. It classifies each person that it has understood in its anthology of human roles and stores every detail.

The Stage figure has a big heart, but is still somehow aloof. To be able to be open to everyone and everything, it protects itself from manipulation and prejudice and is very honest with itself. It can understand other people even in their innermost composition, identify their place in society and explain many things very graphically.

Graphic Analysis

The Stage figure is trapeze-shaped and acts like a bridge that connects two worlds. The special quality of this figure is that it has three different polarities. One polarity appears in the small green lines that symbolise two widely opposing opinions. The second polarity is indicated by the opposition, the acknowledgement of opposites. The third lies in the external red-blue ambivalence.

This figure divides the horoscope into an empty half in which nothing can be reflected or perceived, but is compensated for in the other half by the great blue-green sensitivity. It takes its friends to this soft half and says: "Out there is harsh reality (the public on the other side of the opposition), but we have to learn and practise on the world!" thereby protecting him.

The quadrilateral is symmetrical and the red-blue polarity is connected in several places by green lines. The awareness connections are so strong that the opposites can be joined at any time, although from the outside they are clearly separate. In conversation, it is noticeable how these people strive for harmony. They try to talk away differences and to create a unified picture. The intersection of the quincunxes at the centre is like a double search for authenticity, love and meaning that runs in opposite directions.

The Stage is also composed of two Irritation and two Search triangles. A person with this figure is engaged in a constant search with alert awareness for what stimulates movement. There are two conflicting questions that crop up again and again that call for renewed searching. For every problem, the more sophisticated the powers of discrimination or distinction, the more solutions he finds. This enables all problems to be solved with time. "To each his own" is the motto of the Stage.

Magic Cap

Examples: Walt Disney, Reinhold Messner

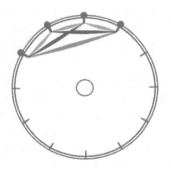

A Magic Cap makes the wearer invisible, and underneath it he can be left alone and in peace. He can pass through groups of people collecting information without anyone noticing or stopping him. The Magic Cap leaves no lasting trace in the hustle and bustle of the world. If a person who meets someone wearing a Magic Cap feels personally affected by the encounter, he has pleasant, positive memories of it. However, the interaction is not intended to be that personal. The person is naturally very sensitive, conciliatory and helpful and is incapable of harming anyone. He likes to let his imagination wander in conversation and in nature, is outwardly approachable, and rather strict with himself. He rarely likes to talk about himself and withdraws in amazement if he provokes a reaction or leaves a trace behind him.

Sometimes he laughs at profile-obsessed egocentrics, but occasionally falls under their influence. He is a selfless server who no-one can pin down. His manner is quick and non-committal, his character neutral, uncomplicated and loving. Discretion is one of his natural talents, and it is noticed by those who put their trust in this perfect listener.

Graphic Analysis

This smallest of trapezes is like a fast-revolving disc, shimmering in the sun like a frisbee. It is hard to catch and acts like a mirror. The two external planets act like ears and are aspected in three colours. They are intelligent and understand everything. The two central blue-green planets act like eyes. The symmetry lies across the dynamic, so that it can dart off in two directions. But if it always escapes to one side when the other side gets too risky, it experiences loneliness and loss of contact.

This quadrilateral is the most concentrated, but also the most distant. This means that its attention and action are concentrated in a specific area, but it is almost unconnected to itself and acts selflessly. That is why it is very important for this person to learn to love himself. By being less influenced by other people and developing his own feelings, an inner emotional fantasy world is created that gives him stability.

The predominantly green aspects indicate a sensitive person, a Love type who likes to communicate. The blue intersection brings balance, harmony and a love of pleasure. Together this produces an artistic type, a hedonist, who can even ward off hardship by virtue of the red line. The basic motivation is the belief and trust in creativity.

The Magic Cap consists of two Eyes and two small Learning triangles. An Eye can absorb varied information and take part in several conversations and discussions at the same time. The Learning triangles mean that he is constantly learning new things and can convey every discovery in diverse ways. His analytical intellect adapts to each emotional situation. It strives for the free flow of information.

UFO

Examples: Alfred Fankhauser, Helmut Kohl

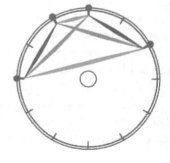

To us, unidentified flying objects seem to be powered by a mysterious force and to possess energies that provide striking lighting effects. We believe that they contain living creatures and technology. No-one knows where they come from and what they want from us, so we don't treat them like an enemy, but with caution. Perhaps we could gain something from them?

We may wonder how the person who owns this quadrilateral with a high-energy consumption still manages to be harmonious, adaptable and sometimes even lethargic. We feel the energy in his words and in his intense concentration. He often says the right thing at just the right time, which can spark something off in another person. He finds support everywhere, because he has a helpful and reliable character and he exudes a fascination that makes him unforgettable.

Graphic Analysis

The UFO is a sizeable trapeze that leaves a lasting impression. One degree larger and it would be a pyramid. The UFO acts like a sphinx in front of a pyramid that attracts inquisitive looks because of the secrets it is hiding within it. A dynamic but symmetrical quadrilateral with equal proportions of all colours, it is a model for further development. This person can take the path of individuation as a loner or help others on their way. The long green line near the centre shows that the inner consciousness is in touch with deeper existential questions. This enables him to create from the heart and to do important things for others.

The blue-green shell behaves like a chameleon that changes colour to match the environment. For the person has a sensitive and harmony-seeking persona and surprises people by the stark contrast if he suddenly speaks very plainly to clear up misunderstandings or to get to the heart of the matter.

Deep in the heart of this figure there is a powerful store of energy, and the two intersecting red blades demonstrate its invincibility. This person wants to manage the most difficult things and looks for special tasks that no-one else can handle. With his will he can achieve anything. He looks for opportunities to develop and checks out all information, gets to the bottom of things and, if possible tries things out. This also enables him to convince other people.

The UFO quadrilateral consists of two medium and two large Learning triangles. The motivation comes from inside, as internal criticism or dissatisfaction cause a large thinking step. The semi-sextile involves the search for further information.

The thinking processes are connected on both levels and lead to satisfying experiences that are released as substance. This also ensures personal development.

Surfer

Examples: Emile Zola, Sergius Golovin

Equipped only with an unstable board and a fluttering sail, the surfer sets out to negotiate the unpredictable wind and waves. He is sensitised to the changing elements and has himself well under control. He can move, turn and adapt fast, all the while keeping on course. His goal is to master unpredictable, dynamic processes and energies. He will manage that too, because he has the ability to recognise natural forces and to reject the artificial and the illusory. He recognises quick opportunities for change when others have already given up, thus making him a kind of orientation flag for those around him when the going gets rough.

The surfer is very sensitive to the balance of power around him. He often tolerates things that others find trivial or even unpleasant. His deeper inner sense of justice forces him to support the underdog, as he always tries to make things fair. He doesn't like it if something is ignored, passed over or neglected, however small it is. According to his sensitive perception, everything is part of a greater whole.

Graphic Analysis

With the very dynamic Surfer figure, this person develops faster than others and his determination is hard to surpass. He sticks almost blindly to his goal and is mostly happy with what he achieves. This can be due to modesty, or the fact that he just doesn't judge his aim.

The planet where three different long aspect colours meet at the apex is quite striking. This planet provides strong, aware and intelligent self-control. The other three-coloured planet in the middle collects, assimilates and occasionally checks what happens in the way of experiences. It is responsible for keeping balance.

The Surfer figure passes right next to the inner centre, which is why this person always remembers his origins, bears them in mind and acts accordingly. He adapts to his environment, but without letting himself be manipulated. He is an individualist with great dedication who is hard to evaluate. He is very sensitive, is happy to let others have their way and only rarely defends himself. In the process, he occasionally forgets to assert himself until unexpected events crop up, in which case his great dynamism makes him unstoppable.

From the outside, the figure appears only to be green and red and gives an impression of perpetual activity. This person is constantly on the go, allows himself no rest and does not like to stay in the same place for long. He communicates extensively, as the exchange of information of all kinds is important to him. The two blue diagonals indicate a deep inner peace. Their existence is only noticed in emergency situations when others are having nervous breakdowns or if a "bomb" has to be defused. He possesses an acquired inner substance and solid experiences on which he can build. He tends to see the world in a positive light and is optimistic, but it also lets him down over and over again.

Oscillo

Example: Fernandel

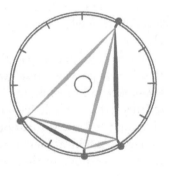

An Oscillo could be a mythical creature that possesses unimagined powers. For many people it is hard to get on with someone who has an Oscillo and to judge him fairly without misunderstandings. He must learn to live with this, for his way of operating and behaving is rather unique.

The oscillograph or the oscilloscope and the oscillator (machine for generating electrical oscillations), as well as the verb oscillate are all well-known in technology. This quadrilateral has a very sensitive reaction to all types of vibration coming from people, places or situations. But even if it does absorb external vibrations, he still retains his integrity and reflects back what he experiences. There is a constant subtle vibration in this person's manner that is not nervous, but is a kind of alert motion like a gyrating radar screen. He periodically returns to previously settled matters to check that they are still OK. He is like the watchdog or supervisor for ongoing projects, developments and activities.

Graphic Analysis

The location of the three green lines in the Oscillo figure is very interesting, as they form a large zig-zag that runs through the whole figure and looks like a pantograph. With the small peak we follow a line that then extends to the long peak. From a psychological point of view, it is the ability to sympathise in a holistic way with all kinds of people.

A person with this Oscillo figure is definitely a very sensitive being (three green and two blue lines) who only rarely defends himself. In his phlegmatic single-mindedness, he is very patient and far-sighted, a lone searcher who, to the amazement of others, manages to achieve his goal eventually nevertheless.

His lovable, harmonious and intelligent persona opens doors. There is very little to criticise in this person, but people sense something disconcerting about him, a kind of inner tension, and they think that he is so well-balanced that something must be wrong with him! It is this quality that provokes criticism in those around him and his own sensitivity enables him to recognise unconscious behaviour patterns in others. He is a kind of pure researcher who can predict a person's reaction through knowledge and experience (not to be confused with clairvoyance!).

Inside, the red-green diagonals make him jumpy, nervous and irritable. It goes without saying that everything is a question of will, awareness and organisation. He is self-critical and is never completely satisfied with himself. From time to time he is susceptible to bursts of energy and the dissipation of substance (tendency to escapism and wastage). As long as there is no emotional tension, he sticks at one thing, and then he suddenly finds an excuse to go before anyone can notice an incipient tension.

6.6 Small Aspect Patterns

By small aspect patterns, we mean those that only occupy a small part of the horoscope. The largest of these is [bounded by] the quincunx, which does not go through the centre. There are other still smaller figures, the largest [bounded by] the trine. Since 1940 (and to an extent in the 19th century), these small patterns have occurred quite frequently [due to the periodic concentration of planetary positions in one half of the zodiac]. In the 1940s, they went up to the 150 degree angle, the long green quincunx aspect. Oppositions are not included. From 1982 to 1985, they were so small, especially in the autumn and winter months, that their largest aspect was still the sextile.

The small aspect patterns are not easy to interpret. The easiest way to understand them is to look at the houses. The planets are concentrated into part of the horoscope: at the top, bottom, right or left. This produces a small visual angle, often a magnifying glass effect, or a subjective perspective in the life area concerned. Instead of seeing the entire complexity of reality, these people only see part of it, or one event. Personal reactions are conditioned by the part of the horoscope in which these small patterns are situated.

Aspect Pattern in the I-space

If it is situated in the I-space, i.e. on the left side of the horoscope, awareness is concentrated on the personal ego pattern. The ego is important here and this is often reflected in a crystallisation, and by ego demands exceeding a healthy level. They usually develop distinctly narcissistic traits.

However, if these people have a spiritual orientation, their concentrated ego strength is used to serve higher ideals, and they have a stimulating and persuasive

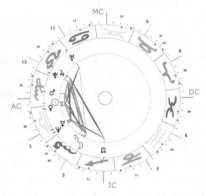

I-space
21.9.1955, 05.55, Bern

effect on their fellow men. It is hard to get away from their spiritual anathema. With great, sometimes uncompromising tenacity, they get the You development process going. They don't let up until the You has changed in line with their ideals or findings. They almost always enable other people to evolve a little. If their ego has become lucid to higher qualities, it acts as a focus for the spiritual energy in the surrounding area. This is why we also often find pedagogues, artists, therapists and counsellors who have a small aspect pattern on the I-side.

However, this position is rather problematic when it comes to a genuine contact with the You, the partner. These people nearly always have problems relating to others. They lack the ability to identify with others because they are predominantly egocentrically to monomaniacally into themselves. They are not truly aware of the You, for they see it as an object. Their life motivation is to assert their ego.

Identity problems usually appear at the start of life, and are initially shown as a lack of ego strength or vitality. These people often form an image of themselves, of the world and of other people which bears no relation to reality, but is actually a product of their own imagination. In certain situations they even make adjustments to reality so that the You, the other person, fits into their subjective world view. There is nearly always an unconscious choice of perceptions, things or people who correspond to their subjective ideas, and which they accept more willingly than other types. The latter are unconsciously rejected, often misjudged and sometimes even turned into the enemy.

Empty Horoscope Space

We should not forget that one half of the horoscope is mostly completely empty. The empty space and unoccupied quadrants almost always cause anxiety, attracting all kinds of extraneous material, which flows in alarmingly as if by suction. Although this increases the ability to attract what is lacking, the exposure to outside influences causes much anxiety. It is therefore not surprising that during a lifetime a hard, often crystallized ego core is built up, which then gives this person problems in his relationships with other people. All influences penetrate through the empty spaces into the unprotected core, right to the centre of the circle. That is also the reason why a chance remark often affects these people deeply – even if the words were well meant. Once they have been hurt in this way, it is hard for them to associate with other people again. They all too easily lose trust and the courage to start a relationship. The principle of complementarity does not always work perfectly for all small aspect figures, which is why such people often also look for a sidekick, i.e. a partner who also has a small aspect pattern. With other people they either have problems or their development is restricted by the You and they become totally dependent, which frightens them.

Aspect Pattern in the You-Space

For everyone with an aspect pattern on the You-side, this small pattern acts like an increased selective mechanism. Awareness is restricted in favour of a one-sided contact with someone by whom the person is often willingly dominated. He has a great longing for love, but usually finds the opposite because he is incapable of cooperation. He is not anchored in his own ego, for in a right-positioned aspect pattern the I-side is empty.

You-space
27.11.1959, 15.15, Bern

If such people have a spiritual disposition, they are often motivated by a philosophy of selfless devotion to the You. They find the greatest satisfaction in a profession in which they can help other people and which therefore allows human contact.

In impersonal contacts they are very sensitive and can react positively to the needs of others. The caring professions are therefore indicated. However, in personal contacts they easily lose their identity and run the risk of being a victim of those around them. They can neither escape nor provide real resistance to the extraneous influences automatically affecting the You-side of the horoscope. In love, they lose themselves to the object of their affections and are unable to assert their own needs. They constantly feel unfulfilled. Automatically, i.e. unconsciously, they are looking for a strong partner to whom they are willing to subordinate and to whom they can delegate the missing ego awareness.

Aspect Pattern in Lower Space

If the aspect pattern is in the lower space or to the right or left of it, it means that the upper space is empty. These people are very close to their families, their relatives. They are emotionally dependent on them and usually only partially develop their potential. Their assessments and judgments are affected by a lack of information, personal attitudes, tradition and preferences. However, it cannot be said that they are always wrong. They are just quite different. For them, the way they evaluate an experience or a situation, however one-sided, is actually correct.

Often the physical strength caused by the concentration of the planets in the instinct or impulse quadrants is very powerful. They can use it to create a new reality for themselves in spite of their attachment to tradition and

Collective space
10.7.1942, 00.15, Zürich

thereby revise the reality that limits them. Creative energy or artistic talent is not uncommon. They may even be able to influence the world around them without making much effort. Their very existence may have a transformative effect on the environment. Their otherness and the prismatic effect of a small aspect pattern at the base of the horoscope can act as a catalyst.

Aspect Pattern in Upper Space

With small aspect patterns in the upper awareness space of the horoscope, all energies are geared to personal individualization. These people's priority is their vocation, finding a meaningful mission in life. For a long time the only things they look for, perceive and experience are those useful for self-actualisation, usually to the exclusion of other opportunities. They are the focus of all their attention. They try their utmost to be perfect in their chosen field and to become specialists. One could say that these people

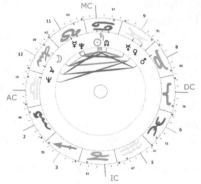

Individual space
13.7.1945, 12.54, Zürich

set their transmitting-receiving equipment to just one station like a radio. Although other stations transmit at the same time, they only tune into one station, namely the one that furthers their own development, whether their goal is spiritual or material. They immediately spot any possibility to move another step up the ladder, as they are so attuned to them. They are also always trying to find their own way, to rise above mediocrity and for this they are attacked by society. Such people need a profession that satisfies them and where they can fulfil their ambition to reach the top. They also make sacrifices in order to reach a professional goal. They can often be an eternal students, constantly striving for more.

Esoteric Point of View

We would like to approach the problem of the small aspect patterns from yet another, more esoteric angle; for this we must expand our awareness and embrace evolutionary philosophy. In esoteric ideology, there is a so-called *deva realm* alongside the human realm, which is comparable to the *angel realm* in the Christian religion. According to Alice A. Bailey, in our time, a connection will be established between the deva realm and the human realm. For this purpose a group of souls should have been incarnated "who have stayed a while in the deva realm". Their task is to collaborate on the manifestation of a new quality of life. Now, if we consider the people with a small aspect figure to be members of this group, we can better understand their deep life motivation and their otherness. We recognise that they have a special role in the world. They contribute a quality that is all too rare in our world, which is why they often feel like aliens on earth.

When this subject is discussed with them, they agree immediately, and feel that their true selves have been acknowledged and affirmed. Usually they are deeply moved. The membership of a special group of souls means a great deal to them, as if they have found their roots in another dimension. Also, connecting with a group of like-minded people who have the same task not only raises their own sense of self-worth, but also gives them a feeling that they are not alone. This compensates to some extent for the ego problems that they nearly always have and the naturally related feelings of inferiority. Also, the knowledge that they have a mission to accomplish in life often helps them to break out of the restrictions of their little lives, to adopt a new attitude towards their own problems and to participate in a large-scale development process.

7. Example Horoscopes

- Roberto Assagioli, Founder of Psychosynthesis
- Mikhail Gorbachev, Soviet Politician

Roberto Assagioli

Founder of Psychosynthesis

by Louise Huber

Roberto Assagioli
27.2.1888, 12.03, Venice/Italy

If we look closely at the aspect pattern of his horoscope, we notice immediately that Roberto Assagioli was a person of exceptional awareness. This intricate formation includes the most well-known four-sided figures, except the Kite. From our pictorial perspective, it resembles a highly-polished diamond with eight corners. Graphically, it looks like a mandala with planets evenly distributed over the whole chart. The large red Achievement Square and blue Righteous Rectangle are linked together, giving the impression of a rotating wheel. Inside, an incomplete Irritation Rectangle extends across the thinking axis (houses 3 to 9). Two large three-coloured Dominant Triangles further enrich the pattern, while an intersecting quincunx from Mars to Neptune and a detached quincunx from Mercury to Uranus break up the relatively static figure and give a certain impression of completeness.

The green-red aspects around the centre indicate a dynamic-creative potential that enables Assagioli not only to activate his inner core but also to awaken the *awareness of the soul* in others. His therapeutic treatment always began with the core personality. He had a special ability to take people back again and again to their inner core, with loving patience and wisdom—sometimes also with the gentle insistence of his bell-like voice. His concept of psychosynthesis held that an effective treatment of the mentally disturbed should begin at the core of their inner being. It was essential for his work that all external manifestations of mental disturbance should be related to spiritual development and the core personality, or the *higher self*, which the person integrates into an active whole.

Such a rich aspect structure is not easy to live with though! Assagioli had to go through inner crises and transformations, as he lived out the complexity of the pattern and addressed the difficulties of integration and synthesis posed by the many layers of his personality. Like many other great people, he searched for satisfactory solutions to his personal problems. One could say that his work of psychosynthesis responded both to the variety of directions and tensions of his aspect pattern and to the universality of his interests and endeavours. There were tasks that he had to overcome, both within himself and the field of psychology, and they made him what he was.

The three oppositions, from houses 2 to 8, 4 to 10 and 6 to 12 were particularly troublesome, keeping him permanently on a high level of tension. The subjects of possession, public virtue and coping with existence, relating to these axes, tormented and controlled him. Assagioli was always materially dependent on his wife, a rich Italian landed aristocrat (Saturn in the second house). She was a maternal woman who held him under her thumb. There is a gap in the aspect pattern in the second house between Saturn and the Moon Node, and Nelly died at the transition of his Age Point over the Moon Node.

Although the propagation of his teachings was very close to his heart, the prominent Pisces Sun at the top of his chart on the MC, occupying one angle of the tense Achievement Square, made him stressed whenever he had to appear in public. Much more important to him were his sensitivity, loving understanding and sympathetic attention to those who sought help from him. He was a born therapist, a true healer whom everyone trusted. Nearest to the DC lie Jupiter sextile Venus. With Jupiter on the cusp of the sixth house opposition Pluto, he was deeply immersed in the subject of existence. Assagioli always raised the mundane to a higher level. He was able to look right into a person's motivations and see much more than some people were comfortable with. It was often really difficult for him to offer practical help.

Dane Rudhyar, who was friendly with Assagioli, wrote about his Achievement Square in *Astrology and the Modern Psyche*, calling it a "perfect square" whose corners linking all four elements are formed by a full-Moon opposition of Sun and Moon— "symbol of extreme awareness and illumination"—and the Pluto-Jupiter diagonal of what he called the "mystic rectangle", sometimes using qualifying adjectives like *sacred* or *integrative* to capture the essence of Assagioli's Righteousness Rectangle. Such rectangles, he wrote, *"can be considered as 'altars' or 'chambers of initiation'... They define a consecrated space within which a process of integration and spiritualization takes place... The perfect square... is more self-contained; while the rectangle configuration of planets emphasizes the resolution of two conflicting natures into a dynamic effort toward a transcendent or sacrificial goal."*

Aspects that stand out from the contained aspect structure of the horoscope, such as unaspected planets or, as in this case, Assagioli's quincunxes from Mercury to Uranus and Mars to Neptune are especially interesting as indicators of a personal profile. They represent a challenge in the development of the personality and always have an unsettling effect, especially if the integrative momentum stands out as much as it does in Assagioli's horoscope. This momentum gives rise to the urge to balance everything and it is frustrating if something prevents this. Creative intelligence (Uranus) is connected to combinational reason (Mercury) by the long green thinking step, and Assagioli's creative intelligence was indeed brilliant. His thoughts, his ideals and his visions were pervaded with a new spirit. He was inspired and motivated to make a contribution to human evolution. The quincunx aspect of Mars to Neptune indicates a strong idealism, a devotion to religious goals. The appearance of his inner objectives and his motivation to love gave him a charismatic aura that helped him in his work. His esoteric knowledge was exceptional, his ideals far-reaching and his efforts to transfer these into concrete methods were always what drove him on. But he always used to say that between the esoteric and the exoteric there had to be a *Holy Wall of Silence*. The Pluto/Neptune position in the signs of Taurus and Gemini in the stress area of the twelfth house cusp makes this anxiety clear. This planetary positioning was also the feature of his generation. Today we can talk freely about the fact that Assagioli was an esotericist, an initiate. Every morning we began our work with meditation. During this time, he gave me the incentive to develop zodiac meditations. He read the books of Alice A. Bailey every day in the search for eternal truths and made numerous markings in the margin of the text. I often had to write out important quotes, on which he meditated for days and which would later influence his exoteric work.

The comparison of his life with his Age Points is interesting (17). Here too it is amazing to see how Assagioli lived out his own horoscope and was able to live it during the course of his life.

Age Point (AP) and Life History

Roberto Assagioli studied neurology and psychiatry at the University of Florence. His Age Point was at that time transiting the signs of Leo and Virgo in the third and fourth houses. It touched the Moon and the opposition to the Sun. Assagioli had wide-ranging philosophical and cultural interests and was a member of many groups of young free-thinking Italians. While a student he ran a bookshop (the sign of Virgo) that was founded by an American. This laid the foundation for international contacts that were so important for his later work.

In **1911** (AP conjunct Uranus, quincunx Mercury) he presented his views on the unconscious in a lecture at the "International Conference of Philosophy" in Bologna. As it approached Mars he further developed his ideas and began to associate and use together the different techniques and methods of psychotherapy in his therapeutic practice.

From **1912** (AP conjunct Mars) to **1915**, he published a scientific magazine entitled *Psyche*. As the Age Point passed through the intercepted sign of Scorpio in the fifth house, he developed techniques of personal rehabilitation which he called *psychosynthesis* as a result of his various clinical and psychological experiences. He himself wrote: *"The start of my approach was already included in my doctorate dissertation on Psychoanalysis (1910: AP Low Point 4, sextile Moon Node), in which I indicated what I saw as the limitations in Freudian Theories"*. He wanted to counter Freud's analytical method with a synthetic, constructive one that incorporated free will and man's higher self.

At the **DC transit at the age of 36**, he began to work openly. The Age Point activated both the mystic blue rectangle and the red square. In **1926**, he founded the *Istituto di Psicosintesi* in Rome, with the aim of developing, implementing and teaching different methods of psychotherapy and psychological training as an educational psychosynthesis resource for patients and young people. In **1927** (AP square Uranus, Sextile Mercury) he published his first booklet in English ("A New Method of Healing – Psychosynthesis"). Again it was the linear aspect, the detached Uranus/Mercury figure, that was the trigger for his prominent creative work. (At the Uranus transit he gave his first public lecture).

After the start of the Second World War, his work in Rome became more and more difficult, as his humanitarian and international ideas and his universal attitude aroused the mistrust of the Fascist movement. In **1941** (AP conjunct Sun and square Pluto), he was even imprisoned and put in solitary confinement for one month. He told his friends that being in prison was an interesting and valuable experience that gave him the opportunity to carry out special psycho-spiritual experiments. It is worth noting that the Sun/Pluto square is often related to war experiences. Pluto on the 12th cusp and the Sun after the MC allow the best understanding of this experience.

In **1943**, at the AP transit of Mercury and quincunx Uranus, he started new activities and came under fire from the fascists once again. He had to go and hide out in the mountains. He managed to escape arrest by the henchmen of the regime that were chasing him, by the skin of his teeth. This is another example of his insecurity in external situations caused by his being a "troublemaker".

The arrival of the Allies freed him from this difficult situation in **1944** (AP sextile Neptune).

After the end of the war, he began to transfer his Institute from Rome to Florence. The AP had passed the "zero point of the zodiac" and in January **1945** it entered the sign of Aries. The fiery strength of Aries enabled him to risk a new start. It was in Florence that he first really developed the concept of psychosynthesis. His first writings, treatises and pamphlets date from this time. He was very active and held many courses and lectures on psychosynthesis in Italy and abroad (Switzerland, England, America). His short articles and pamphlets were also published in different languages.

In **1957** (AP in Low Point 12), the *Psychosynthesis Research Foundation* was founded in Valmy, Greenwich, Delaware in the USA with the help of a group of foreign friends. Here too, on the way to the AC, the Age Point was waiting with a new life cycle, a diversification. In **1958**, Assagioli was invited to a psychology conference in the USA and at this event he gave a lecture on psychosynthesis at the University of Brandeis.

The *Istituto dei Psycosintesi* continued its activity in Florence (via San Dominio). Two international conventions on psychosynthesis were held in Capolona, near Arezzo, Italy, in **1956** and **1957**, with lectures and participants from eight nations. Bruno Huber visited this symposium in **1957** and there it was decided that we should help Assagioli to publish a book on the *Techniques of Psychosynthesis*. From **1958** to **1961** we worked with him on a daily basis and, with a lot of new knowledge and great satisfaction, finished work on his book in the English language.

In **1973**, when the AP aspected Uranus once again (Sextile), Assagioli produced his greatest work: his second, notable work *The Act of Will* was published. It was interesting that this aspect of Uranus to Mercury was present at the origin of all his writings. This shows how important such detached aspects are in life.

After a very active period, Roberto Assagioli died in **1974** at the ripe old age of 86. The Age Point had reached the halfway point between the Moon Node and the Moon. Shortly before his death he called us to see him once more. He gave his blessing to our work and supported us in the foundation of the *Institute of Astrological Psychology*, for which we are very grateful to him.

Mikhail Gorbachev

Soviet Politican
By Bruno Huber

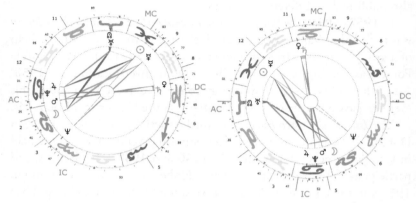

Mikhail Gorbachev	Mikhail Gorbachev
2.3.1931,12.34 Privolnoye/	2.3.1931,8.00 Privolnoye/
Stavropol/USSR	Stavropol/USSR

A political phenomenon or Gorbi, the man who made peace acceptable to the power politicians.

I have thought a great deal about Mikhail Gorbachev, the politician and the man, and of course I know that everyone who cares a little about this world does the same thing. He cannot just be dismissed, he obviously exists and he finds his way into every living room. He was a politician who worked successfully in high office as leader of the largest nation in the world and changed the history of the world (and more) with a couple of handshakes. A man who did not just do the "done thing" in the world of politics. "What kind of man is he?" and "How did he do it?" are questions we astrologers must ask. "And can he make it last?" was then, the apprehensive or sardonic question according to the person's attitude.

Initially we astrologers had a handicap: we had a birth date and a place but no birth time. The place also proved to be one of many with the same name in the USSR. Even the media could not agree whether Gorbachev was born in the Ukraine or the Russian Socialist Soviet Republic (whose capital was Moscow). Speculations were raised, and attempts to establish the birth time were made; I myself participated in this with a suggestion in issue 42 of *Astrolog* of February 1988 (7).

A Moscow psychologist and astrologer alleged that she had received the exact time from a high-ranking official in the Kremlin, and now there are at least two versions of Gorbachev's horoscope. Below I will try to weigh up one against the other. As a researcher, I am just not convinced by the accuracy of the above source reference without careful and detailed verification.

What stands out immediately ...

With a time difference of six and a half hours, the two birth charts remain almost exactly the same in terms of planetary position and hence aspect pattern. What strikes us immediately is the two- or three-fold oppositional tension in the "political axis" Capricorn/Cancer – a prominent feature in leaders' horoscopes. This indicates a highly active awareness of the experience dimension of two naturally polarised archetypes: government (Capricorn) and people (Cancer), or even: ruler and ruled. Expressed more simply: since his childhood, Gorbachev must have experienced the sharp contradiction between the dictatorial Soviet rulers on the one hand and the resulting helplessness of the people on the other. Apparently, though, in his consciousness he differentiated and processed the two main polarities Saturn/Pluto and Venus/Mars present in the opposition. This is proved by his revolutionary philosophy of perestroika.

Saturn opposition Pluto is a powerful contradiction between the static need for order and security in life and the dynamic will to take control of one's own world. This is a contradiction that in history was apparently often solved with a doctrinaire and/or dictatorial control system that was developed along markedly paranoid and expansive lines. Let me repeat again in simple words: Gorbachev has inside him, as a part of his character, a "built-in dictator".

But...

This one opposition is cemented (conjunctively bound) to a Venus-Mars opposition, which on the one hand has a very good affinity with the one mentioned above (masculine-feminine polarisation), but on the other hand makes it unlikely that this planetary configuration operates unscrupulously as power (or even authority). Mars and Venus at their maximum possible angle (180°) ensure that one is dependent on the opposite sex to be able to live fully. In other words: it is hard to believe that "Gorbi" could have become the person we know without his wife Raïsa. His wife will always have a moderating influence on him, in the human sense, whatever her personal character may be. This is also clearly demonstrated by the fact that he is always seen with his wife, even when etiquette does not demand it.

The morning horoscope (Asadullina version) incidentally shows a small difference compared to the midday birth chart (12.34). It features an additional one-sided opposition, from Venus to Pluto that disappears at midday. To be sure this is just a detail, but one which could have a corrective effect if it were possible to clarify the following point from the life story of both: the one-sided opposition would mean that Raïsa blindly worshipped her Mikhail, but was also jealously watchful as to whether he really corresponded to her ideal, larger than life man. According to what she herself said, as a student, she had chosen him from a large number of suitors, because he was the "most sensible".

The Aspect Pattern

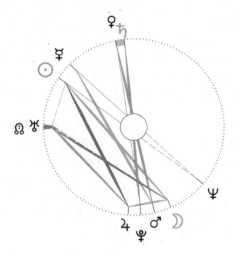

The aspect pattern consists of a coherent whole in which two qualitatively different parts can be distinguished. First there is a flat Trampoline, containing the Sun, Moon, Jupiter and Uranus/Moon Node and in the way of aspects a red square, two blue trines and three green – a quincunx and two semi-sextiles. This is joined to a red-green purely linear figure: Sun-Neptune-Mercury-Mars-Venus-Saturn-Pluto (plus, in the 8am version, an opposition back to Venus).

Both figures are positioned *carefully* next to each other, so that there is neither an impression of conflicting nor collapsing, they are two different function circuits that must work in harmony. Gorbachev could not therefore measure his life and his actions by two different standards, in the way that people with divided figures usually do. That requires a high level of self-knowledge and self-control, for one figure is characterised by sensitivity and humanity (the Trampoline) and the other is endowed with rigour, great toughness and determination (the linear figure). Gromyko (former Foreign Minister) put it like this: "he has a nice smile, but iron teeth".

The base of the Trampoline, a special and quite rare figure, is a Square, which as usual shows solid basic stability (a lot of energy), and on top is a flexible, springy structure. The two opposing, intersecting Trines are like steel springs (compact substance), while the three green aspects that form the other three sides of the quadrilateral resemble the flexibility and elasticity of rubber bands or sheets. Together they form a very dynamic figure that has nothing of the blocked awkwardness common in figures with squares. On the contrary, the three green sides make the figure highly sensitive to what is happening around it. But as they are stretched over a strong frame (red and blue aspects), the whole thing reacts like a trampoline, whose jumping surface (quincunx) can indeed be pushed in deeply (impressed), only to promptly spring back again. Gorbachev's ability to treat both friends and enemies with sensitivity, but then to show certain inconsistent reactions, is genuine and is confirmed in this figure.

Planets and Signs

If the components (planets) of these figures are incorporated, they show another peculiarity, and indicate a special personality profile that gives the ego unusual strength and adaptability. In the red-green linear figure the ego planet is Saturn, and in the three-coloured Trampoline figure the Sun and the Moon. This accentuates the typical nature and qualities of both figures mentioned above. For it is obvious that Saturn in its domicile Capricorn, with its stability and sometimes necessary toughness, can work better in a predominantly red linear figure than in one that is mainly green (Trampoline), which would be expected to be more nondescript and sensitive than Saturn's nature actually is. On the other hand, both ego planets in the three-coloured trapezium find themselves in an environment that gives them plenty of opportunities for action. In addition, their planetary configuration possesses quite special qualities that make a vital contribution to the profile of this man.

The Good Man (The Trampoline)

The Sun in Pisces tends towards idealistic human kindness and in all signs generates the urge at least to visibly distinguish themselves. That produces two possible ways of playing in the development of children, which we can determine from the birth chart. Which of the two goes on to be educated, we can only establish for sure in the adult personality.

The first form is an unconditional subjugation of the ego to the prevailing systems and ambitions current when the child is growing up, because the Pisces child, in his naturally inoffensive way, believes in man's competence and noble character. The adult is consequently put under strong pressure to prove himself according to collective rules, which can take him very far from his true nature (heteronomy). Excessive pressure to do well can lead to a partial loss of high innate sensitivity, dependency on the environment and gradual loss of identity.

The other effects (clearly manifested in Gorbachev's current personality) can be instinctively recognised even in childhood, i.e. that the world wants us to be other than we really are. This leads to a uniquely external adaptation to the requirements of the environment, while – already in childhood – bottling up humanitarian ideals in his own inner world and quietly maturing his own plans for the distant future. In this process, the child learns very early on to be endlessly patient and to keep his inner world to himself, or only to share it with people he can trust (in the case of Gorbachev, with his closest friends and later with his wife). This can give the impression that he is a moral coward, a secretive or even devious, if not dishonest person. Such labelling by his fellow men can only be avoided if his character also contains enough diplomatic intelligence and ability to perform and to assert himself. Gorbachev has these qualities in his linear figure.

The Moon in Leo

The position of the Moon suggests a very conflictive disposition, i.e. the expansive extroversion of his need for contact, clearly shown in Gorbachev's spontaneous "get out of the car and shake the people's hands" attitude. With this lunar position, there is also a pronounced need for human dignity both for himself and – with typical leonine generosity – also for others.

The position of the two lights, Sun and Moon, in their exclusively blue-green aspect and their reciprocal quincunx connection, expresses very clearly the idealistic component of his spiritual ideology, as expressed in his book *Perestroika*. Particularly for the "humanisation of politics" and for the ensuing Politics of Peace that led to reactions in the Western world: initially to the loss of the good old Red enemy, then also to the changing of norms, to the breakdown of mistrust and to the politics of genuine rapprochement.

The substructure of this idealistic Sun-Moon position in the Trampoline figure gives Gorbachev the sense of the reality of experience of the people (Jupiter in Cancer: public spirit, social sensitivity) and intellectual strength and determination in the construction of suggestions for improvement (Uranus/Moon node in Aries), which most idealists and reformers lack.

The Man with the Iron Teeth (the linear figure)

I mentioned the other face of Mikhail Gorbachev, expressed in the dominant red line figure, already at the start of this article. It is conspicuously – but not uniquely – highlighted by the strong multiple opposition in the zodiac vertical line Cancer – Capricorn. The rather static Saturn-Venus conjunction with its strong and hyper-dynamic opponents Mars and Pluto (which do not lie in a conjunction though) may initially startle a beginner. As described above, it is already caught up inside him though, so at worst it is expressed as threatening gestures or sabre-rattling. In addition, the two *aggressive* components Mars and Pluto are already gently nestling in Cancer and controlled by the two sensitive planets Jupiter and the Moon, which belong to the Trampoline figure.

The hard vertical figure also has its *dangerous* feet in the space of the peace-loving Trampoline and is therefore at its service, so to speak. What is more, in this hard line figure, there is a soft and idealistic component in the second, less noticeable opposition bundle with Neptune and

Mercury. This figure, which goes from the Sun in the Trampoline with a one-way opposition that extends towards Neptune in the You-sign of Virgo, and on the other side from Mars to Mercury also returns it back to the space of the Sun along a second one-sided opposition, has a kind of bridging function between the hard vertical components and the sensitive trapezium. It shows a kind of repetition of the topic of the above-mentioned Peace Figure.

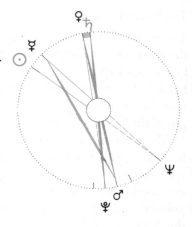

Synthesis

Neptune also plays a leading role of mediator that should not be underestimated. It is strange that this role has been at the least undervalued, if not misconstrued, by both political commentators and horoscope interpreters.

Neptune (the ideal of love) in its exposed position in Virgo could be termed the call to freedom, justice and equal opportunities for all. For it demands genuine commitment if it encounters social injustice, blameless weakness or incompetence, selfish exploitation and its negative consequences for the oppressed. This sympathetic and compassionate philanthropy is the transpersonal dimension of its indestructible idealism and optimism. On the one hand, it makes the more personal need for human dignity and quality of life, as called for by the qualities of the Trampoline planets, a requirement that applies to everyone. Which the Sun in Pisces has less trouble achieving. On the other hand, the hard figure becomes an unflinching fighter for good things. Mercury's role is important here: it is the interpreter of the Neptune ideal – in its position it can even do it very well right up to the end of Aquarius (typical border position: last or first degree = mixed quality), where it not only has access to the polished verbal intelligence of this air sign, but also to the intuitive flexibility of watery Pisces.

It is safe to assume that Gorbachev was not always balanced in synthesis between the two figures on his long/short journey to power. The Neptune bridge is a weak structure made up of only one-way aspects. Many times he could have fallen into one extreme or the other, and then had to either overcome the needs of his ego for peace and love (Sun) or revise the aggressive and power-oriented ideas of the red figure with Mercury. The result is an unusually integrated personality with a wide scope, whose integration would always be possible by the orientation towards a transpersonal ideal. So Gorbachev is and was an example of not only personal, but also spiritual psychosynthesis, which will have worldwide influence only so long as it can be treated as a spiritual mission.

Houses, Fields, Places (both house orientations)

So far I have dealt with the aspect pattern, the planets and the sign orientation of Gorbachev's horoscope. It is therefore only a representation of the character the man was born with and brought into the world. If we do not have a birth time, this is all that can validly be said about a person. That is his potential. How successfully he can actually put it into practice in his life depends on the house positions, for they indicate how well his upbringing has prepared him to be effective in the world.

If we compare the two versions that are presented at the start of this horoscope description, we notice straightaway that in my original version (on the left for 12.34pm) the aspect figure is more horizontally inclined and the hard Cancer-Capricorn opposition lies directly on the horizon. That means an accentuated orientation of the mental dynamic when it comes to personal contact, and therefore a pronounced manipulative and monopolising attitude towards the You. That clearly contrasts with the orientation of the Trampoline figure to the ninth and tenth houses, i.e. to the individuation space. All in all, this positioning emphasises philosophical rather than political thinking.

In the case of the Assadulina version (08.00 am, on the right), the hard opposition structure comes in the vertical axis 4-10 (political axis in the house system = ambitious individual aspiration), which directly confirms the innate Cancer-Capricorn tension, and therefore strengthens his philosophy of power. If a man has climbed the political ladder as purposefully and successfully as Gorbachev, then this version is preferable. Even the anchoring of the Trampoline figure in the twelfth and first houses (I-space) corresponds very well to the quality of the planets and signs it contains.

Basically, in this version the signs and houses do correspond mutually, which enables a more direct transfer of innate behavioural patterns. Only the house axis 5/11 makes an exception, in that the fifth and eleventh signs (Leo and Aquarius) do not lie on the house cusps, but are enclosed in their space (intercepted). This is only correct though, if the very rounded-sounding birth time of 08.00 am is accurate. For even eight minutes later the eleventh cusp enters Aquarius and the fifth enters Leo – so that the correspondence would be perfect, as Uranus would lie exactly on the AC and would therefore be stronger, but on the other hand, Mercury and Mars would move even more clearly in the shadows of their axes which weakens them noticeably.

In my attempt to establish a birth time for Gorbachev, my main starting point was a particular characteristic of his: he never actually willingly demonstrated his aspiration for power. On the contrary, even more frequently he compromised his opportunities for power in order to maintain consistency in his idealistic demands (e.g. in the issue of a future democracy). The Pisces Sun on the Low Point of nine corresponds very well to this attitude. But in the cusp area of the twelfth house it would best fulfil the requirement that the idea is always more important than the person. This puts the whole aspect pattern in a position where it can be actualised more easily. Not only because of the accentuated power axis, but particularly due to the strong points of contact with the collective space, as represented in the three-fold occupation of Cancer in the fourth house.

There are still quite a few single positions whose different situations could be looked into. Perhaps with questions like: does Uranus' position, intercepted in the tenth house correspond better, or the strong AC-situation? Or: is he more a manipulator of people (Saturn on the DC) or a powerful man (Saturn in the tenth house), who also knows the fragility of power from the Low Point position in the house.

However, I would like to stop these thoughts here by introducing two more overriding considerations. One concerns the sign occupation of the main axes, which determine the worldly motivation, which one perceives as a mission for life. In the new version (08.00 am), the cardinal signs on both main axes reveal a strong-willed person who wants to create new things and is well-suited to politics, for example. The occupation of the main axes by two different crosses provides a different pattern though: in the 12.34 pm version, there are cardinals on the horizon (AC-DC), but mutable signs on the Meridian (MC-IC). That indicates an out-and-out idealist, who can easily fantasise (crusader mentality) and who would naturally be more at home with philosophy and religion.

House Horoscope for two Birth Times

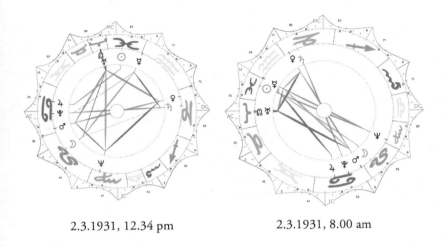

| 2.3.1931, 12.34 pm | 2.3.1931, 8.00 am |

The last thing to consider is the aspect pattern in the house horoscope. In the midday version, the aspect pattern is more spread out, and, in comparison to that of the natal chart, the concentration of strength and therefore dynamism are clearly reduced. The upbringing has rather weakened the innate potential. In the morning version (on the right) though, there is not only a visible increase in dynamism but also a richer substance (more aspects), which can be attributed to the influence of the upbringing, or the effect of education and the collective influence.

All things considered, on comparing with the features of Gorbachev's personality that I know up to now, it seems to correspond more to Mrs Asadullina's new version. One may try to use isolated planetary configurations to "prove" that only this version could be considered, but this always remains a special case and is therefore hardly convincing. If we return to the apprehensive question at the start "Will it last?" the above mentioned comparison of house positions does, however allow us to state with certainty that it is clear that the new version shows a Gorbachev who is much stronger in worldly terms, whose astonishing staying power enables him to endure a lot, but that ultimately the political intrigues were not up to it. Gorbachev has undoubtedly made history. He is still working on his peace mission and will continue to do so for a long time to come.

Pictorial Index to Aspect Figures

Triangles

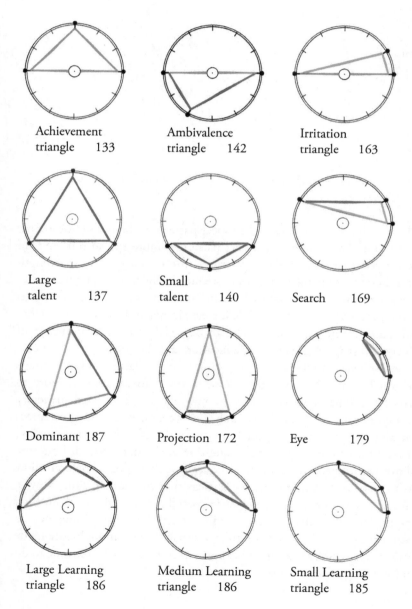

Achievement
triangle   133

Ambivalence
triangle   142

Irritation
triangle   163

Large
talent   137

Small
talent   140

Search   169

Dominant 187

Projection 172

Eye   179

Large Learning
triangle   186

Medium Learning
triangle   186

Small Learning
triangle   185

Opposition Quadrilaterals

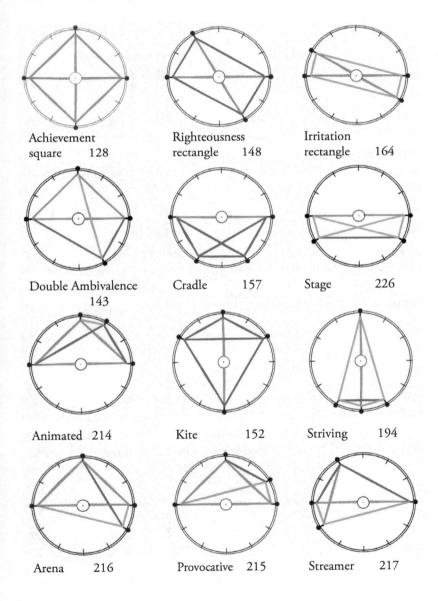

Achievement
square   128

Righteousness
rectangle   148

Irritation
rectangle   164

Double Ambivalence
143

Cradle   157

Stage   226

Animated 214

Kite   152

Striving   194

Arena   216

Provocative 215

Streamer   217

More Opposition Quadrilaterals, Trapezes

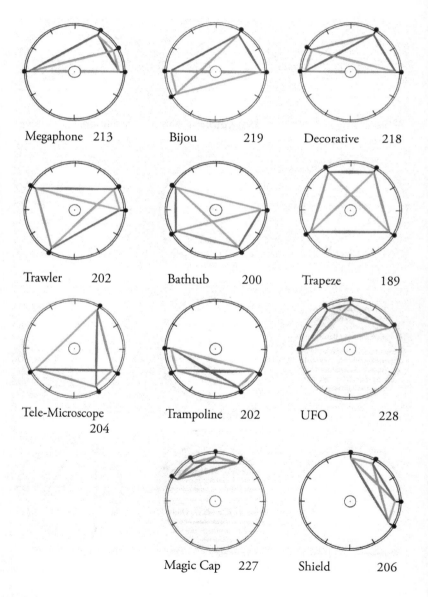

Megaphone 213

Bijou 219

Decorative 218

Trawler 202

Bathtub 200

Trapeze 189

Tele-Microscope 204

Trampoline 202

UFO 228

Magic Cap 227

Shield 206

More Quadrilaterals and Other Figures

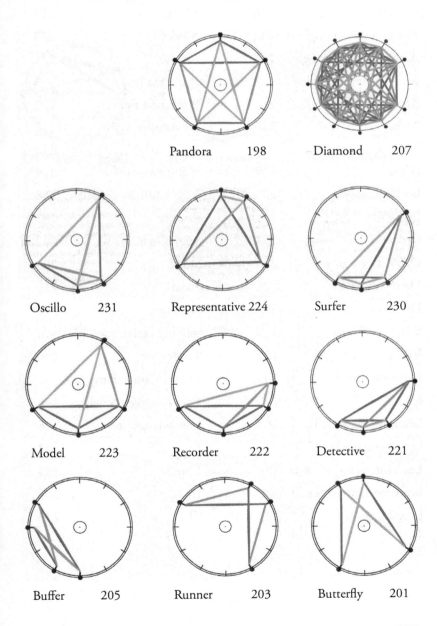

Pandora   198

Diamond   207

Oscillo   231

Representative 224

Surfer   230

Model   223

Recorder   222

Detective   221

Buffer   205

Runner   203

Butterfly   201

Alphabetical Index to Aspect Figures

Bibliography

References to books in the English language are given where possible.

(1)   Huber Bruno: *Astro-Glossarium, Band I, API-Verlag, CH-8134 Adliswil, 1995*

(2)   API study materials. Equivalent information is contained in English in the book *Astrological Psychology: The Huber Method*, HopeWell 2017.

(3)   *API-Computer "CORTEX", Adliswil*

(4)   Software for Huber-style charts is published by Cathar Software. Programs include AstroCora, MegaStar, Regulus. See also www.astro.com.

(5)   Arroyo Stephen: *Astrology, Psychology and the Four Elements*, CRCS Books

(6)   Assagioli Roberto: *Psychosynthesis Principles and Methods*

(7)   *Astrolog*, German language magazine of astrological psychology.

(8)   Bailey Alice A.: *Esoteric Astrology* and *A Treatise on White Magic*, Lucis Trust, London

(9)   Brunton Paul: *The Wisdom of the Overself*, Rider, 1943

(10) Durckheim Karlfried Graf: *"Vom doppelten Ursprung des Menschen"*, Herder-Verlag, Freiburg, 1973

(11) Gauquelin Michel: *Cosmic Clocks*, Paladin 1973

(12) Hamaker-Zondac Karen M.: *Aspects and Personality*, Weiser

(13) Huber Bruno und Louise: *Transformation: Astrology as a Spiritual Path*, HopeWell 2008.

(14) Huber Bruno: *Astrological Psychosynthesis*, HopeWell 2006. For click horoscopes, see also *Astrolog II*, HopeWell 2009, "Relationship as a Developmental Process", Luise Huber.

(15) Huber Bruno und Louise: *"Horoskop-Berechnung und Zeichnung"*, Verlag Astrologisch-Psychologisches Institut 1973, 4. Auflage 1982

(16) Huber Bruno und Louise: *The Astrological Houses*, HopeWell 2011.

(17) Huber Bruno und Louise: *Life Clock*, HopeWell 2006

(18) Huber Bruno und Louise: *Moon Node Astrology*, HopeWell 2005

(19) Huber Bruno: *Astrological Psychosynthesis*, HopeWell 2006

(20) Huber Louise: *Reflections & Meditations on the Signs of the Zodiac*, AFA 1984

(21) Huber Louise: *"Was ist esoterische Astrologie?"* API-Verlag 1976,2. Auflage 1984

(22) Huber Michael A.: *"Dynamische Auszahlungen"* API-Verlag 1997,2. Auflage 1984. ["Dynamic Calculations" are covered in *Astrological Psychology: The Huber Method*, HopeWell 2017]

(23) Huber Bruno: *Astrological Psychosynthesis*, HopeWell 2006

(24) Jung C.G.: *Memories, Dreams, Reflections*, Fontana 1967 etc

(25) Kandinsky Wassely: *Concerning the Spiritual in Art*, Dover 1977

(26) Ptolemy Claudius: *Tetrabiblos*, Kessinger 1997

(27) Thomas Ring: *"Astrologische Menschenkunde"*, *Kombinationslehre*, *Bauer-Verlag*, *Freiburg*, *1994*

(28) Dane Rudhyar: *Astrology and the Modern Psyche: An Astrologer Looks at Depth Psychology*, CRCS, 1976

(29) Jean Claude Weiss: *"Horoskopanalyse Bd. II, Aspekte im Geburtsbild"*, *Edition Astrodata, Zürich 1984*